THE WAGES
OF PEACE

⚹ PRIO

International Peace Research Institute, Oslo
Fuglehauggata 11, N-0260 Oslo, Norway
Telephone: (47) 22 55 71 50
Telefax: (47) 22 55 84 22
Cable address: PEACERESEARCH OSLO
E-mail: info@prio.no

The International Peace Research Institute, Oslo (PRIO) is an independent international institute of peace and conflict research, founded in 1959. It is governed by an international Governing Board of seven individuals, and is financed mainly by the Norwegian Ministry for Education, Research, and Church Affairs. The results of all PRIO research are available to the public.

PRIO's publications include the quarterlies *Journal of Peace Research* (1964-) and *Security Dialogue* (formerly *Bulletin of Peace Proposals*) (1969-) and a series of books. Recent titles include:

Nils Petter Gleditsch & Olav Njølstad, eds: *Arms Races: Technological and Political Dynamics* (1990)

Knud S. Larsen, ed.: *Conflict and Social Psychology* (1993)

Robert Bathurst: *Intelligence and the Mirror: On creating an Enemy* (1993)

THE WAGES OF PEACE

Disarmament in a Small Industrialized Economy

NILS PETTER GLEDITSCH,
ÅDNE CAPPELEN
AND
OLAV BJERKHOLT

PRIO
International Peace Research Institute, Oslo

SAGE Publications
London • Thousand Oaks • New Delhi

© International Peace Research Institute, Oslo, 1994
First published 1994

SAGE Publications Ltd
6 Bonhill Street
London EC2A 4PU

SAGE Publications Inc
2455 Teller Drive
Thousand Oaks, CA 91320

Sage Publications India Pvt Ltd
32, M-Block Market
Greater Kailash – I
New Delhi 110 048

HC
370
.D4
G54
1994

British Library Cataloguing in Publication data

A catalogue record for this book is available from the British Library.

ISBN 0 8039 7750 6

Library of Congress catalog card number 94-066826

Typesetting by Håvard Hegre, PRIO, Oslo
Printed in Great Britain at the University Press, Cambridge

Contents

Foreword

With the end of the Cold War, many governments started to cut military spending, raising expectations of a vast 'peace dividend'. Some of the optimism that greeted the breaching of the Berlin Wall in November 1989 has since dissipated, with the Gulf War in 1990/91, the wars of Yugoslavia's disintegration beginning in the summer of 1991 and the instability and conflict accompanying the break-up of the USSR. But the end of an era of intense and prolonged great power confrontation has made possible smaller military budgets and establishments.

There have been numerous studies of the economic effects of arms cuts, including by the authors of the present work. The International Peace Research Institute, Oslo (PRIO) has been involved in such studies for some three decades. There are three reasons for adding to the literature now.

The first is that economic circumstances change, as do fashions in government economic policies; both affect the context in which military cuts will be made. Whether world trade is buoyant or depressed, for example, can have a major impact on the prospects of realising a prospective peace dividend. The outcome will also be influenced by whether governments prefer to plan the reallocation of resources out of the military sector (and, if so, in what direction) or to leave the process to market forces.

The second reason is that earlier studies were conducted as abstract exercises: what the advantages *would* be *if* armed forces were cut by such and such percentage. Today, these studies can be taken as necessary input to policy formation. Although military preparations remain one of humanity's largest enterprises, consuming about one-twentieth of the world's production of goods and services, more than either education or health care, arms spending is already being cut in some countries and there is a much higher probability than before that it will be cut in others.

The third reason is that most earlier studies were set at a very general or a very detailed level. The former have focused on the world scene and on making a normative case for disarmament. The latter have tended to focus on conversion of single industries, firms or areas from military to civilian production. These studies have been very useful, yet also limited for they have generally failed to set their conclusions within the context of how national economies actually work. There have been relatively few macroeconomic studies and fewer that are comparable across national boundaries.

This book therefore adds to a rather small collection of studies that use macroeconomic models to assess the economic consequences of reduced military spending. Drawing on a wide range of sources, it offers a highly detailed and systematic view of the possibilities for a peace dividend in one country. As such, it is intended not only to shine a light on Norway but also to contribute to the development of comparable studies in other countries. It is equally hoped that the new ground broken here by modelling the environmental effects of disarmament measures will also set an example that others will follow.

The principal author of this work is Nils Petter Gleditsch, a Senior Research Fellow of PRIO and Editor of the *Journal of Peace Research*. His co-authors are Olav Bjerkholt and Ådne Cappelen, Assistant Director General and Research Director respectively at Statistics Norway (formerly the Central Bureau of Statistics). The three have worked together for a decade to produce scholarship of the highest standard on the economics of disarmament, of which this is the latest example.

Dan Smith
Director, PRIO
December 1993

1

The Burden of Arms

1.1 A Major Project of Humankind

As this is written, in the early 1990s, the world is spending about 1,000,000 million USD annually on armaments.[1] This is almost 5% of the total global output, and represents about one-sixth of total public spending. Arms expenditure exceeds world spending on public education by 10% and health spending by 25%. Global arms spending is 20 times higher than foreign aid and more than 2,000 times higher than what is spent on international peacekeeping. There can be no question, then, that the arms race remains one of the major projects of humankind.

In wartime, of course, military spending may reach much higher levels. Towards the end of World War II, for example, the four major combatants in the European war – the USA, the UK, Germany, and the Soviet Union – were spending about 50% of their national products on the war effort.[2] Even for countries with relatively little actual fighting, war can be quite costly. For Norway it has been calculated that the war and the German occupation cost about 45% of projected national income for the war years.[3] For countries in the middle of major battles, the effects of war can be devastating, in human as well as economic terms.[4] This book, however, will focus on peacetime effects of military spending.

The mobilization of major peacetime resources for armaments is a relatively recent phenomenon. Traditionally, military resource use was low between wars. In wartime a major share of a nation's resources might be mobilized, but after the war the military establishment would shrink again. However, it might not fall to the prewar level: a 'ratchet effect' has been observed in data on military resource use for many countries.[5]

World War II produced clear long-term effects on the peacetime military spending of many industrialized countries. Postwar demobilization was interrupted by both the Cold War and particularly the hot war in Korea, followed by substantial rearmament in Europe and North America. US military expenditure peaked at 14% of the Gross Domestic Product (GDP) during the Korean War; the ratchet effect is clearly visible in the postwar level of military spending. More recently the Indochina War also had a marked effect on military spending in the USA, peaking at 9.6% of GDP. But this war had only a limited effect, if any, on military spending in Western Europe. And the end of the war occurred during a period of detente, so US military spending declined in absolute terms to slightly below the prewar level.

The first Strategic Arms Limitation Treaty (SALT) was the backbone of detente in the 1970s. Following the ratification failure of SALT II and the Soviet invasion of Afghanistan in late 1979, relations between the superpowers cooled considerably. In the area of intermediate-range weapons, arms competition continued, unchecked by any treaty, and the superpowers competed for allies in the Third World. Arms expenditure rose rapidly as the USA set out to overcome the 'Vietnam syndrome' – the humiliating experience of having lost a major war to a second-rate military power.

Towards the end of the 1980s this process was reversed. The superpowers agreed to ban intermediate-range missiles; for the first time in the history of their disarmament efforts, they actually engaged in the physical elimination of an entire class of weapons systems, including some highly modern weapons. Progress was made across the board in global as well as regional European arms control and disarmament negotiations. Two treaties limiting nuclear testing, originally signed in 1974 and 1976, were finally ratified in 1990. In the same year, the 22 member-states of NATO and the Warsaw Pact signed the Treaty on Conventional Forces in Europe (CFE), establishing ceilings on such major non-nuclear weapons systems as tanks, artillery, and combat aircraft.

Even more significantly, the political basis of the East-West conflict evaporated. In the final months of 1989, all the Communist regimes in Eastern Europe tumbled as if to confirm the late domino theory. German reunification suddenly reappeared on the political agenda and was carried out in less than a year from the breaching of the Berlin Wall. Soviet military forces started to withdraw from Eastern Europe, a process due to be completed in 1994. In March 1991 the Warsaw Pact was formally dissolved. At the end of the same year the Soviet Union itself became history, followed by 15 independent republics with only a loose superstructure – the Commonwealth of Independent States, encompassing 11 of them. The Cold War was over and the Soviet threat gone. However precarious 'The Long Peace' in Europe after World War II might have appeared in times of crisis, and whatever its causes, it seemed to have developed into a lasting peace, 'peace for our time' and even beyond.[6]

Outside Europe as well there were grounds for optimism about human conflict. The world's wealthiest 44 countries have, with one exception, avoided war among themselves since World War II,[7] and wars remain unlikely among these countries. As of 15 May 1984, the major countries of the developed world had remained at peace with each other for the longest unbroken period since the days of the Roman Empire (Mueller, 1989, p. 3). The number of on-going major armed conflicts – those involving a cumulative total of at least 1,000 battle-related deaths – declined slightly in the late 1980s.[8] The ending of the East-West conflict in Europe seemed to make it highly unlikely that the two superpowers would engage in serious rivalry over local conflicts in any region; instead, they started to work together to contain such conflicts. By 1992 it seemed dubious to speak of more than one superpower, except in terms of strategic nuclear weapons.

That, of course, does not mean that perpetual peace is close at hand. The slight decline in major armed conflicts in the late 1980s followed a 35-year period of increasing internal conflict (Lindgren, 1991, p. 16). With a lower threshold – 25 annual deaths – Wallensteen & Axell (1993) have recorded 54 armed conflicts within or between states during the period 1989-92, some of them with a potential for escalating into war. The 30-odd major armed conflicts reported annually are regularly claiming thousands of lives. Altogether, by the end of the 1980s armed conflicts after World War II are said to have claimed civilian and military losses on the order of 22 million lives,[9] fewer than World War II (51 million), but more than World War I (10 million).[10] The Gulf conflict of 1990-91 served as a reminder that local conflicts can escalate to massive use of violence, involving major powers and sophisticated weaponry, and causing great loss of human lives as well as extensive environmental damage.

Violent ethnic and other internal conflicts are raging on all continents except North America. In Europe, conflicts that predate the Cold War are re-emerging, mainly because of the removal of what Buzan et al. (1990) have termed the 'overlay' of the East-West conflict, although so far only the conflict in the former Yugoslavia has erupted into large-scale violence. Pessimists have predicted a future as violent as Europe's past, but while the probability of minor war has increased, the potential for escalation is all but gone.[11] Outside Europe, the prospects of ethnic violence are even greater. To illustrate the global potential for ethnic violence, we may note that there are 3,000-5,000 distinct communities which might claim nationhood on the basis of shared territory and characteristics such as language, beliefs, and institutions. At present, there are 234 'countries' in the world (encompassing independent nations and separate dependent territories).[12] This number has been increasing, with potential for much secession and conquest, and for associated violence. Indeed, Nietschmann (1987) claims that a 'Third World War' has already started between indigenous nations and states in the Third World. Of the 196 independent nations in the world by mid-1993 (184 of which were members of the United Nations as of August 1993), only a handful – including Norway – are conventionally classified as ethnically homogeneous.[13] Although even Norway has a small ethnic minority, the Sami, as well as a growing number of immigrants from the Third World, the probability of ethnic warfare must, however, be classified as extremely low; the same applies to most ethnically divided nations. And the lack of great-power rivalry to exploit local conflicts and the increasing role of the world community in peacekeeping and conflict settlement, provide grounds for cautious optimism although the fear of escalation may also have worked towards defusing local conflicts during the Cold War.

Another reason for caution with regard to Mueller's thesis about 'the obsolescence of major war' is that we need to understand *why* the leading industrialized nations are not fighting each other. Mueller sees this in part as a normative and cultural change – war as an institution is becoming as illegitimate as slavery. In fact, some of the countries which have not fought each other (notably the Soviet Union and China) have until quite recently had human rights records corresponding to slavery in all but the name, so there must be some factor at work beyond a normative respect for human life. 'Realist' thinkers would attribute the lack of war to deterrence – and nuclear deterrence in particular – but Mueller puts more stock in what we might call 'economic deterrence', the mutual fear of economic destruction of interdependent and economically advanced states. As Milward (1977, p. 3) reminds us, the economic effects of war are hard to predict in advance; a country with highly destructive weapons will not necessarily use them in all wars. Thus, when Arrow (1992, p. 66) writes that the major economic case for cuts in defense spending is the reduction in the probability and cost of war, 'the costs of which are only too easy to predict', he is probably referring to full-scale nuclear war between the two superpowers, and not to the 'normal' type of war, the several hundred major and minor wars – international and civil – of the 'postwar' period. To Milward the idea that modern warfare is becoming costlier and deadlier and therefore has priced itself out of the market, is an idea that has little foundation in history (p. 1). However, regardless of how many cheap wars advanced indu- strialized nations have engaged in against lesser opponents, they have clearly refrained from going to war *against each other*, as Mueller points out, and economic deterrence may indeed be a factor. A competing perspective is that the establishment of a durable peace has occurred primarily among democracies: most empirical research on this issue agrees that democracies rarely if ever fight each other, even if they are no less prone to participate in war than non-democracies.[14] The long-term trend towards the wider diffusion of democratic government is probably the best ground for optimism about the future of the international system.

The end of the Cold War led to renewed debate about the size of the peacetime military establishment. Several nations have started unilateral cutbacks of their military forces, and others have imposed a de facto freeze on military expenditure. World military expenditure has declined in real terms every year since 1988.[15] For 1991, SIPRI reported lower military expenditure than the preceding year for 70 of the 123 countries. For many of those with small increases in 1991, the long-term trend was still downward; for only 29 countries did the 1991 figure exceed the highest figure of the preceding decade. For 1992, SIPRI estimated a decline in world military expenditure of 15%; this was mainly due to a sharp cut in the military spending of Russia and the other states of the former Soviet Union. A clear anticipation has developed that further cuts in military spending are on the cards. The arms trade, according to US ACDA (1994), is dropping more sharply than military spending.

On the other hand, not many countries will be prepared at short notice to dispense entirely with the option of threatening military force in self-defense as a last resort. Few are likely to join the ranks of Iceland and Costa Rica, with no domestic military forces. But among those countries previously affected by the East-West conflict, and particularly in Europe, the size of the military establish- ment is coming under very serious discussion. Increasingly, pressing public and private needs will compete with national security requirements for public funds: responsible environmental policies, such as more efficient and less polluting means of transportation, social welfare (especially care for the increasing cohorts of the aged), and effective policies to combat drug abuse. Many of these civilian priorities will even be formulated in terms of 'security' – as in the popular notion of 'environmental security' – with the deliberate purpose of signaling to policy- makers that environmental and other threats to industrial societies should be viewed on a par with national security in the traditional sense.[16] In Eastern Europe and the former Soviet Union, consumers will be pushing hard for improved standards of living, and public funding will be needed to ease the transition towards a market economy.

1.2 An Overview of this Book

Much of the existing literature on conversion is divorced from the mainstream of studies of economic change and adjustment by means of macroeconomic models. Various such models have been developed over the past 50 years and are now being used by research institutes and government agencies alike to forecast economic developments, discuss policy options, and to simulate various scenarios for change. In this book we have based our analysis on the macroeconomic models developed for the general purpose of macroeconomic planning. Similar studies have been carried out in Australia, Belgium, Canada, Finland, France, Germany, the Netherlands, Sweden, Switzerland, the United Kingdom, the United States, and possibly a few other countries.[17] However, this literature is still fairly small and the comparability of the studies low. Thus, we believe that a fairly detailed study of Norway may be of interest above and beyond the results for that particular country, as a source of hypotheses for parallel studies in other countries.

The literature on conversion has tended to proceed from much more scattered evidence, such as case studies of single industries. Naturally, in selecting cases for study, writers will often choose the more challenging and difficult cases, and this may in turn lead to an overly dim view of the prospects. For instance, some recent studies on conversion have focused on the high cost of weapons destruction (as with chemical weapons) or verification (as in the case of the agreement to ban intermediate-range nuclear forces).[18]

The macroeconomic models used in this are briefly explained in the main text, and more extensively in Appendix B. The use of such models links our work to a host of other studies of the Norwegian economy and other economies which have been studied with similar models. Some controversy has attended the use of large-scale models, and not only for the analysis of military spending. Within the discipline there are competing schools of macroeconomic beliefs, but less so in Norway than in many other countries. The user (and, indeed, the reader!) may lose track of the main model structure and even more so the various auxiliary assumptions. We are well aware of these problems[19] and have tried to take into account how robust the results may be to changes in the models. The Norwegian models used for analysis in this book are in our view the best ones available. They are also highly relevant because they have been so extensively used by government agencies for a wide variety of purposes over many years.

The focus of this book is the economic effects of reduced military spending in one small industrialized country, Norway. We begin by taking a broad overview of the effect of arms spending in industrialized countries more generally (Chapter 2). We review the international debate about the effects of military spending on employment and economic growth, and examine the evidence for competing hypotheses about spinoffs and crowding-out effects.

The Norwegian military sector is described in Chapter 3, and in Chapter 4 we discuss the effects of national conversion. Although such national conversion may be conceived as part of an international disarmament effort, the cross-national ramifications are not explored here. Here it should be noted that we use the term 'conversion' in the broad sense of reallocation of resources from the military sector to civilian sectors of the economy. Public discussion is frequently limited to industrial conversion, i.e. the retooling of military industry to serve civilian needs. In major arms-producing countries, such as the USA and the Soviet Union, military industry comprises a major portion of total employment in the military sector. In many other industrialized countries, however, military industry represents only a limited component of the military sector. For Italy, the figure is about 20%, for Norway perhaps 10%. The bulk of defense-dependent employment concerns uniformed personnel and civilians employed in the armed forces. For a country like Norway, the major conversion problem relates to the closure of major military bases in remote areas with few prospects of alternative employment nearby.

Through international trade and other international economic linkages, disarmament in one country will have some economic effects in other countries as well. In particular, small countries with open economies are likely to be influenced by disarmament in the major powers. Although the modeling framework for analyzing such cross-national effects is not as well developed as that which analyzes the national effects. In Chapter 5 we use the World Model developed by Wassily Leontief and associates to study the global effects of international disarmament and also its effects on the Norwegian economy. We find that global disarmament is likely to have a limited but positive effect on the world economy. Over and beyond this, Norway stands to gain from world disarmament because the country has low arms production and will earn more from the alternative resource use in a disarmed world.

Chapters 4 and 5 are the model-based chapters. Readers who are unfamiliar with macroeconomic models should nevertheless be able to digest most of our results with relatively little trouble. Those who would rather not make the effort may skip these sections without any great loss of continuity. However, it should be kept in mind that the models contain assumptions which shape the results.

A large literature outlines the negative social and economic effects of the arms race – notably a series of UN reports – and these studies imply considerable potential gains from disarmament. On the other hand, much of the writing on the economics of defense conversion emphasizes the *problems* involved: Resources cannot always be transferred from one sector to the other; plants involved in specialized defense production may have to close down when the demand for weapons disappears; defense-sector employees may have to be retrained or seek early retirement; entrenched interests, whether representing labor, capital, or local communities with tax revenues from firms and defense employees, may resist disarmament – as epitomized in the concept of a 'military-industrial complex'. In Chapter 6 we examine some of these disaggregate effects. Even though they are of greatest concern to those who are directly involved, such pressure groups may act to block a process towards national disarmament.

Overall, the available research indicates that, regardless of transition problems, the effects of conversion in the medium to long term are clearly positive, for employment as well as for economic growth. Our own research largely supports those positive conclusions. Moreover, the fundamental changes in international relations are likely in the long run to outweigh national economic and political resistance to conversion. This book is itself intended as a contribution to the process of overcoming that resistance.

Decisions on disarmament and conversion will not be determined by economic factors alone. In Chapters 6 and 7 we briefly examine public opinion and the politics of conversion. Because the military establishment in Norway is relatively limited, it is unlikely that disarmament measures would be blocked because of misleading expectations about their economic effects. Decisions on the size of the military establishment in Norway are likely to be made primarily on the basis of analyses of 'the threat' and how to counter it. Nevertheless, exaggerated fears about the negative economic adjustment involved in disarmament may influence the debate in a negative direction. In this sense we hope that our book may contribute not just to analyzing disarmament, but to achieving it as well.

The positive expectations about the likely savings from the decline of the East-West conflict have been epitomized in the slogan 'the peace dividend'. The likely *size* of this dividend remains a controversial issue.[20] Moreover, it is arguable that the peace dividend that seemed within reach with the demise of the Cold War has already been lost – or at least that it has been consumed for several years in advance – as a combination of the international recession, the war in the Gulf, the economic chaos and disintegration in the former Soviet Union and Yugoslavia, and the environmental disasters left behind by the Soviet military and others. An international analysis should take into account the opportunities lost, but also focus on the potential peace dividend that may be realized if major regional wars can be avoided and if the former Soviet Union can succeed in transforming its heavily militarized command economy. In the case of Norway, there is clearly a peace dividend – and the Norwegians have already started spending from it. We anticipate that the actual decline in military expenditure will outpace any decision-making on how to spend the freed budgetary resources.

In developing models for alternative defense spending, we will look at various forms of alternative spending. In this way we hope to transcend the single-issue discussion of 'guns versus butter' promoted by groups that advocate particular causes. One of these issues, and a particularly important one, is *development*. Among others, the United Nations has promoted the idea of channeling funds from disarmament to development. As early as 1962 a UN report stated that a 'much larger volume of resources could be allocated to investment for productive development in [the developing countries] even if only a fraction of the resources currently devoted to military purposes were used in this way. Disarmament could thus bring about a marked increase of real income in the poorer parts of the world' (United Nations, 1962, p. 51). In discussing national conversion in Chapter 4 we discuss in greater detail how development may be given priority in a Norwegian package of countermeasures. In Chapter 5 we take up the issue of how much development can be bought for global disarmament.

Another important special issue is *the environment*. The idea of coupling conversion with the environment has also been promoted by many groups, including the United Nations Environment Program (cf. Gleditsch, 1992a). To date, there has been rather little modeling work in this area. But environmental variables are being built into national planning models, and some results are reported in Section 4.10.

Notes

1. Estimates for total arms spending vary considerably because of official secrecy, misleading account-ing procedures, and varying exchange rates. For 1986 Sivard (1989) reports a world total of USD 858,635 million, while US ACDA (1989) uses the figure USD 983,800 million. In 1990 the *SIPRI Yearbook* stopped providing a figure for world military expenditure, mainly because it was too difficult to provide reliable estimates for such major arms spenders as China and the Soviet Union. However, the press release to the 1990 edition of the *Yearbook* gave an estimate for 1989 'of the order of' USD 950,000 million. US ACDA (1994) reports a peak figure of USD 1,215,000 million (in 1991 dollars) for 1987, declining to 1,038,000 in 1991.

2. Cf. Harrison (1988) and Milward (1977), pp. 63-76. A major difference between the USA and other major war combatants pointed out by Milward was that the US could mobilize much greater overall resources. Thus, consumer purchases of goods and services in the USA *rose* by 12% between 1939 and 1944, while in Great Britain they *declined* by 22% between 1938 and 1944.

3. Cf. Aukrust & Bjerve (1945, pp. 41-49); Gleditsch et al. (1983, pp. 190-191).

4. For an excellent study of the economic determinants and effects of World War II, see Milward (1977).

5. Cf. Russett (1970); Diehl & Goertz (1985).

6. Contrary to popular myth, Neville Chamberlain's famous utterance on his return to Britain after the Munich agreement proclaimed peace *for* our time, rather than 'in'. Cf. *Oxford Dictionary of Quotations* (2nd edn., Oxford University Press, 1955, p. 75) and Melko (1990), p. 1. The term 'The Long Peace' was coined by Gaddis (1987).

7. Mueller (1989, p. 4). Wealth is measured by GNP per capita. The exception is the Soviet invasion of Hungary in 1956, a major political event but a minor war. The figure 44 would be greater if it were not for Iraq's various wars in the 1980s and 1990s. For a brief discussion of borderline cases, see Mueller's note 5, p. 271.

8. Annual surveys have been published in the *SIPRI Yearbook* since 1987. For the two most recent ones, see Heldt (1992); Amer et al. (1993).

9. For data casualties, cf. Ahlström (1991) and Eckhardt (1989). Some of Eckhardt's conflicts should perhaps be classified as massacres rather than as wars. In a study of 'genocides and politicides' Harff & Gurr (1988, p. 370) estimate that the aggregate civilian death toll in massacres from World War II to the mid-1980s adds up to between 7 and 16 millions, considerably exceeding the number of battle deaths in all wars during the same period (Small & Singer, 1982). Rummel (1994) has estimated the number of people killed by their own governments in the 20th century at an amazing 170 million, more than four times as many as have been killed in war in the same period.

10. Data on the number of casualties in the world wars are cited from Beer (1981), pp. 37-38.

11. For a clear (even extreme) statement of the pessimistic position, see Mearsheimer (1990). For various counter-arguments see five letters to the editor in the following two issues of *International Security*.

12. For a definition of 'country', see Gleditsch (1988), p. 17. The number of countries is from Gleditsch, Hegre & Nordhaug (1993).

13. Cf. Nietschmann (1987), Nielsson & Jones (1988), Gurr & Scarritt (1989). For statistics, see also Gleditsch (1988), Chapter 9.

14. For a review of some of the relevant research, see Russett (1993), Gleditsch (1992e) and other articles in the same issue (4/92) of *Journal of Peace Research*, as well as numerous articles in recent volumes of *International Interactions*, *Journal of Conflict Resolution*, *World Politics*, and other international relations journals.

15. According to US ACDA (1994, p. 47) the peak year was 1987. The *SIPRI Yearbook 1990* also reports declining global military expenditure from 1988, although precise estimates have not been provided annually.

16. For a discussion of environmental security with many references, see Gleditsch (1992b).

17. For studies of *Australia,* see Liew (1985) for *Belgium,* Proost et al. (1981); for *Canada,* Centre for Studies ... (1983), Galigan (1984), Maxwell (1984); for Finland, Forssell (1966), Forssell et al. (1968), Joenniemi (1970), Lindén (1987); for *France,* Aben & Smith (1987), Fontanel (1980), Fontanel & Smith (1985), Martin et al. (1987); for *(West) Germany,* Berger et al. (1991), Brömmel-hörster (1991, 1992), Bundesministerium der Verteidigung (1972), Elsner & Voss (1991), Filip-Köhn et al. (1980), Kiy & Löbbe (1990), Schloenbach (1973), for *the Netherlands,* Duisenberg (1965ab); for *Sweden,* Forsberg & Hedberg (1978), Brundin (1985ab); for *Switzerland,* Hofmeister (n.d., 1976); for the *UK,* Aben & Smith (1987), Barker, Dunne & Smith (1991), Brown (1964), Dunne & Smith (1984), Economist Intelligence Unit (1963), Martin et al. (1987); for the *USA,* for instance Benoit (1962), Benoit & Boulding (1963), Bezdek (1975), Congressional Budget Office (1992), Klein & Mori (1973), Leontief & Hoffenberg (1961), Leontief et al. (1965), Roland-Holst et al. (1988), Thomas et al. (1991). Attempts at modelling the economic effects of the centrally planned economies of the (then) Warsaw Pact countries are found in Gronicki & Klein (1992), Klein & Gronicki (1990) and Klein et al. (1992).

18. Cf. Kireev (1991); Lock (1992).

19. Cf. Smith (1990) and two books edited by Bjerkholt & Rosted (1987), Bjerkholt et al. (1990).

20. This debate has been particularly keen in the United States. Cf., for instance, Adams (1986), Anderson et al. (1986), Adams & Gold (1987), Oden (1988), Gold (1990), and Dumas (1990).

2

The Economics of Military Spending

2.1 Main Effects of Military Spending

As one of the major projects of mankind, the arms race is bound to have considerable economic impact in peacetime.[1] Military spending allocates resources to an unproductive endeavor. The case against military spending has been put succinctly in a series of UN reports, for instance in this statement from 1982:

> The arms race represents a waste of resources, a diversion of the economy, a hindrance to national development efforts, and a threat to democratic processes ... military outlays have no long-term positive effects on economic growth. (United Nations, 1982, p. 6, p. 47)

Seen from a *global security perspective*, the effects of military spending are generally unfavorable: one country's security is another country's perceived threat. Thus, it is hardly surprising that the global perspective adopted by the United Nations should involve a particularly critical view of the arms race.

At the *national level*, any negative consequences of military spending must, of course, be balanced against positive effects in terms of fulfilling national security needs. Such considerations lie outside the scope of this book. We are concerned only with the *economic* effects of military spending; it is assumed that disarmament is undertaken when national security permits it, regardless of how this assessment is made or by whom.

Like most other forms of government consumption, military spending may serve in the short run to stimulate demand, with favorable consequences for employment and other measures of economic activity. In a longer-term perspective, however, military spending influences economic growth and development through various channels. The military sector draws resources away from non-military use. The importance of this effect will depend on the scarcity of various resources. The financing of military spending may have a negative influence on the overall savings rate, which in turn may lead to lower investment and less growth. On the other hand, certain components of military expenditure may yield non-military benefits toward economic growth. This might be true particularly in less developed countries for certain kinds of infrastructure (roads, airports) and for education of military personnel, and in mature industrialized economies for technological progress resulting from military R&D expenditure.

Because military spending is so centralized, it can also be used as an instrument of economic policy. Any significant economic *effect* represents a possible *motive* for increasing or reducing arms spending. In the short term, arms spending may be used to boost the economy just prior to an election, to the advantage of the government in power. In the long term, arms spending may be used to promote full employment or the development of a national high-technology industry. This is not to say that there are not more effective national policy instruments for achieving the same ends. But such policy instruments may not be politically feasible or economically sufficient. Moreover, *beliefs* about economic effects of arms spending may influence defense policy decision-making regardless of how they actually work (Lindgren, 1984, Section 6).

Even if arms spending in the long term is harmful to the economy as a whole, it may still benefit vested interests such as business and professionals with special-ized skills in military production. With effective lobbying, such groups may exert disproportionate influence on the formulation and execution of national policy. This makes it all the more important to focus the attention of decision-makers as well as the general public on the national and global effects of the arms race.

The literature suggests that military spending may have a significant effect on several important macroeconomic aggregates: the level of employment, the sav-ings rate, economic growth, inflation,[2] the volume of imports and exports, the balance of payments, and income distribution[3]. It is beyond the scope of this chapter – or indeed of this book – to review every economic effect of military spending. Instead, we shall concentrate on the effects of two key national indica-tors: *employment* and *economic growth*, and pay particular attention to *military R&D*. The international literature on these issues is quite extensive; some of it is summarized in the next three sections, while the impact of military spending in Norway on employment and economic growth is dealt with in Chapter 4.

It is a far from trivial task to establish the interrelations between military expenditures on the one hand and macroeconomic indicators such as the unemploy-ment level and the rate of growth on the other. Moreover, most of the contributors to the literature would like to interpret their findings as causal links. For many of the studies using fairly simple analytic techniques such as correlation studies, this is a farfetched claim, although it has not restrained an intensive debate over the issues. More advanced recent statistical techniques especially designed to analyze causal links have also been adopted, but the concrete uses of these as well as the more traditional techniques are often prone to criticism and may have less validity and reliability than is frequently claimed.

The reasons for this are several: Economic growth and unemployment are not explained within the economics discipline by widely shared coherent theories. Many different factors influence both growth and unemployment – both phenom-ena can be viewed as a final outcome of the functioning of the economic system – hence, causal analyses may differ with regard to the factors they encompass. The data available as measures of growth and unemployment as well as military expenditures may often have severe weaknesses prone to introduce biases in the analyses. Comparison of contributions to the literature gives abundant examples showing that the results are sensitive to sample, specification, estimation method, and the use of cross-section vs. time-series data. In the analysis of the effects of military spending ideological factors may also be at work. Our own view on the methodological issues is eclectic, and we have tried to avoid ideologically influ-enced interpretations. In the survey of the literature which follows below we have tried to take account of the interchange which has taken place over time, as well as the improvements in analytic techniques, and tried to extract consensus or majority views.

2.2 Military Spending and Employment

Worldwide, direct employment in the armed forces in the late 1980s has been estimated at 28 million. Additionally, the arms industry is said to employ another 22 million, for a world total of 50 million.[4] In the OECD area, total armed forces number about 7 million at the end of the Cold War. To take proper account of the indirectly generated employment, one would have to add more than military industry to the figures for the armed forces. Here, a multiplier between 1.5 and 2 might be appropriate. The military establishment is, indeed, a major source of employment in today's world.

Instant disarmament, releasing to the labor market all those directly or indirectly dependent on military demand, would create major unemployment. Total unemployment in the OECD countries stood at about 30 million in 1992. Complete and rapid disarmament might increase it in the short term by as much as one-third, if we count the direct as well as indirect effects. In the long term, the picture would be very different. By alternative public spending, by tax reductions, or simply by reducing the deficit, other sectors would eventually absorb much of the excess labor. Studies in various countries indicate that although the military sector is labor-intensive, it has gradually become less so, and other forms of public expenditure can easily support higher employment. In Norway, central government civilian expenditure generates almost as much employment per unit of expenditure as does the military, conscripts included; local government consumption yields nearly 30% more (Cappelen, 1986, Table 4).

In the United States, with a much larger economy and a military establishment not subsidized by conscription, studies also indicate that more employment can be generated by non-military spending. DeGrasse (1983, p. 41) cites figures showing that the number of jobs created by military industry contracts falls slightly below the median for industry. US Department of Labor studies in 1976 indicated that civilian government spending created 30% more jobs per dollar than military spending, and that increased private consumption through tax cuts would create 47% more jobs.[5] On the basis of such evidence, Congressman Ted Weiss, sponsor in the House of Representatives of H.R. 101, a national plan for conversion, feels that there is 'compelling evidence that military spending generates significantly fewer jobs than comparable spending in the civilian sphere' (Weiss, 1992, p. 156). Recently, the Congressional Budget Office (CBO) of the US Congress, using two different models of the US economy, concluded that the use of the peace dividend to reduce the federal deficit would benefit the economy in the long run, although it would lower employment as well as GDP in the short run. If the peace dividend were applied instead to increasing private or public consumption (by tax reduction or increasing federal civilian spending) the adverse short-term effects could be offset – but the CBO feels that this would harm the long-term promise of the deficit reduction (Congressional Budget Office, 1992, p. 9).

For Belgium, Proost et al. (1981, p. 599) concluded in a study using input-output techniques that the employment effect of Belgian military spending was 'rather weak', when compared to other categories of public spending, such as education and health caie. Similarly, Barker et al. (1991, pp. 355f.) concluded in the case of the UK that halving military spending in eight years would by itself increase unemployment by approximately 0.5 million, but that if the released spending was allocated to other government expenditures, the net effect would be to *decrease* unemployment by about the same number. These overall results hide various transition problems, but these need not be as difficult as in the past, since the armaments industry is already being restructured for other reasons. For Australia, Liew (1985) found in an input-output study that by shifting military expenditure to health, education, or welfare (or vice versa) would leave the Australian economy largely unchanged. However, with increasing emphasis on purchases of sophisticated weaponry and little expansion of the armed forces, he saw this changing in the future. Even a 'Buy Australian' procurement campaign would not be able to compensate for the loss in employment caused by such a shift in defense spending, unless Australia were willing to move more forcefully into arms exports. Studies for several other countries in Paukert & Richards (1991a) show similar results. On the whole, the evidence from national studies does not support the idea that high military spending is necessary for full employment. It is even possible to conclude from many of these studies that military spending may contribute in a small way to unemployment by reducing public expenditure in sectors that could generate more employment.

Regardless of the strictly economic effects, military spending may be *politically* more acceptable than other forms of public spending. In certain countries or at certain times, increasing military spending may have provided the *only* acceptable form of Keynesian state intervention. Baran & Sweezy (1966, p. 53) have developed this 'underconsumptionist' argument with reference to the US economy:

> This massive absorption of surplus in military preparations has been the key fact of postwar American economic history ... If military spending were reduced once again to pre-Second World War proportions, the nation's economy would return once again to a state of profound depression.

As late as the 1970s, comparing the situation in the 1930s with high unemployment and low arms spending with the opposite state of affairs (on both variables) in the postwar period might also inspire the idea that high military spending was responsible for the postwar boom. However, as Smith (1977, p. 65) pointed out, to complete the underconsumptionist view it would also be necessary to argue that military spending was motivated primarily by the desire to maintain high demand. In fact, some Marxists have argued precisely that military spending represents a form of covert capitalist planning.[6] Smith, however, rejected the underconsumptionist thesis. Using data for eight OECD countries for 1973 he found a high positive correlation between relative military spending and unemployment. Later, following a critical comment by Chester (1978), Smith (1978) concluded that this eight-country sample was not representative. Smith (1977) had also found that time-series evidence for the UK and the USA strengthened the case for military spending being a burden rather than a boost. In a longitudinal perspective, 'it is not military expenditure which has generated full employment, but war' (p. 68) – a view also given empirical support in Klein's study of the US economy (1971, p. 511). Of course, by the 1980s the simultaneous occurrence of rising military expenditure and rising unemployment in many industrialized countries made the prewar/postwar comparison less compelling as evidence for the traditional underconsumptionist argument.[7] The thesis lives on, however; for a recent defense of it see Pivetti (1992) and for a rejoinder Smith & Dunne (1993).

Other studies of military expenditure and employment have reached somewhat contradictory conclusions. Szymanski (1973) tested Baran & Sweezy's argument using rank-order correlations of military expenditure and economic performance for the 18 wealthiest capitalist countries over the period 1950-68. He found total government spending to be negatively related to unemployment, but found non-military expenditure to be less effective than military in reducing unemployment. This view, however, is contradicted by most national studies.

Dumas (1986, p. 174) posited a negative relationship between military expenditure and employment in arguing that the military burden in the USA 'surfaced mainly in the form of simultaneously high inflation and high unemployment, through the intervening variable of deteriorating productivity.' (We shall look at the influence of military spending on growth and productivity in the next two sections.)

Lindroos (1981) reviewed a great deal of national case material and concluded (pp. 155f.) that the arms industry tended to be capital-intensive and research-intensive, and while it might stimulate economic growth it was not efficient in creating growth. This he saw as one of the central arguments for conversion. Lindgren (1984, pp. 380f.), in a review of half a dozen studies, concluded that the results regarding military spending and employment are contradictory and that the relationship between the two is too complex to capture by simple correlation or regression. In other reviews Chan (1985, 1987) failed to find convincing evidence for the view that military spending promotes higher employment in the long run. He advocated research which would try to separate the short-term and the long-term effects. In his own correlational study of the OECD countries for 1961-80, Chan (1984) found high per capita levels of military spending to be associated with various indicators of deteriorating economic health. Unemployment was one of them, but that link was not strong. High *rates of increase* in military spending, on the other hand, were positively related to improving economic health.

Dunne (1986, 1991) in reviewing national conversion studies for seven industrialized countries for the ILO, found them so different in questions asked, types of models used, and in frameworks of analysis that they did 'not invite comparisons across countries'. In the same volume of ILO studies, Paukert & Richards (1991b) concluded that, in the Western industrialized countries at least, a limited share of total employment is generated by the military establishment, that any conflict between disarmament and employment was likely to be short-term, and that defense conversion could be seen as a particular case of industry conversion.

In a recent study of military spending and unemployment in the OECD countries, Dunne & Smith (1990) fault earlier studies of unemployment for not testing the impact of military expenditure, and earlier studies of military employment for not providing a consistent comparative framework. On the basis of longitudinal studies of the UK and the USA and cross-sectional and pooled analyses for eleven OECD countries, they conclude that the share of military expenditure does *not* seem to exert a significant influence on the unemployment rate. As a general conclusion, they suggest that in analyzing unemployment, no special account needs to be taken of military expenditure (p. 70).[8] (However, they do confirm Smith's earlier view that major wars do tend to generate full employment.) Of course, their conclusion does not imply that we can ignore (un)employment effects in the analysis of military expenditure, particularly in the short and medium term. Their conclusion is consistent with input-output analyses from a number of countries. In addition to those already cited, we might add that for Germany, even the drastic cuts in domestic and foreign military spending in the country after the Cold War were judged unlikely to have more than a marginal overall effect on employment, although they would entail considerable restructuring.[9]

Quite apart from national and cross-national effects, *local* employment problems are likely to be more severe than national ones. We return to this issue in Chapter 6.

2.3 Military Spending and Economic Growth

The case for the harmful effect of military spending on economic growth rests on the premise that the arms sector is unproductive and that a reallocation of resources to the civilian sector is likely to improve the performance of the economy. Lloyd Dumas, for instance, argues that the dogged pursuit of the worldwide arms race has 'undermined the productive competence and economic wellbeing of even the strongest and most developed economies', and that both 'our physical security and our economic wellbeing require that a significant fraction of the productive resources currently being poured into the militaries of the world be shifted to productive, civilian-oriented activity' (1989, p. 3).

Such a view is not novel, as concern about the costliness of military spending can be traced back to the classical economists. Adam Smith noted in his *Wealth of Nations* (1776) the increasing costs of providing weapons for war, and expressed views on how to organize a military defense and distribute the economic burden.[10] David Ricardo, who wrote during and in the immediate aftermath of the Napoleonic wars, was concerned with finding ways of restraining the government as well as war profiteers from embarking on military adventures detrimental to economic prosperity. Tax financing (with Parliamentary approval) was much to be preferred over loan financing because 'when the pressure of the war is felt at once, without mitigation, we shall be less disposed wantonly to engage in an expensive contest, and if engaged in it, we shall be sooner disposed to get out of it unless it was a contest of some great national interest' (Ricardo, 1820). Neither Smith nor Ricardo were iconoclasts in their views of defense like the French economist Jean-Baptiste Say, who made a sweeping attack on the economic uselessness of wars and raised an important issue in extending the military cost concept to include human capital, i.e. the loss of forgone earnings of war casualties: 'War costs more than its expense, it costs what it prevents from being learned' (Say, 1803, Book II, ch. XI, section 1).

More specifically, military spending is likely to hamper economic growth in at least three different ways:

First, it may decrease investment and thus negatively affect the renewal and expansion of civilian industry. This raises the issue whether military spending crowds out investment or consumption or uses resources otherwise left idle as underconsumptionists seem to imply.

Second, if military spending leads to lower employment, as argued in the previous section, labor resources will be utilized in an inefficient way.

Thirdly, military spending may create bottlenecks in the demand for highly qualified labor, and take resources away from civilian R&D resources, thereby impeding non-military innovation and growth.

On the other hand, it has also been claimed that military spending is conducive to economic growth. One basis for this view is the 'underconsumptionist' argument cited in the previous section. If military expansion leads to a fuller use of national resources, then it will support growth, even if the basic purpose of the military establishment is unproductive.

Another line of reasoning stresses that military research and development have significant spinoffs which lead to innovation and improved productivity in the civilian sector. This is probably what Harold Brown had in mind when, as US Secretary of Defense, he argued in 1980:

> Our research suggests that [military expenditures] are beneficial in the long term to the civilian economy, since much of the additional spending promotes domestic production in our most capital and technology intensive sectors.[11]

The spinoff argument is examined more closely in Section 2.4.

Cross-national comparisons indicate that industrialized countries with high military spending tend to have lower economic growth. An analysis of this kind is found, for instance, in *World Military and Social Expenditures* (Sivard, annual). The 1982 edition claimed that 'countries with the highest military burdens compete less well in world markets' (p. 23). In the accompanying chart, the military burden (military expenditure as a share of GDP) was compared with the annual growth rate in manufacturing productivity for the period 1960-80 for nine industrial countries. The chart showed a negative relationship between the two variables. We have calculated the correlation coefficient to be -0.81.[12] In a study from the Congressional Budget Office (1983, pp. 38-40) the same point is made: 'International comparisons seem to support the notion that high defense spending retards economic growth.' For the six major industrial nations, the correlations between military burden and growth of productivity were -0.73 (1960-70) and -0.53 (1970-79).

Szymanski (1973, p. 10) found military expenditure to be negatively correlated with economic growth for his sample as a whole and for the subgroup of the six largest economies. For the smaller 12 countries, he found a slight positive relationship between defense spending and growth.

Benoit (1973, pp. 147f), although primarily interested in developing countries, also performed a regression analysis of 19 developed countries for two separate periods between 1950 and 1965. He found an inverse, although not significant, correlation between military burden and growth of GDP. This he attributed largely to the competition between defense spending and investment.

In a more elaborate cross-sectional regression analysis of 17 industrialized countries for the period 1967-80, DeGrasse (1983, Chapter 2) found that countries with high military spending tended to invest less and experience lower growth in total manufacturing capital. This negative relationship held in separate analyses for the period prior to the 1973 energy crisis and the period after 1973. For the first period, but not for the second, this study also found a negative relationship between military burden and productivity growth. For both periods there was a weak negative relationship between military spending and growth of GDP. The report discussed the alternative possibility that the sluggish growth of advanced industrialized countries might be due to their economic maturity rather than their high military spending as such. A regression analysis found both notions to be consistent with the data, but military spending accounted for more of the variance than economic maturity. Finally, DeGrasse et al. (1983) found no evidence for a hypothesized negative relationship between military spending and civilian consumption. The study concluded that:

> while numerous factors influence economic performance, America's heavier military burden seems to have stifled investment, and reduced our economic and productivity growth over the last few decades. (p. 73)

As noted, Smith (1977) rejected the underconsumptionist argument. He concluded that military expenditure competes with investment and therefore reduces the growth rate. Smith argued that military expenditure is necessary in order to counter threats from national liberation movements and other challenges to the established order. But at the same time military expenditure has negative long-term consequences for the economy which serve to undermine the system it is intended to defend.[13]

In a later time-series analysis of 14 large OECD countries for 1954-73, Smith (1980a) found that reduced investment was a major opportunity cost of military expenditure. He found that the negative association between military expenditure and investment held up in time-series, cross-sectional, as well as pooled analyses and that the crowding-out was close to one to one. In a correlation analysis of 15 OECD countries for 1960-70 and 1973-78, Smith & Georgiou (1983) found a strong negative association between military expenditure and investment for both time periods, but an ambiguous relation between military expenditure and growth (negative in the first period, close to zero in the second). In a time-series analysis of the USA, the UK, and West Germany for 1954-78 they did not obtain very clear results for the relationship between military expenditure and growth.

In his correlational study of the OECD countries, Chan (1984) found high per capita levels of military spending to be associated with lower growth, while high *rates of increase* were associated with higher growth. These two patterns appeared to characterize, respectively, more mature industrial states and newly industrialized countries.

Finally, in our own analysis of 17 OECD countries for the period 1960-80, we found a negative correlation between the military burden and the rate of growth;

the figure was -0.23.[14] As a note of sobriety we reiterate that correlation does not show causation. In many of the studies reviewed above, Japan and West Germany, both fast-growing with a low military burden in the post-World War II period, exert a strong pull in the direction of a negative relationship between growth and military expenditures. The importance of these two countries in the world economy adds emphasis to the observation. There are, however, counterexamples of fast-growing countries with a high military burden, although not within the OECD. The most prominent 'anomalies' are South Korea, Taiwan, and to a lesser extent, Singapore.

Rothschild (1973) suggested that export-led growth may be hampered if high military expenditure leads to domestic consumption of technologically advanced goods which are in strong international demand. He proposed this in addition to the more common argument that military expenditure impedes growth by reducing investment. In a preliminary cross-sectional study of 14 OECD countries for 1956-70, he found this idea to be confirmed.

Longitudinal (diachronic, time-series) studies tend to yield the opposite result. The Congressional Budget Office Study (1983) cited above pointed out that time-series data on productivity do not support the view that defense spending retards economic growth. On the contrary, in looking at the three decades 1950-79, one finds for five of the six countries considered a *positive* relationship over time between the military burden and growth in manufacturing productivity; for the sixth country there is no relationship. The CBO report therefore concluded that 'elementary statistical tabulations provide mixed evidence on the relationship between defense spending and trends in productivity growth' (p. 38). The study further argued that no causal link can be inferred from these studies, since they do not isolate the effects of defense spending from other important factors, such as the accumulation of capital, the training of labor, the country's stage of development, etc. One of the UN reports on the economic and social consequences of disarmament has also acknowledged that in the past, high military spending has coincided with high rates of economic growth for some of the developed countries. But the same UN report also argued that this does not provide evidence for the positive role of high military spending. On the contrary, 'the causality was probably reversed, that is, higher military spending was made possible due to high rates of growth, and not vice versa' (United Nations, 1982, p. 41).

In our own analysis of 17 OECD countries for the period 1960-80 from which we have reported a negative cross-sectional correlation between the military burden and the rate of growth we found mostly *positive* correlations longitudinally by country. The correlations were positive for 13 countries (all above 0.3), including Japan, the USA, and the four major European powers; three correlations were negative and one was positive but close to zero.[15] The correlations were calculated over periods which consisted of a whole business cycle, in order to eliminate short-run variations in demand. The number of periods for each country varied from three to five (Cappelen et al., 1984a, pp. 31-36).

Thus, we find that for industrialized countries simple correlational analyses of the military burden and economic growth yield a consistent but also somewhat paradoxical result: cross-sectional analyses indicate a negative relationship, while longitudinal analyses point in the opposite direction. A weakness in the longitudinal studies just cited is that they have not included time-lags and that it is unreasonable to expect high defense spending to result in lower economic growth in the same time period. While investment may be curtailed immediately because of competition for funds, the effects on growth can only be expected later. Therefore, it is frequently argued that long-term effects are better measured by cross-national comparisons than by longitudinal comparisons for single countries and without time-lags. Recent developments in time-series analysis and 'co-integration' methods (Engle & Granger, 1987) show how long-term effects may be analyzed using longitudinal data, if certain time-series properties of the data are met.

In recent analysis and debate the causality issue has been faced more directly, based on Granger's (1969) operational definition of causality and its application by means of vector autoregression (VAR), introduced in a seminal contribution by Sims (1980). The VAR approach implies fewer preconceptions about the structure of the causal links than the traditional regression type econometric analysis. Kinsella (1990) analyzed the causal links in both directions between military spending, output (GNP), consumer prices, the rate of unemployment, and the interest rate using annual US data 1939-89. His carefully phrased conclusion was that there were no substantial causal links in either direction between military spending on the one hand and the price level, the rate of unemployment, and the rate of interest on the other. An immediate causal link between military spending and the output level could not be ruled out, but could not be ascertained from annual data. Baek (1991) criticized Kinsella's use of Sim's unrestricted VAR technique as atheoretical, and applied instead a more recent adaptation of the same methodology called structural VAR (or SVAR). Beak arrived at somewhat less definitive conclusions and also argued that the war years were better left out of the causal analysis.[16] Payne & Ross (1992) obtained confirmation of Kinsella's results of no corroborated causal links by using quarterly data, which – although covering a shorter period (1960-88) -provided longer time series and thereby a better basis for reaching conclusions on the causality issue. Obviously the discussion within this methodological framework is still at an early stage. Payne & Ross suggested that further analysis within the same framework ought to incorporate the open-economy nature of the US. Within the same methodological VAR framework Mintz, Huang & Heo (1992), using US data for 1955-80 in an analysis of disaggregated military expenditure, found that unemployment 'caused' military spending, but only for procurement, suggesting the interpretation that 'policy-makers use procurement expenditures to regulate unemployment' (p. 33). Other recent contributions by Huang & Mintz (1990, 1991) have aimed at more sophisticated modeling and estimation within the traditional single-equation regression approach. Huang & Mintz (1990) tackle the notorious multicollinearity of explanatory variables of economic growth by applying ridge regression, confirming earlier results of no significant trade-off between military spending and growth. Huang & Mintz (1991) try to distinguish 'externality' and 'productivity' effects of government expenditures upon the rest of the economy, distinguishing military from non-military expenditures. Their results are interpreted to confirm earlier findings of no direct defense-growth tradeoff while showing that non-military government expenditures do have positive externality effects and (almost significant) productivity effects.

We have focused here on studies of industrialized countries. Far greater controversy has surrounded the question of the effects of military spending on growth in developing countries. Benoit (1973, 1978) found, contrary to his own expectations and in contrast to his results for developed countries, a positive correlation between the military burden and economic growth for 44 developing countries for the period 1950-65. He explained this result by arguing that military infrastructure (roads, airports, etc.) would also benefit the civilian economy and thereby stimulate economic growth. In addition, the personnel trained by the military could later be employed in civilian sectors and increase labor productivity and growth. His conclusion was nevertheless very cautious: he suspected that the net growth effects of defense expenditure had been positive, 'but we have not been able to prove it' (Benoit, 1973, p. 4). Despite this caution his study has generally been interpreted as arguing for a causal link, and a large critical literature has developed. The burden of the evidence is now against the Benoit thesis.[17]

An interesting variation on this theme has been made by Weede (1983), who argues that the military contribution to growth is made not by military spending, but by 'military participation', particularly through national service. Military service teaches social discipline and thereby improves human capital, which in turns stimulates growth, and also decreases income inequality. Weede tested the effect of military participation. In a cross-sectional regression analysis of nearly 100 countries for 1960-77, he found that the military participation ratio (i.e. military personnel as a fraction of the working-age population) made a positive, if not critical, contribution to growth, while military spending as a share of GDP made no contribution at all. All of this, however, seems less relevant to developed countries, although it might shed some light on their economic history.

A famous historical argument about how military spending may weaken the economy of a hegemonic power was made by Kennedy (1987), who saw high military spending as part of an imperial overstretch. While the bulk of his acclaimed book is a historical study of the post-Renaissance period, he became an instant celebrity because of the concluding chapter in which he prophesied the eventual demise of the US and Soviet empires. His views on US defense spending were expressed as follows:

> If the United States continues ... to devote 7 percent or more of its GNP to defense spending while its major economic rivals, especially Japan, allocate a far smaller proportion, then *ipso facto* the latter have potentially more funds 'free' for civilian investment; if the United States continues to invest a massive amount of its R&D activities into military-related production while the Japanese and West Germany concentrate upon commercial R&D; and if the Pentagon's spending drains off the majority of the country's scientists and engineers from the design and production of goods for the world market ... it seems inevitable that the American share of world manufacturing will steadily decline, and also likely that its economic growth rates will be slower than in those countries dedicated to the marketplace and less eager to channel resources into defense. (p. 532)

Very similar views have been expressed by Dumas (1986) and by US industrial economists such as Ullmann (1983) and Melman (1983, 1987).

While Kennedy's views of US imperial overstretch remain controversial and have inspired a host of book-length rejoinders, his dim view of the future prospects of the Soviet Union came to pass rather more quickly than anyone had foreseen. But precisely because the Soviet military burden was so enormous, in a system with many other inefficiencies, his thesis was more suitable for the Soviet empire than for the US-led international system. In the longer run, US hegemony will certainly be challenged by Germany, Japan, and presumably by other Asian countries, but differences in relative military spending will probably play but a minor role (Gold & Adams, 1990).

A common shortcoming of many previous studies of military spending and growth is that they rest on weak theoretical underpinnings, do not control for third factors, and do not put forward a comprehensive model for explaining growth. Most economists share certain views as to which factors influence economic growth, as embodied in theoretical growth models. In the well-known Harrod-Domar model, for instance, the growth rate of GDP is a simple function of the saving or investment rate of the economy (i.e. investment as a share of GDP). If the saving rate is also closely associated with the military burden, there will be a correlation between the military burden and the growth rate of GDP. However, this bivariate correlation gives a biased impression of the effect of military spending on GDP growth, because the effect of the saving rate is not explicitly taken into account. Objections along these lines have played a role in the debate about Benoit's findings.

A few studies have attempted to develop a more systematic modeling framework for the study of military expenditure and growth. Faini et al. (1980) argued that the relevant variable is not the *level* of the military burden, but rather *changes* in its proportion of GDP. They analyzed the growth rate of GDP as a function of the growth of exports, population growth, growth rate of capital stock, GDP per capita, changes in capital inflow from abroad, and changes in arms spending relative to GDP. Analyzing 69 countries for the period 1952-70 they found changes in the military burden to have a positive but insignificant impact on the growth rate. This result was explained by suggesting that these countries may – at least for some periods of time – suffer from lack of effective civilian demand, which is compensated by military spending, canceling out the negative effect of spending in an unproductive sector. For the developing countries, increases in arms spending significantly *reduced* economic growth. In some contrast to the conclusions of Faini et al., Smith & Smith (1980) found no effect on growth in developing countries, while there was a significantly negative effect in the OECD countries. Their model consisted of three equations. The first was a production function including employment, capital stock, and a total factor productivity term. The second equation related changes in the capital stock to growth, military spending, and the rate of unemployment. According to the third equation, growth in total factor productivity (as measured by R&D as a percentage of GDP) was supposed to depend on military spending only. Thus the question of whether or not military spending is more efficient than private investment in promoting total factor productivity was not tested. The estimation results indicated that while the R&D effect of military spending was positive for the OECD countries, this positive effect was counteracted – and dominated – by a negative effect on investment of military spending; thus, military spending was associated with lower economic growth when both factors were taken into account. In a more recent cross-sectional article, Deger & Smith (1983) concluded that military expenditure had a small positive effect on growth through modernization but a larger negative effect through savings. The net effect on the growth rate was negative.

A different approach was taken by Leontief & Duchin (1983ab), using an input-output model of the world economy. Comparing a scenario for reduced growth in military spending to a baseline scenario essentially continuing present trends, they found that the former scenario led to increased growth in GDP in all of their seven regions of developed countries and in five out of their seven regions of developing countries. The additional GDP generated was modest (generally a few percent), but of course the degree of conversion in this scenario was also very modest. (The World Model used by Leontief & Duchin is described in Appendix B; our study using the World Model is reported in Chapter 5.)

In our own work on the OECD countries for the period 1960-80 (Cappelen et al., 1984ab), we combined cross-sectional and longitudinal analysis, using a model originally developed by Kaldor (1966) in an attempt to explain the slow rate of growth in the United Kingdom and further elaborated by Cornwall (1977). The model takes the manufacturing sector as an 'engine of economic growth' and postulates a linear relationship between the growth rate of GDP and the growth rate of manufacturing output. If we regard economic growth as a process of transformation of resources (as distinguished from the notion of balanced growth with increasing amounts of factors of production), the importance of manufacturing may be explained partly by its high level of productivity. When surplus agricultural labor is employed in manufacturing, there is an increase in the overall level of productivity in the economy; this creates more income, demand, and production. Furthermore, the manufacturing sector is characterized by increasing returns to scale, i.e. the growth of labor productivity increases when the growth of output increases (Verdoorn's law). A third factor is that the manufacturing sector produces goods that promote growth in the non-manufacturing sectors as well. New technology is embodied in new capital goods produced by the manufacturing sector, and their use increases the productivity of other sectors as well – as when fertilizers increase agricultural output or computers increase the productivity of the service sector. Finally, since the manufacturing sector is usually the most important producer of tradable goods, manufacturing growth is important in financing the growth of imports – assuming unchanged terms of trade.

To the Kaldor/Cornwall basic model we have added two more explanatory variables: the military burden and the gross investment ratio. Here we will not go into detail with the theoretical justification for the model, which is described fully in earlier publications (Cappelen et al., 1984ab). The structure of the model is depicted in a simple way by means of the arrow diagram in Figure 2.1.

Figure 2.1 A Growth Model for the OECD Countries

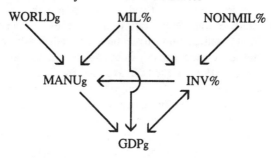

WORLDg is the annual growth of world exports of manufactured goods. MIL% and NONMIL% are military spending and non-military government final consumption, both relative to the gross domestic product. MANUg is the average annual growth rate of manufacturing output. INV% is the gross fixed capital formation relative to the gross domestic product. GDPg is the annual growth rate of the gross domestic product (averaged over a period covering a business cycle). A detailed description of the model and its derivation is given in Appendix B.

When the coefficients of the formal model were estimated, the military burden was found to have a very small but positive direct influence on growth in GDP, a stronger direct positive influence on manufacturing growth, and an even stronger negative influence on investment, as in Smith (1980a). Manufacturing growth and the investment rate in turn have a strong positive influence on GDP growth. Investment has only a slight direct influence on GDP growth, but a strong influence on manufacturing. The net effect of the military burden is that it has a negative overall effect on GDP growth for the sample as a whole, for a subsample of four large countries, and for a subsample of seven small stable democracies in Northern and Central Europe. For a subgroup of five Mediterranean countries, the net impact of the military burden on GDP growth was estimated to be slightly positive. These are, of course, the European countries which are closest in many ways to the developing countries. For the most modern economies, the net impact of the military burden is clearly detrimental to GDP growth. Non-military public spending also has a negative net impact on GDP growth, for the sample as a whole and for all the subgroups. For the whole sample the equation for GDP reads in reduced form:

$$GDPg = 4.64 + 0.36WORLDg - 0.14MIL\% - 0.24NONMIL\%$$

This may indicate that a simple transfer of military spending to other forms of government spending will not necessarily lead to increased growth. For the sample of small countries in Northern and Central Europe, the negative coefficient is smaller than for military spending. Hence it looks as if transfers to government non-military spending generally may increase growth (Cappelen et al., 1984b, pp. 370f.). The explanation for this may simply be that these small countries have very limited arms production and that military spending is therefore more import-demanding than other forms of public spending. Therefore, conversion improves the balance of payment in these countries and thus the possibility for stimulating investment and increasing growth.

In a follow-up study of four neutral European countries for the period 1960-87, Maneval et al. (1991) tested the same model but only on the basis of time series for the individual countries. Contrary to our study, no clear pattern emerged from the data. A critique by Gold (1990) argued that averages for a number of countries 'do not necessarily apply to any single country'. He argued that there were some discrepancies in the US case, but did not suggest an alternative model.

In evaluating studies of military spending and growth it is important to take note of how the models are specified, explicitly or implicitly. Faini et al. (1980) assume that *changes* in military spending affect *changes* in GDP, while others try to explain changes in GDP by the *level* of the military burden. Most studies relate the *share* of military spending in relation to GDP to the *growth* of GDP. Of these three 'models', the second is doomed to failure in normal circumstances because the level of military spending in constant prices has a trend-like development (i.e. it is a stationary series after taking the first difference or dividing it with GDP), while the growth rate of GDP is a stationary variable. Regressing these two variables after including other possible 'explanatory' variables that are stationary will normally produce an insignificant estimate of the link between the two variables. The only way to arrive at a significant relation between changes in GDP and the level of military spending is by including at least one other variable which has a trend-like development and which correlates highly with military spending, so that a linear combination of these two variables is stationary.

Fagerberg (1988) has constructed a model where military expenditure enters the investment equation in the same way as in Cappelen et al. and Smith. He confirms that military expenditure crowds out investment, even to a greater extent than found in the earlier studies. The rest of his model is not directly comparable with the other studies. His results for the net effect of military spending are not significantly different from zero; they also depend on the method of estimation.

2.4 Growth Effects of Military R&D: The Question of Spinoffs

A common argument for the growth-inducing effect of military spending is that military R&D has significant spinoffs (or spillovers) to the civilian sectors – that research in the military field yields civilian applications as a byproduct. Radar, computers, and electronics are often cited as examples. Two MIT scientists have stated the case for spinoffs clearly in these terms:

> Missile guidance systems were an early source of support for integrated circuit development; requirements for satellite-tracking radars have supported the development of surface acoustic-wave technology and charge-coupled devices, as well as modern signal-processing techniques ... Finally, we should mention such significant second-order developments as radio and radar astronomy, microwave spectroscopy, and instrumentation for earth resources satellites and for modern health care, all of which are heavily dependent on concepts and components derived from military electronics.[18]

Specific examples of spinoff include commercial aircraft: the Boeing 707 was developed from the B-47 bomber and the 747 was developed from the losing design submitted for the C-5 cargo plane (Tirman, 1984b, p. 18).

A variant of the spinoff argument is that even when innovations are not made originally through military R&D, the military establishment provides the extensive 'first use' of a new technology which makes it commercially viable. The transistor has been mentioned as an example where heavy purchases for military purposes led to an improved product and reduced prices (DeGrasse, 1984, pp. 77f).

Spinoff from the military to the civilian sector was also used as an argument for the Strategic Defense Initiative. For instance, John McTague, former Deputy Science Advisor to the US President, has argued that 'the research being conducted under the Strategic Defense Initiative is right now rolling back the frontiers for continued economic growth' (McTague, 1987, p. 7). It was also claimed that this made West European participation in the program necessary.[19] European participants would gain insight into modern technology which would be difficult to obtain otherwise. This, it was held, would strengthen the high-technology sectors in Western Europe. In the 1980s the USA became increasingly restrictive in releasing sensitive data from R&D and in exporting civilian technology which could be exploited for military purposes. These restrictions made it especially important to have good relations to the US military-industrial establishment. With the end of the Cold War, this whole line of argument has become less important, although there are still restrictions on exports of technology, for instance to aspiring nuclear powers.

The basic case against spinoffs is that military R&D results in crowding-out of civilian R&D expenditure and that the latter is economically more productive. Qualified scientists and engineers are attracted to the defense sector and become scarce or too expensive to civilian industry. In a frank statement in 1987 the UK government explained the crowding-out effect of military R&D:

> Britain's resources of qualified scientists and engineers, and the skilled manpower supporting them, are not inexhaustible ... defence and civil work are in competition for the same skills, and it would be regrettable if defence work became such an irresistible magnet for the manpower available that industry's ability to compete in the international market for civil high technology products became seriously impaired.'[20]

Spinoffs do not, of course, occur on a one-way street from military R&D to civilian products. Inventions made in civilian R&D can produce spinoffs for the military sector as well. An important example is the development of metallic paint to shield microwave ovens, later exploited for the military purpose of creating a radar-absorbing surface for stealth aircraft and missiles (SIPRI, 1983, p. 215). The COCOM restrictions on selling militarily useful technology to the East are evidence for a firm belief within the Western national security establishments of the dangers involved in such reverse spinoffs. The US military establishment benefits domestically from the advanced civilian sector. Indeed, Christensen (1989, pp. 22f.) argued there are probably more spinoffs from the civilian sector. Military production emphasizes extreme performance rather than mass production, essential for success in civilian markets. Military R&D focuses more on *product R&D* than *process R&D*, while the latter is more important for productivity (Griliches, 1987, p. 34). And military procurement cycles tend to be very long (Zegweld & Enzing, 1987, p. 110), while commercial profitability requires short time-lags between invention and commercialization. Secrecy also impedes spinoffs from military R&D. The greater openness of civilian R&D, including free publication, encourages institutional cooperation and diffusion of knowledge. With the rapid growth of civilian R&D which we shall document in the next section such reverse spinoffs will increasingly dominate the traditional spinoffs from military R&D to the civilian sector.

The yield of publicly-funded R&D projects has been questioned in several econometric studies in the USA by Griliches, Lichtenberg and others,[21] which have found much higher positive returns to privately financed R&D than to federally financed R&D. These studies did not specifically single out military R&D, but since such a large part of US federal R&D is military these studies point in the direction of higher returns to civilian R&D than to military R&D. Other studies, however, have emphasized the positive role of Japan's Ministry of International Trade and Industry (MITI) in promoting the growth of knowledge-intensive industries (DeGrasse, 1984, p. 95). This role has been favorably compared to the role of the Department of Defense in the US economy (Tirman, 1984c, p. 221).

Udis (1978) interviewed various professionals in Western European military institutions and in firms producing military goods. Their opinions were divided. Some believed that military and civilian production are quite similar in many fields and that substantial spinoffs occur. Others were more skeptical and felt that the spinoff argument was frequently used as an excuse to justify high defense spending.

Dumas cites a 1974 report of a committee of the US National Academy of Engineering. While not commenting directly on military R&D, this report was very critical of the alleged spinoffs from federal R&D programs, of which military programs constituted a major share:

> With a few exceptions the vast technology developed by federally funded programs since World War II has not resulted in widespread spinoffs of secondary or additional applications of practical products, processes and services that have made an impact on the nation's economic growth, industrial productivity, employment gains, and foreign trade. (Cited in Dumas, 1981, p. 3)

A major weakness of the spinoff argument is that it builds on selected examples. With military R&D after World War II a major share of all publicly-funded R&D, it would be surprising if no examples of benefits to the civilian sector could be found. A convincing case for spinoffs would have to rest on some form of proportionality in the civilian benefits derived from this enormous appropriation of science and technology resources.

Two case studies of the US nuclear power and semiconductor industries argue that, in these areas, heavy military funding has been less than successful in promoting innovation. Commercial nuclear power was led down the wrong trail by pursuing a design especially developed by the US Navy for submarines

(Thompson, 1984). In electronics, the three military services backed – each with heavy funding – three different approaches to the problem of miniaturizing electronic components, none of them successful. Meanwhile, a commercial firm developed the integrated circuit – without military funding. Later, the development of a process for the mass production of silicon chips was also achieved without military funding. As with the transistor, the military provided a mass market for the production of these inventions. However, it has long been argued that military spending is less necessary even in this role since 'semiconductors have become so cheap and standardized that they can be profitably used in a wide array of civilian products'. Hence it is civilian rather than the military demand that primarily stimulates further technological development (DeGrasse, 1984, p. 93).

The importance of spinoffs from military production has probably declined because of a highly specialized military production with fewer civilian applications (Chalmers, 1985, p. 120). Military technology may become so complex that it does not even work very well for the military establishment itself; it becomes 'baroque technology' (Kaldor, 1982). But even if it does work for its primary purpose, cost considerations widen the gap between engineering feasibility and operational practice in the civilian sector compared with the military sector. The military sector is characterized by highly sophisticated production and small quantities, while civilian products need to be inexpensive and are often produced in large quantities. Nuclear submarines and supersonic aircraft are two examples of well-established military products with scant promise of civilian use.

Chalmers (1985, pp. 120f) has examined the evidence for spinoffs in British military industry and argues that at least for some military R&D they may actually be negative. Attempts to make use of spinoffs from military R&D have led to investments in civilian sectors which in themselves are uneconomic and in need of government subsidies. Major examples are the aerospace industry and the nuclear power industry. Both have received large subsidies and both derive, at least partly, from Britain's strong emphasis on military R&D in these fields. In both industries US firms have a dominant position, and Chalmers concludes that military and military-related production requires large resources. Small and medium-sized countries may lose in this competition; they are probably better off researching in areas where they have a long-term comparative advantage. Japan and (West) Germany have avoided the aerospace industry, concentrating instead on consumer electronics – with impressive results.

In a recent quantitative study of military R&D, Buck, Hartley & Hooper (1993) provide new estimates of UK military research resources and discuss the evidence for the crowding-out of government-funded civil R&D. Within a cointegration framework Buck et al. find 'no simple and naive form of crowding-out between government-funded UK defense and civil R&D expenditure' (p. 170). The time span in this investigation covers a period of falling military R&D efforts. The authors duly recognize difficulties related to the definition of research expenditures and data shortcomings in evaluating crowding-out hypotheses. The crowding-out issue can hardly be separated from the issue of enterprise conversion. When enterprises lose defense contracts with a substantial R&D element, what do they do? To replace military contracts with civilian government contracts calling upon the same skills is not an easy task. Smith (1993) discusses British experiences and emphasizes that the reason why enterprise conversion often fails may be that the organisational skills called for in defense contracts ('performance maximization') differ from what is required in the civilian market place ('cost minimization').

Lerner (1992) tried to test hypotheses about spinoff and crowding-out effects by looking at a vast US survey of scientists and engineers. He found that there was substantial mobility between military and civilian activities, particularly for the industries with the least defense activities and with dual-use technologies. The switch from civilian to defense activity was more likely to be accompanied by unemployment and less likely to be accompanied by a substantial pay rise than mobility in the opposite direction. Lerner concluded by expressing some concern about the effects of projected cuts in military R&D, but did not discuss a potential program of public countermeasures which presumably could compensate for the negative effects.

Similar points were raised at the first Chinese conference on conversion issues (Chai & Zhang, 1992) following the massive changes in the military-industrial complex of China towards a more commercial arms exports policy and large-scale conversion to civilian products both for import substitution and export promotion. Wang (1992), in particular, noted advantages and disadvantages China's military industrial enterprises were facing in the conversion towards civilian products. While the official statements on this policy tend to gloss over the difficulties, Wang gives an unusually succint expression of the problems. After noting the advantages the Chinese defense industrial enterprises have in comparison with civilian ones by the higher proportion of scientists and engineers, the more intensive use of R&D, more integrated production, strict quality control, and the hi-tech character of many of their products (Wang, 1992, p. 215), he also notes the disadvantages:

(1) As the defence enterprises have been run in a highly mandatory planning system for a long period, their motivation for competing in the market is weak.
(2) The defence enterprises are usually less conscious in cost and profit, and the cost management system in these enterprises is usually far from perfect.
(3) As most of them were long in a self-reliance system, they are less intended to cooperate and combine with the companies outside the defence fields.
(4) The team of market research in the defence company is usually not strong enough.

Bergsgard et al. (1989) studied the economic effects of military R&D in Norway, using the electronics industry as a case and relying on interviews as the main source of information. Military contracts were found not to have much effect on the internal organization of a company. Most companies regarded the military like any other customer, and argued that the oil industry had at least as exacting requirements. In most cases, technology transfer within the company was not impeded because of secrecy. Military contracts were hard to obtain, but once established they provided a long-term stable source of income. On the marketing side, military contracts were a sign of prestige with a positive effect in civilian markets. Bergsgard et al. also found that a number of new companies were established in the 1950s and 1960s as a result of military R&D. Several such companies were off-shoots from the Norwegian Defence Research Establishment, which held a dominant position in Norwegian electronics research, had close contact with the universities, and was eager to transfer its new inventions into industrial production. The relative importance of military R&D was, however, regarded as declining and after 1967 this study could not find any new examples of electronics companies originating from military R&D. Finally, with regard to the transfer of products, processes, and basic knowledge, the results of the study were ambiguous. Transfers of process technology had taken place in connection with Norwegian subcontracts for foreign companies, for instance in the F-16 fighter aircraft program, but transfer of basic knowledge through military R&D now seems to be less important. Job mobility from military R&D to civilian industry seemed to be high and would imply some transfer of knowledge.

In a case study of the introduction of servo technology in Norway after World War II, Wicken (1988b) found that in the semi-industrialized conditions in Norway at the time Norwegian industry was very slow to pick up the new technology. By the mid-1950s only the Norwegian Defence Research Establishment (NDRE) was conducting advanced research in servo technology. This can be interpreted as a result of 'demand pull', or the lack of such (there was no demand for control equipment from Norwegian industry), but also as a result of the NDRE sucking up the few qualified Norwegian scientists in this area. In effect, the military sector contributed to the transfer of high technology to the civilian sector.

Several studies emphasize the important role of small firms in the process of innovation. These are generally not the kind of firms which receive the greatest support from the military. Large firms with major defense contracts tend to be risk minimizers, rather than innovators.[22]

Dumas (1986, p. 184) comments on a deteriorating 'patent balance' for the USA in the period 1966-73. Foreign patents in the USA increased while US patents abroad decreased, and this development seemed to continue in the 1970s. Dumas blames the high share of military R&D for this. One problem with this argument is that military R&D in the USA stagnated throughout the entire period 1963-80. During 1966-73 military R&D fell, in absolute terms as well as relative to civilian R&D. The trend may, on the other hand, be explained by a long-term deterioration of US innovative capacity because of continuous high spending on military R&D.

The most fundamental objection to the spinoff argument, however, lies in the unpredictability of the spinoffs. In deciding on the desirability of an R&D program it seems more prudent to evaluate only the direct costs and benefits. Lester Thurow has put this point succinctly: 'Hoping that a solution for a known problem will come from some project focused on a completely different goal makes no sense at all' (Thurow, 1978, p. 69). He goes on to argue that the benefits of spinoffs should be ignored in allocating research funds, as should the prospects of multiplier effects. Since all R&D projects produce approximately the same multiplier effects per dollar, such multipliers do not help to differentiate military from civilian projects.

As a general rule it is more efficient to use money directly on a civilian R&D project, instead of hoping for unintended and unpredictable bonuses from military R&D projects. Military R&D is carried out for military reasons; chance byproducts to the civilian sector can at best provide a marginal justification for such programs.

Military R&D – like any military activity – might be beneficial in an economy with considerable unutilized resources. Any alternative use of those resources would have zero value. This is hardly the case with military R&D, however. Military R&D competes with civilian R&D for highly qualified personnel. Even when unemployment is high, there may be a shortage of personnel required in the military establishment, such as computer engineers or electrical engineers. Thus an expansion within military R&D may cause bottlenecks in the civilian sector. Fewer are left to teach in the universities and to work on product innovations in civilian industries. To quote Thurow again:

> If the brightest engineers in Japan are designing video recorders and the brightest engineers in the United States are designing MX missiles, then we shouldn't find it surprising that they conquer the video market.[23]

Or, for that matter, that the USA corners the market for MX missiles.

2.5 Military R&D and Growth: Quantitative Studies

The economic performance of countries with different levels of military R&D spending can be compared cross-nationally, as has been done for military spending generally. However, we are aware of only a few cross-national assessments involving military R&D spending. Before turning to these, it may be useful to look briefly at the postwar trends in civilian and military R&D spending. Given the technological character of the East-West arms race, many have attributed great importance to military R&D not only as a driving force in that race but also as an increasingly important element in science and technology generally (Thee, 1986, p. 104). Yet, as Figure 2.2 shows, military R&D grew much less rapidly than civilian R&D through most of the Cold War. The idea that military R&D consumes the lion's share of R&D spending generally, probably derives from a narrow focus on *public* R&D spending, and particularly in the United States.

DeGrasse (1984, p. 126) presents data for productivity growth in manufacturing industries and military and civilian R&D efforts relative to GDP. Six countries are investigated for the period 1970-79. His chart shows that countries with highest military R&D (the USSR, the USA, the UK) have the slowest productivity growth, while countries with lower military R&D (West Germany, France, Japan) have higher productivity growth. The relationship between civilian R&D and productivity is less clearcut. DeGrasse argues that the negative relationship between military R&D and productivity growth can be explained partly by the low share of military R&D spent on basic research. This share was only 3% in the USA from the early 1960s to the early 1980s. He considers basic research important for broad innovations and productivity growth .

DeGrasse's empirical finding is borne out by our own data. Table 2.1 gives a fourfold classification of postwar economic growth (1964-83) by the level of

Figure 2.2 Civilian and Military R&D Expenditures 1963-84 for Thirteen OECD Countries (USD Million, 1975 Prices and Purchasing Power Parities)

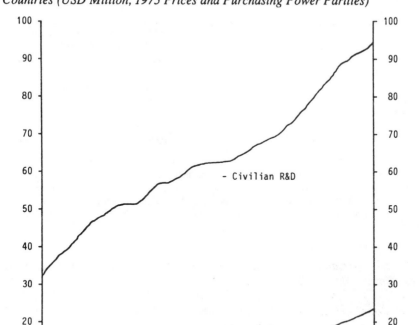

Source: Gleditsch, Cappelen & Bjerkholt (1988), p. 210, based on OECD statistics

military R&D spending (as a percentage of manufacturing value-added) for the same period. There is a clear negative relationship between the two variables, although most of the correlation is accounted for by the four outliers: Japan, West Germany, the USA, and the UK.

The division into high and low on the two axes in Table 2.1 is made at the arithmetic mean of the extreme values. A scatter diagram of the relationship reveals that Japan, the Federal Republic of Germany, Sweden, the UK, and the USA lie close to a regression line with a negative slope, while Canada, Finland, and Norway lie clustered together off to the side.

The longitudinal relationship between R&D and economic growth was not studied by DeGrasse. For our own data, the correlations are given in Table 2.2. For civilian R&D, five out of the eight correlations are positive, whereas for military R&D the correlations with productivity are mostly negative (six out of eight countries). The three negative (and thus anomalous) correlations for civilian R&D are smaller than those for military R&D for the same countries.

Table 2.1 Publicly Financed Military R&D as a Share of Manufacturing Value Added by Average Growth of Total Factor Productivity, Eight OECD Countries, 1964-83

		Military R&D as Percentage of Manufacturing value-added	
		Low	High
Average annual growth in	High	Japan Germany, Fed. Rep. Sweden	
manufacturing productivity	Low	Canada Finland Norway	UK USA

Correlation: gamma for grouped data = -1.0; r for ungrouped data = -0.51.

Sources: Total factor productivity and Manufacturing value-added: Christensen & Torvanger (1986). Military R&D: Mainly from OECD statistics, supplemented by national statistics for a few countries and other sources. For a detailed list of sources, see Gleditsch, Cappelen & Bjerkholt (1986), Appendix II, pp. 55-61

Table 2.2 Correlations between R&D Spending and Growth of Factor Productivity over Time, Eight OECD Countries, 1964-81 (r)

| | Correlation between growth of Total factor productivity and | |
Country	Military R&D in % of GDP	Civilian R&D in % of GDP
Canada	-0.92	-0.43
Finland	-0.83	0.61
Germany, Fed. Rep.	-0.76	0.87
Japan	-0.42	-0.33
Norway	0.77	0.64
Sweden	-0.87	0.77
UK	0.48	0.25
USA	-0.91	-0.55

Sources: See Table 2.1

Thus, unlike the case with military burden and growth, the cross-sectional and longitudinal correlations do not point in the opposite direction. This strengthens our confidence in the empirical relationship. However, it is still a weakness of these analyses that they do not build on a theory-based model.

An attempt at a model-based analysis was made by Christensen & Torvanger (1986). Their model sought to estimate the effects of military R&D and civilian R&D on 'total factor productivity growth' (TFP). This latter term was defined as the residual in a constant returns to scale production function in labor and capital. TFP was then modeled by assuming a relation between the capital stock of civilian and military R&D. Using the same data as in Tables 2.1 and 2.2, they performed separate cross-sectional, time-series, and pooled analyses. In the time-series analyses, using their first model they found military R&D to have significant positive influence on TFP for two countries and negative influence for two. Their second model yielded mixed results: a negative correlation for four countries. In the cross-section analyses there were also few significant coefficients. Using the second model, they found military R&D to have a significant positive influence on TFP in the periods 1964-69 and 1974-76 and a negative influence in the period 1977-80. Surprisingly, the coefficients for civilian R&D were largely negative. A plausible interpretation for this finding is that civilian R&D data include basic as well as applied research, whereas military R&D consists mainly of applied research. Thus, the comparison is biased in favor of military R&D; a 'fairer' comparison would be between the applied parts of civilian and military R&D. However, the available data do not permit such disaggregation.

Some authors discuss 'growth-oriented' R&D as a separate category, excluding not only military R&D, but also, for example, medical R&D. It has been shown that such growth-oriented R&D has stagnated in the USA, and this might explain the slow growth.[24] Data are not available for enough countries to permit a comparative study, so we must end this section on a somewhat inconclusive note.

2.6 War and Productivity

While few researchers in this area would argue that military spending is *beneficial* for the economy, there is a widespread sense that whether military spending is harmful or beneficial many other factors are more significant for economic growth. Gold (1990, p. 77), for instance, maintains that 'the economic success of Japan is largely the result of factors other than the size of its defense burden', such as Japan's high rate of capital formation, its highly educated labor force, its ability to adapt foreign technology, and its unique business-government partnership.

Many of the studies comparing the defense burden and productivity place at the extremes countries which were on opposite sides of World War II. In the chart used by Sivard, for instance, countries which lost the war (mainly) to the USA – i.e. (West) Germany, Italy, and Japan – had average manufacturing growth rates 1960-80 of about 6.5%. Those which were occupied but suffered little war damage (Denmark and France) had average growth rates of 6%. Sweden which stayed out of the war entirely, also had a high growth rate of 5%. The low performers are those Western countries which fought the war to victory (the USA, Canada, and the UK, with growth rates averaging 3%). The data for the growth of GDP used in our own study (Cappelen et al., 1984ab) show that the war losers had an average growth rate of 5.0%, those that were occupied 4.9%, those that stayed outside the war 4.6%, and the victors (the USA and the UK) 3.0%. This suggests that the long-term economic effects of war may be more important than the short-term effect of peacetime defense spending.

Boulding (1986) has argued that wars of conquest do not pay off very well for the conquering power. The contrast between the victors and the vanquished in war has been analyzed by Organski & Kugler (1980), who pointed to a 'Phoenix effect' which permits the defeated countries to catch up with their victors in less than two decades and sometimes even to surpass them. Organski & Kugler suggest that we do not know why this effect occurs, but suggested that it may be related to the motivation to rebuild which improves the work ethic of the population of a defeated country. Kahn (1979) and Weede (1983) have suggested that the work ethic also can be improved by a strong outside threat to national security, as exemplified by the economic miracles of South Korea and Taiwan. Olson (1982) explained the Phoenix effect by referring to the destruction of social rigidities created by the accumulation of institutionalized special interests.

Thus it may be an economically efficient strategy to conduct a war which destroys a substantial part of the means of production, and then to receive substantial aid to rebuild the economy.[25] However, a political elite which loses a war is quite likely to lose power after the war and it does not seem very likely that such a series of moves would be deliberately pursued by any country.[26]

*

Summing up this chapter, we note that the main thrust of the literature on the economic effects of military spending is that the military establishment represents a diversion of resources away from activities which could lead to higher employment and greater economic growth. However, the results are not always completely clearcut and there is a lack of model-based studies. The main objective of this book is to subject the Norwegian case to closer scrutiny. With this end in mind we now start with an examination of the military sector in Norway.

Notes

1. General surveys of the economic effects of military spending in peacetime are found in Cappelen et al. (1984a), Chan (1985, 1987), Isard & Anderton (1992b), Lindgren (1984, 1988), Mosley (1985), Renner (1991), UNIDIR (1993), as well as a series of UN reports from 1962 onwards, listed under United Nations in our list of references. For a comprehensive but already dated bibliography of work in English, see Hartley & Hooper (1990a). Recent useful collections of articles include Bischak (1991), Chan & Mintz (1992), Chatterji & Forcey (1992), Isard & Anderton (1992a), and Mintz (1992). More uneven, but with some useful contributions, is Brunn et al. (1992). Good overviews and case studies of arms industry and industrial conversion are found in Anthony et al. (1991), Wulf (1993), and Paukert & Richards (1991a). Useful surveys of conversion research and peace economics in German and French respectively are found in Köllner & Huck (1990) and Fontanel (1993). Hartley & Sandler (1990) contains an international survey of the determinants of defense spending and Mintz (1992) is a collection of articles on the political economy of US defense spending.

2. For studies of the effect of arms spending on inflation see Mosley (1985, Chapter 6) and Starr et al. (1984).

3. For studies of the effect of arms spending on the income distribution see Abell (1990, 1994).

4. Renner (1991), p. 15; cited from UNIDIR (1993), p. 23. Renner builds in turn on data from US ACDA (annual) and, for military industry, on Wilke & Wulf (1986) and other sources. For earlier estimates, see Renner (1989), p. 10; Renner (1990), p. 13. Updated figures for employment in arms industry can be found in Wulf (1993), Table 1.1, pp. 14-15. The figures for the 1990s indicate a decline for most countries. Wulf acknowledges that many of his figures are 'rough estimates only'. The table provides no total but on p. 13 the author indicates a world total for arms industry employment at 15 million, down from a 1980s peak of 16 million. Since such totals are heavily dependent on estimates for the former Soviet Union and China, they remain highly uncertain.

5. The US Department of Labor Studies are cited in Lindroos (1981), p. 116. A number of other US studies are cited in Mosley (1985), Ch. 5. All the studies point in the same direction, although there is some dispute about the number of jobs lost through military spending.

6. In particular, Cypher (1974, 1987) and a series of articles by the same author. Cf. also Reich (1972). In his historical study of World War II, Milward (1977, p. 4) argues that Germany and Japan 'were influenced in their decisions for war by the conviction that war might be an instrument of economic gain'.

7. Much earlier, Weidenbaum (1964, p. 173), had also pointed out that an 80% demobilization after World War II occurred with no increase in employment. More recently Alexander (1994) has argued that the 1945-46 demobilization is not a viable model for what would happen today, since there was a tremendous pent-up civilian demand and that most women who had been mobilized for defense industry and other non-combatant work during the war once again became housewives without being registered as unemployed.

8. This was also the conclusion of the section on employment in a recent survey by Isard & Anderton (1992b), p. 24.

9. Kiy & Löbbe (1990). Cf. also Brömmelhörster (1991), p. 16.

10. For this and the following two references we have relied on Kennedy (1975), pp. 23-26, p. 29, and p. 32. Cf. also Goertzel (1985).

11. Secretary of Defense Harold Brown in testimony before the US Senate Budget Committee, 27 February 1980; cited from DeGrasse (1983), p. 55. DeGrasse also indicates that three other US defense secretaries had made similar statements in the preceding decade.

12. Japan and the USA are extreme outliers in the chart. When we remove the USA we obtain a correlation coefficient of -0.59, and when Japan is also removed r drops to -0.48.

13. Cf. Smith (1977), p. 76. See also the ensuing debate, Chester (1978), Hartley & McLean (1978), and Smith (1978).

14. Cappelen et al. (1984a), p. 17; (1984b), p. 367.

15. Ibid.

16. In a rejoinder Kinsella (1991) accepted some of Baek's points, but remained skeptical of Baek's imposition of theoretical presuppositions.

17. For critiques of the Benoit thesis, see Ball (1981, 1983) and references therein. For more recent model-based studies see Adams & Gold (1992), Biswas & Ram (1986), Chowdury (1991), Deger & Smith (1983), Faini et al. (1984), Grobar & Porter (1989), and Lim (1983).

18. Dinneen & Frick (1977), pp. 82f.

19. Cf. Christensen (1989, 1990). A moderate version of the case for West European participation in SDI is found in a report to the Norwegian Prime Minister's Office (Ministry of Foreign Affairs, 1985).

20. UK Ministry of Defence (1987), para 522, quoted from Buck, Hartley & Hooper (1993), p. 162.

21. Cf. Terleckyj (1974), Griliches & Lichtenberg (1984), and Lichtenberg (1988).

22. Cf. Gansler (1980, p. 101); Tirman (1984b, p. 19); Moe (1985).

23. Lester Thurow in Los Angeles Times, 10 July 1983. Quoted from Chalmers (1985), p. 122.

24. See Mosley, 1985, pp. 75f. for a review of such studies.

25. While Organski & Kugler (1980, pp. 132f, 142ff.) report evidence for the Phoenix effect, they reject the notion that aid from the winners to the losers plays an important role in the recovery.

26. In the novel and movie The Mouse that Roared the Grand Duchy of Fenwick declared war on the USA precisely in order to exploit the effect of aid after being defeated. Unfortunately, the declaration of war was misplaced in the Department of State, and when the Grand Duchy attacked it won the war – with unforeseen and amusing consequences (Wibberley, 1955).

3

The Norwegian Military Sector

3.1 Towards a Peaceful Corner of Europe

The Nordic countries today form a peaceful part of the world. But this has not always been the case. The military establishment has played an important part in the national history of these countries, as in any other part of Europe.

Historians disagree as to *when* it becomes reasonable to speak of a Norwegian nation. Traditionally, Norway's unification is said to have taken place some time in the 880s – the exact year is in dispute – when Harald Fairhair defeated other local Viking kings and chieftains, winning a decisive victory in the battle of Hafrsfjord. By then he had united most of Western and Central Norway under his rule. Over the next several centuries a succession of kings and royal pretenders battled each other regularly for regional and national leadership, with some intervention from Denmark and from pretenders who had sought refuge abroad. Centralized royal power increased, from the eleventh century under the banner of Christianity. In 1387 Norway entered into a personal union with Denmark, which Sweden joined two years later. After a protracted struggle, Sweden finally withdrew completely from the union in 1521, but Norway remained in what was increasingly becoming a center-periphery relationship. Norway had been seriously weakened by the Black Death in 1349-50, losing up to one-third of its population, although the causes of the long-term decline continue to be debated. Denmark did not have to take military action in order to discipline or pacify its Northern province, but there were several wars between Denmark/Norway and Sweden, including wars with military action on Norwegian territory.

In 1814 Denmark found itself on the losing side in the Napoleonic wars. The Congress of Vienna awarded Norway to Sweden, which had fought briefly on the winning side. Norway thereupon declared its independence and passed its own liberal constitution. Independence quickly yielded to union with Sweden, but virtually the entire constitution remained in force, and Norway achieved considerable home rule. In 1905 Norway unilaterally ceded from the union and after two referenda gained full independence with a Danish prince as King. The secession followed a period of increasing tension and arming on both sides. There was some belligerent talk at the time of independence, but the more conciliatory elements prevailed on both sides.

After independence Norway, like the other Nordic countries, sought to pursue a policy of neutrality. This was successful in World War I, when the three independent Nordic countries managed to stay out of the European war (Finland did not become independent until after the war). It was less successful in World War II, when Denmark and Norway were invaded simultaneously on 9 April 1940. During the war the Norwegian government took up residence in London, and strong ties were formed between the British government and the Norwegian government in exile. Military cooperation became close at all levels. After liberation in 1945, Norway nevertheless resumed a quasi-neutral policy of 'bridgebuilding', coupled with strong support for the newly formed United Nations and low emphasis on rearmament.

With the intensification of the Cold War, the bridgebuilding policy came under increasing strain. The Prague coup in February/March 1948 and Soviet pressure on Finland were followed by rumours that Norway might be 'the next country on the list' for Soviet expansion. Military collaboration increased between Norway and major Western powers, in particular with the United Kingdom. Norway joined NATO as a founding member in April 1949.

The origins of the Norwegian military establishment go back beyond the 'Danish period'. In the Viking age, chieftains would regularly raise small armed bands to man warships and raid neighboring communities, even other countries. These raids eventually brought the Vikings as far afield as the Mediterranean, the interior of Russia and the Black and Caspian Seas (sailing their longboats on the Volga, the Dniepr, and other major rivers), Iceland, Greenland, and North America. Norse settlers at various times between the eighth and the tenth centuries controlled areas as far apart as Kiev, Rostov, the British Isles, Normandy, Iceland, and Greenland. Military power was extensively used in nation-building, and in fighting civil wars and wars between the Nordic countries. In the 1260s 'Norwegian' reign reached its maximum extent with Greenland, Iceland, the Faeroes, the Hebrides, the Isle of Man, the Orkneys and the Shetlands all under the Norwegian king. Several of these possessions followed Norway into the union with Denmark, remaining as Danish possessions until this century.

In the seventeenth century Sweden rose to become a major military power in Europe, fighting not only in Scandinavia but also on the Continent and to the East (with Muscovy, later Russia). Denmark, too, had ambitions beyond its present territory, and Norway was pulled into the rivalry between its two neighbors. The union of Denmark and Norway lost major portions of its Norwegian territory to Sweden in 1645 and in 1658.

Swedish territorial expansion was reversed from the late seventeenth century. King Charles XII suffered a major defeat against Russia at Poltava in 1709. Later he failed to conquer Oslo, and in 1718 was killed in a battle at Fredriksten fortress in Southern Norway. Swedish military power declined, although war activity – mainly with Russia – continued until the Napoleonic wars. Ever since the Congress of Vienna, however, war activity in the Nordic area has been minimal. In the mid-nineteenth century Denmark fought two wars with Prussia over its southern border, finally settled in its present form by a plebiscite in 1920 following the Treaty of Versailles. Finland fought a bloody civil war in 1918 and two wars with the Soviet Union in 1939-41. Denmark and Norway were occupied by Germany in World War II.

Sweden has not fought in any war since the Congress of Vienna. Overall, the past 175 years can be characterized as a generally peaceful period in Nordic history. In the four preceding centuries there had been about 40 international wars among the Nordic countries or between them and outside powers, and over a dozen civil wars. Since the Napoleonic wars only one civil war (in Finland) and four international wars are recorded. Sweden has a record of unbroken peace since the Napoleonic wars; for Norway World War II represents the only interruption in a similar long peace.[1]

In 1931-32 a conflict between Denmark and Norway broke out, with Norwegian nationalists and later the government 'occupying' parts of Greenland. There was no violence and the two countries agreed to submit the conflict to the International Court at the Hague. Norway lost the case in 1933 and thus failed in its half-hearted attempt to reemerge as a true colonial power. It remained in possession of the Svalbard archipelago and several uninhabited Arctic islands. But the Svalbard Treaty of 1920 had demilitarized the islands and the other Norwegian possessions were too small or too remote or both to make military defense a realistic or attractive option. Thus, the Norwegian 'empire' has no military significance today.

After World War II Denmark and Norway participated in the occupying force in Germany. Since then, the Nordic countries have exercised military power only in support of United Nations objectives. By 1993 a total of 38,000 Norwegian personnel had participated in 13 UN peacekeeping operations in Kashmir, Greece, the Middle East, the Congo, Angola, Korea, Somalia, and the former Yugoslavia – more than half of them in UNIFIL in Lebanon since 1978. In the Korean War, also defined in Norway as peacekeeping, Norway participated in a non-combatant role in the UN-sponsored multilateral force, mainly with a field hospital. Norwegian authorities offered to send combatant forces, but the offer was declined by the USA, which considered Norway to be overextended in preparing for a possible war in Europe. In the Gulf War in early 1991 Norway contributed to the multilateral force fighting in support of UN-defined objectives. The closest thing to a direct military contribution was a Norwegian Coast Guard ship, which acted as a supply ship to a Danish frigate; in fact neither ship saw combat.

If NATO's area of operations is extended or if a more informal alliance of Western nations engage in operations similar to the Gulf War, Norway is likely to come under increasing pressure to participate. However, the major political parties are in agreement to limit any such participation to non-combatant roles. Agreement on this policy spans more or less the same spectrum as in Norwegian security policy debate generally, i.e. from the Conservative Party on the right to somewhere left of the center of the Labor Party, with the left criticizing this policy for being overly militaristic and the far right arguing the opposite.

3.2 Comparative Indicators of Military Spending

Discussions of military expenditure suffer from reliance on a plethora of different indicators. In order to discuss the development of Norwegian military expenditure over time and to compare it across nations we need a conceptual framework for comparison.

One such framework might be provided by asking what military spending is for: *what is being defended?* We may distinguish between four different bases for defense:

- defending the *population*
- defending the *territory*
- defending the *national wealth*
- defending the *social structure*

The first of these, *defending the population*, leads to comparisons on the basis of a per capita measure: Two countries are equal in their military spending if they spend the same amount per individual. And a country's military spending is constant if it spends the same amount per individual at different times.

The second concept, *territorial defense*, leads to a variety of comparative measures. The most obvious is military spending per unit of territory – a measure used, for instance, by the Norwegian Defense Commission of 1974 in order to show that Norway's military spending was lower than that of some of its Western European allies (*NOU*, 1978: 9, p. 112). In Norway's case, *sea territory* (or *undersea territory*) would yield even lower comparative figures, and with some justification: patrolling vast economic zones at sea in peacetime and defending them in wartime does require major resources. The symbolic value of defending sea territory is hardly equal to that of land territory, but the economic value can be considerable, for fishing as well as the extraction of oil and gas. A country does not have the same degree of sovereignty over its economic zone as over its actual territory; e.g., 'innocent passage' is permitted within territorial waters even for military forces. On the other hand, defending ocean territory may involve a new set of opponents. Norway's fishing rights in its economic zone are more frequently challenged by fishing vessels from its military allies than from its presumed military enemy. Territorial defense is also associated with *boundary defense*: to compare the effort put into border defense, military spending per unit of boundary length might be appropriate. Again, the boundary might be defined on the basis of the land territory, or the combined land and sea territory.

The third defense concept, *defending national wealth*, is not so easily translated into an operational measure for comparison. If we assume that the national income is proportionally related to national wealth, an appropriate indicator might be e.g. the most common comparative measure of military spending, namely as a percentage of the gross domestic product (GDP).

The fourth concept, *social defense*, involves even greater measurement problems. This notion of defense must be more closely linked to *wealth* or *people* than to *territory*. But neither lifestyle, culture, nor system of government is directly measurable by people or money. Some aspects of lifestyle may be closely linked to territory -- as is the case with a nomadic people, or even with a country like Norway which places a high premium on undisturbed wilderness, quiet, and outdoor activities in unspoilt nature. But most of all, the social structure is linked to institutions, and these do not lend themselves to simple counting rules. In any case, successful defense of the territory is usually understood as a sufficient condition for social defense, if not a necessary one.

An entirely different basis for comparison would involve asking *how much effort* a country is putting into its military defense. Such effort might be measured in at least three different ways:

- military effort per individual
- military effort per unit of production (or income)
- military effort per unit of government expenditure

Of these, the first leads to comparisons on the basis of military spending per capita, the second to comparisons on the basis of military spending as a proportion of national income, and in the third the denominator is government (or, more commonly, central government) spending. As an alternative numerator, the effort might be measured by the number of people in the armed forces rather than the amount of money spent.

A third basis for comparison might be based on the *national security threat* to a country. This might also be measured by a physical concept, such as the length of the boundary. A more appropriate measure would take into account the military spending of a possible opponent, his military capability, or his intentions. In a simple two-country situation, numerical comparisons can be made, as in the classic case of the Anglo-German naval race preceding World War I (Richardson, 1960). In the case of Norway, whose only plausible opponent is a superpower, this approach raises an apparently insoluble measurement problem: what part of the superpower's military spending or capability can be directed against its small neighbor rather than against the opposing superpower?

We have surveyed these different measures – not in order to argue that one of them is the best measure under all circumstances, but to show how arguments can be adduced for quite different indicators of relative military spending, yielding very different results in comparisons over time as well as across nations. Generally, per capita measures show rich countries to be relatively higher spenders than do measures relative to the national product. Sparsely populated countries like Norway seem more modest in their military spending when compared per unit of area than on a per capita basis. Countries with a single military threat may seem more modest in their military preparations than countries which prepare for possible armed conflict on two different fronts. A case in point is the Soviet Union, which has had forces deployed against separate perceived threats from the United States and Western Europe in the West and against China in the East.

Standard reference works on military spending employ many of these different indicators, usually without much discussion of their meaning. Besides absolute measures (in local currency and current prices as well as USD in constant prices and exchange rates) the *SIPRI Yearbook* compares military expenditures in percentage of GDP. Ruth Leger Sivard's *World Military and Social Expenditure* gives expenditures per capita, per soldier, in percentage of GDP, and in relation to area, as well as extensive comparisons with education and welfare expenditures. *The Military Balance,* from the International Institute of Strategic Studies in London, reports military spending per capita, in percent of GDP, and in percent of public expenditure. *World Military Expenditures and Arms Transfers*, issued by the US Arms Control and Disarmament Agency, relates military spending to population, GDP, and public expenditure, as well as to health and education expenditure. This source also regularly reports armed forces in proportion to population, and arms imports and exports as a share of total imports and exports. Finally, *NATO Review* regularly publishes comparisons for the NATO countries, per capita as well as in proportion to GDP. None of these sources uses a geographical basis for comparison.

Summing up, the most commonly used measure – military spending in proportion of GDP has a rationale mainly as a measure of *military effort in relation to the national output* – although it can also be considered a measure of the type of defense (in terms of national wealth or social structure). Military spending per capita can be interpreted as a measure of national effort by the population, as well as an indicator of population defense. Military spending in relation to (central) government spending can be seen as a measure of effort relative to the government's available resources. Of the geographical measures, measures relating to the length of boundaries can be justified both in terms of territorial defense and in terms of potential threat; the same goes for measures in relation to area. To some extent we shall rely on all of these, except for measures relating to the length of boundaries, for which we are not aware of available data. Instead, in one case we use a simplified measure – the length of the country, measured as the maximum distance between two points on the land territory.

In this discussion, we have assumed that the numerator in most of these comparisons, military spending, is unproblematic. Unfortunately, 'military spending' is not in fact such a simple concept. In Norway, as in other countries, we find separate figures for initially budgeted military spending, revised budgeted military spending (which takes into account budget changes during the year), actual military expenditure (as measured in the Fiscal Accounts), and military consumption (as measured in the National Accounts). In Appendix A, we outline the differences between these concepts, as used in Norway. Generally, we are most interested in the resources actually consumed by the military, and will use national accounts data where available. The choice of spending concept does make a difference in over-time comparisons for Norway, to be discussed in the next section. For instance, during periods of rapid military buildup, military budgets will frequently be ahead of actual spending. For the broad international comparisons undertaken here, the choice of spending indicator makes little difference. A much greater problem in the international context is the question of exchange rates.

Finally, we have assumed that there is only one source of military spending – the fiscal budget – and that all spending is overt and publicly accounted. These conditions do not hold perfectly. During much of the postwar period, Norway has received extensive military aid from its allies, in particular from the United States. Since the early 1950s the NATO infrastructure program has maintained an extensive building program in Norway; the expenses in Norway have always exceeded Norway's contribution to the program. Moreover, some de facto military spending is hidden in the budgets of other ministries, and the conscription system has made labor power available for military use at far less than its market value. There are also some covert military subsidies from abroad, which will be discussed in Section 3.5.

3.3 The Growth of the Military Establishment

While data on wars are available back through several centuries, it is much harder – in the absence of specialized studies – to be precise about the size of the military establishment. The Norwegian national accounts have been calculated backwards into the nineteenth century, and statistics can be reported for military employment from 1865 and military consumption from 1887.

Of the various relative measures of military spending discussed in the previous section, we shall limit our discussion here to those which have a changing basis. For most countries, the geographical measures tend to change very little. Norway added the Svalbard archipelago to its territory in 1925 and the island of Jan Mayen in 1930. Since then, there have been only minor changes in land territory. The sea area was appreciably widened in 1977, when Norway claimed a 200 nautical mile economic zone. However, only a minor share of Norway's military spending is specifically related to the exercise of jurisdiction over its economic zone.

Figures 3.1-3.5 provide a long-term view of the Norwegian military sector. Figure 3.1 gives the absolute level of military consumption over the past 100 years in constant prices and Figures 3.3-3.5 report military employment and military consumption in relative terms. The data underlying these figures are reported in detail with other military indicators in Appendix A.

Figure 3.1 Norwegian Military Consumption 1887-1993, Constant 1970 Prices (NOK Million)

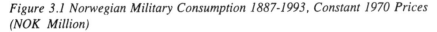
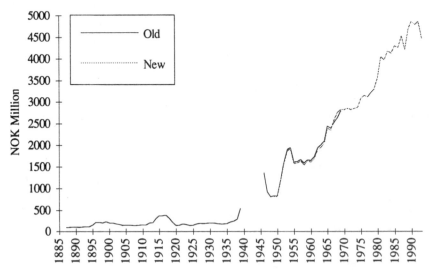

For the period 1949-69, there are two overlapping curves – New (= new definition) and Old – due to a change in definitions in the national accounts. There are no meaningful data for the period of the German occupation (1940-45).
Sources: National account publications of Statistics Norway, cf. Table A.1 in Appendix A

Up until World War II Norwegian military consumption remained at low peacetime levels, around 1-2% of GDP (Figure 3.4). Military consumption rose rapidly in absolute and relative terms just before the turn of the century, reflecting the increased tension between Norway and Sweden in the final years of the union and the struggle between the Norwegian Parliament and the Swedish king. Norwegian independence was accompanied by a measure of disarmament in that the border fortresses between the two countries were shut down.

A second hump on the curve for military consumption as a share of the national product is found around World War I. The Nordic countries successfully pursued a neutral policy, but the neutrality was accompanied by a certain amount of rearming. However, the long-term trend from 1887 until the late 1930s is towards slightly lower military consumption as a share of GDP.

Norway started arming more intensively just before World War II, but this process was interrupted by the German occupation in 1940. Immediately after liberation in 1945 military spending dropped sharply, but the emerging tension between East and West and eventually Norwegian membership in NATO drove it back up and well beyond the prewar level. Except if we compare a brief period at the end of the bridge-building period with the maximum spending of the two previous peaks, the entire postwar era has seen higher peacetime military consumption as a share of GDP than ever before.

Figure 3.2 World War II as a Shift in Military Consumption

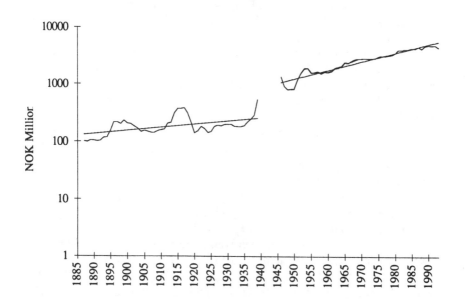

The curves represent the logarithms of military consumption as depicted in Figure 3.1. Separate trend lines have been fitted to the prewar and postwar periods, representing an average growth of 1.3% and 3.6% respectively.

World War II clearly represents a turning-point in military consumption, as illustrated in absolute terms in Figure 3.1 and in logarithmic terms in Figure 3.2, with the trend-lines added. The postwar trend line is located higher up and rises more than twice as steeply than the prewar trend line.

NATO in its first years was mainly a paper alliance, a mutual expression of solidarity. After the outbreak of the Korean War in 1950, this changed very rapidly, with the establishment of an integrated military command in peacetime.[2] In Norway, as in most other NATO countries, military spending rose very rapidly. After the Korean War, military spending decreased and then leveled out until the mid-1960s, but at a level unprecedented prior to Korea. Since then military spending has continued to rise in absolute terms, while there has been a slight downwards trend relative to GDP.

In 1978 the NATO Heads of Governments agreed to increase military spending by 3% per annum in real terms. For a long time Norway adhered to this decision, through changing governments and shifting economic fortunes. In the late 1980s the Norwegian Labor Party altered the growth rate to 2.5%, an adjustment initially left unchanged by the most recent non-socialist government, which held office from September 1989 to November 1990. Under the Labor government in office since late 1990, however, there has been wide agreement on zero growth in the military budget.[3] In 1993 there was a clear reduction in military consumption.

The cuts, relative to what might have been undertaken under the assumption of 'business as usual', affect both labor and equipment costs. On the equipment side, for instance, a decision was made in April 1990 not to replace fighter aircraft that crash, and so the Norwegian fleet of F-16s is slowly being depleted. Originally, 72 were purchased; by 1990 61 were left. Norway has joined the Mid-Life Update Program, a collaborative effort of the US Air Force and the air forces of four European countries to prolong the life of the F-16 fleet.[4] Another major program for new equipment, the German-Norwegian submarine program, completed its deliveries to Norway valued at NOK 6,500 million before the spending freeze took effect. It seems doubtful if any similarly large equipment programs will be initiated in the near future.

On the personnel side, preparedness has been lowered, in order to reduce labor costs. Since an attack out of the blue is now completely unlikely, around-the-clock vigilance is no longer so urgent. Shorter and more intensified training has also been introduced for parts of the conscript force.

Figure 3.3 depicts – for an even longer time-period than the two previous figures – the use of labor resources by the military, in percentage of the labor force. Military use of manpower accompanied the rise in military spending after World War II, but leveled off after the Korean War. Military service, of just 2-3 months' duration in the 1930s, made a jump to one year after liberation in 1945, amended to 9-14 months in 1947, and was then progressively lengthened until 1954, when the initial service in the Army was set at 16 months. In 1964 this was reduced to 12 months, the current level.[5]

Military spending is, of course, an absolute measure, while the military use of manpower is depicted relative to total employment. Thus, one would not expect the military manpower indicator to continue to rise. However, the absolute level of manpower consumed by the armed forces also stopped rising in 1952 and has remained about level since then.

Figure 3.3 Military Employment as a Share of Total Employment 1865-1993 (%)

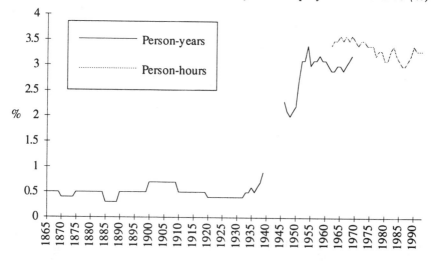

For 1865-1930 we have data for five-year intervals only. The Figure assumes that the level is constant between these years. There are no meaningful data for the period of the German occupation (1940-45). The curve for person-years corresponds to the old definition in the national accounts.
Sources: See Figure 3.1 and Table A.3 in the Appendix

Figures 3.4 and 3.5 give two commonly used relative measures for military spending – as shares of the Gross Domestic Product, and of General Government Consumption. With about 3% of the GDP and 15% of General Government Consumption going to military purposes, the military establishment can be seen as a major project in resource terms. On the other hand, this is very far from being a wartime economy, in which a country might spend 40-50% of its national product on the military sector. Over the past 30 years, after the peak rearmament of the early Cold War, military consumption as a share of the national product has stayed at about the same level. Military consumption as a share of General Government Consumption has decreased steadily since the 1950s, and is now almost as low as in the interwar years.

There have been no special studies of the long-term determinants of Norwegian military spending. However, visual inspection of the curves indicates that external determinants must have played a major role. One long-term influence is the East-West conflict; short-term influences are the events leading to Norway's secession from the union with Sweden in 1905, the World Wars, and the Korean War – possibly also the Indochina War and the 'New Cold War' in the early 1980s. Norway was not an active combatant in the traditional sense in any of these wars. During World War II, Norway's conventional military role in defending itself against the German invasion ended within two months and gave way to a five-year occupation. In the other wars Norway did not participate at all. In 1905, war was a real threat, but was averted. On the other hand, because Norway has been a close ally of the USA, even remote wars can have been perceived as indirect threats, in that they might escalate into worldwide conflict.

Figure 3.4 Norwegian Military Consumption 1887-1993 as a Share of GDP (%)

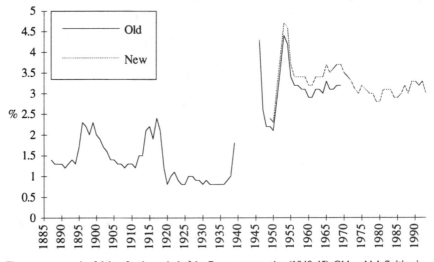

There are no meaningful data for the period of the German occupation (1940-45). Old = old definition in
the national accounts. New = new definition.
Sources: See Figure 3.1

The rapid rise of Norwegian military spending in the early 1950s was accompanied by considerable debate. Nevertheless, most opposition to high military
spending came from the Communist Party (represented in the Storting until
1961), from the left of the Labor Party, and from scattered radicals in other parties
and did not give rise to any mass movement. (Such a mass movement did arise,
however, in opposition to nuclear weapons.[6]) Annual real increases in military
spending became the order of the day in the thriving Norwegian economy, with
relatively feeble opposition. Not till the 1980s did the issue of military spending
cause any divergence between the major parties, with the Labor Party favoring
2.5% real annual increases and the non-socialist coalition parties (in government
in 1981-86 and again in 1989-90) sticking to 3%. Today, for the first time since
World War II, there seems to be broad consensus that military spending must be
curtailed. It remains to be seen if this sentiment will lead to a real long-term
reduction, or simply peter out, or result in one-shot cuts followed by new annual
increases. The military establishment has argued consistently that Norway has a
'minimum defense' which cannot be reduced without irreparable harm to the
defense effort. However, such perceived 'national minima' tend to adjust to the
actual level of spending; in the future the military establishment will have to come
up with an improved rationale for continued high spending if it is to be heard.
    In 1989 the Norwegian government appointed a broadly composed Defense
Commission – only the third such commission after World War II – which
reported in early 1992. Initially the government tried to refer the question of the
level of military spending to the Commission, but the tide could not be stemmed
and the 1991 and 1992 budgets were proclaimed as zero growth budgets. This is
confirmed by the figures for military consumption in the national accounts for the

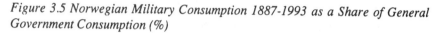

Figure 3.5 Norwegian Military Consumption 1887-1993 as a Share of General Government Consumption (%)

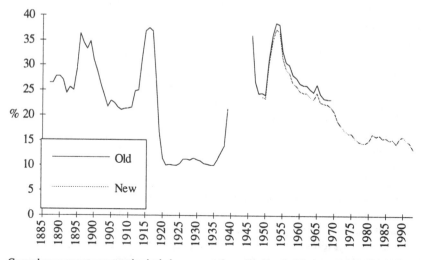

General government consumption includes consumption at local levels. There are no meaningful data for the period of the German occupation (1940-45). Old = old definition in the national accounts. New = new definition.
Sources: See Figure 3.1

years 1990-92. For 1993 the government budgeted with a 2% decline. Similar zero growth periods have been found in the past (for instance 1970-74, when military consumption increased in real terms by less than 2% in four years). Changes in consumption are frequently delayed relatively to budgeting, because of inertia in individual defense programs, and unless there is a drastic change in the threat perception or new major tasks are assigned to the military establishment, a decline should soon be visible in military consumption.

3.4 The True Costs of Defense

The defense budget does not necessarily represent the true cost of maintaining a military establishment in defense of national security. Costs may be hidden in the budgets of civilian ministries or may be extracted from the private sector by unrealistically low prices on goods and services purchased by the military establishment. Estimating these hidden costs raises many conceptual issues about what is and what is not a defense cost. We shall not attempt a complete calculation here, but shall briefly discuss some of the more obvious limitations of the defense budget.

A major issue in the true cost consideration is the use of conscripts who are paid less than the real value of their labor power. In a comment on an official report on the pricing of conscript labor *(NOU*, 1989), Christensen & Torvanger (1989) concluded that the present pricing system obscures the real costs of conscription. They estimated that if the conscripts were to be paid equivalent wages to the same cohorts in civilian sectors, the labor costs of the military establishment would have risen by 30-40% and the defense budget by 10-14%. A Swedish study in the late 1960s (Ståhl, 1968) estimated the hidden cost of conscription at 5-10% of military spending. If the military establishment were forced to pay competitive wages, it would probably have to restructure and cut down on personnel in the peacetime armed forces. But conscription permits the military establishment to pass on the extra costs to the private sector. Today, with higher unemployment in the relevant age cohorts, the social costs of conscription might be lower, since many of the conscripts would not have found alternative employment but would have drawn unemployment pay or social welfare from public funds.

Other hidden costs of the military establishment relate to various preparedness measures. Norway subscribes to a concept of 'total defense', which involves civilian defense and various civilian preparedness measures, in addition to military defense. According to the official *Facts and Figures* of the Ministry of Defense (1993, pp. 10f.) 'All sectors of the community are under obligation to render assistance to the defence of Norway.' To our knowledge, the cost of this assistance has never been estimated in Norway, but a Swedish study in the 1960s estimated that the defense budget must be expanded by about 15% if these other preparedness measures were included. But preparedness can be viewed in an even wider perspective. The agricultural policy heavily subsidizes small farm units all over the country with wartime food supply as an explicit rationale. A Swedish economist guesstimated in the early 1960s that Sweden maintained uneconomic agricultural production in order to secure self-sufficiency in wartime. The cost of this he estimated at one-fifth to one-fourth of the defense budget. The corresponding cost for Norway can be no less.

A telling illustration of the kind of costs passed on to the private sector relates to the question of air-raid shelters. Norway had until recently regulations which made it compulsory to build shelters in private buildings above a certain size. In 1967 the added cost for private builders was about NOK 60 million, exceeding the total amount budgeted for civil defense that year (Thue, 1969).

On the positive side of the accounts, certain civilian functions such as rescue operations, disaster relief, assistance to major sports events, education of conscripts and enlisted men, etc. are undertaken by the military establishment. These are hidden civilian costs in the Defense Budget. We are not aware of any estimates of the total value of these services for the civilian sector. Although some of these activities are quite visible and provide good publicity for the armed forces, it is hard to imagine that they could amount to more than a few percent of the defense budget.[7]

3.5 Foreign Income

Most military spending in Norway comes from Norwegian sources. However, Norway has received very substantial military assistance from its major allies throughout the postwar period. Of particular importance in an economic sense is the US Military Assistance Program (MAP) between 1951 and 1970. The financial value of this program cannot be calculated exactly, since most of the assistance was in the form of weapons, whose value is debatable. Estimates from the Norwegian Ministry of Defense indicate that the value of assistance from the USA and Canada amounted to about 20% of domestic military spending from 1951 to 1970 and as much as two thirds in the period 1951-55.[8] Even after the termination of the MAP program, parts of the military establishment have been funded by external sources. NATO has funded military construction in Norway through the military infrastructure program – a program for airfields, air defense radars, communications facilities, etc.; many of these installations are meant for allied military forces which would be operating in Norway in wartime. Like most other NATO members, Norway pays for a share of the infrastructure program – currently 3.17%. But the volume of projects in Norway has always exceeded Norway's contribution to the program; thus Norway has always been a 'net recipient'. Apart from NATO programs, the US Department of Defense has funded several military installations, such as the Loran-C navigation stations (Wilkes & Gleditsch, 1987) as well as dozens of research projects in the Norwegian Defence Research Establishment (Gleditsch et al., 1978). The amounts involved can be quite significant as a proportion of funds for that particular activity, but are now relatively small in comparison to the overall Norwegian defense budget. In 1990 the foreign contributions to military construction and opeating expenditure amounted to about 5% of total expenditure.[9]

The net benefit from the joint infrastructure programs is accounted for as export of services in the Norwegian national accounts. At first glance this may seem odd, as it would appear that such income pays for labor, buildings, and equipment consumed in Norway rather than abroad, but it is firmly in line with national accounting conventions (United Nations, 1968, Sections 6.77-6.78). And if outside support for infrastructure in Norway is conceived as an export of defense services from the Norwegian military establishment to Norway's allies, it makes sense conceptually.

The bulk of the exports of defense services are included in the defense budget. However, some projects are hidden in other budgets. A well-documented example is provided by the Omega navigation system, a US military navigation system now extensively employed by civilian users as well. Control over the Omega transmitter in Norway, fully funded by the USA, was transferred from the Norwegian Defence Communications Agency to the Norwegian Telecommunications Agency in 1971 in order to make it appear that the station's civilian functions were predominant. Thus the operating costs for the station no longer appear in the Norwegian defense budget, and the exact size of the US military contribution has become invisible in the budget because it has been lumped with non-military items. The US subsidy for the period 1986-90 averaged NOK 5.3 million per year, which is insignificant in economic terms.[10] The R&D contracts from the Pentagon to civilian research institutions in Norway also appear under civilian ministries, notably the Ministry of Church and Education Affairs and the Ministry of Foreign Affairs. In recent years such contracts have at most added up to a few million kroner. Thus, they are uninteresting in economic terms, even if they may be significant in political terms.[11]

The US contribution to intelligence activities in Norway, notably equipment and salaries of a series of signals intelligence activities (Wilkes & Gleditsch,

1979, 1981) appears to be in a separate 'black budget', i.e. outside the published official defense budget. Since these establishments are operated mostly by Norwegian personnel, their salaries may well be lumped within the large amount (almost NOK 6,000 million in 1991) budgeted for salaries within the Norwegian Defense Staff. However, since the income cannot be included under the budget item 'foreign contributions',[12] a discrepancy would arise between outlays and incomes. This may be adjusted somewhere else in the budget, or the budget item for expenditure may simply be too low. If it is assumed that the USA covertly reimburses the salaries of 400 persons in the signals intelligence establishment – probably a conservative assumption – the total expenses might be about NOK 100 million or less than 0.5% of military expenditure for 1992. After the end of the Cold War US purchases of signals intelligence from Norway was reduced, and – according to newspaper leaks from a secret session in Parliament – about 350 jobs were lost.

While the overt and covert subsidies for military installations, R&D projects, and intelligence activities have been the subject of much secrecy – attended by much political controversy on the few occasions when the secrecy has been broken – all of these activities are insignificant in economic terms, with a slight possible exception for the covert intelligence funding.

3.6 Arms Production and Exports

Military industry in Norway has traditionally been limited to two firms, Kongsberg Våpenfabrikk (KV) and Raufoss Ammunisjonsfabrikker (RA). KV was established by a royal decree in 1814, with the sole purpose of producing weapons for the Norwegian defense sector. A slack in demand after World War I made it necessary to take up production of civilian goods as a supplement. From the mid-1950s the firm established itself as a participant in NATO co-production arrangements, in addition to domestic military deliveries. RA dates back to 1886 and – as its name indicates – was established to produce ammunition; civilian production is of more recent origin. Both firms are located in East Central Norway, within 100 km of Oslo.

The Norwegian government stimulated the growth of a Norwegian defense industry. This policy rested on two pillars. First, the authorities encouraged close collaboration between the Norwegian armed forces, industry, and military R&D – mainly concentrated in the Norwegian Defense Research Establishment (Forsvarets Forskningsinstitutt). The collaboration was facilitated by the public ownership of Raufoss Ammunisjonsfabrikker and Kongsberg Våpenfabrikk. Military-industrial cooperation led to product development for the Norwegian armed forces, as well as to exports, particularly within the NATO alliance. Initially, the development of a Norwegian defense industry was hampered by low domestic production and high imports of weapons from Norway's allies – particularly weapons provided free or cheaply through US military assistance programs. Military assistance dwindled in the late 1960s.

Secondly, as US military assistance to Western Europe dwindled, European arms production picked up. The USA encouraged Western European cooperation and standardization in defense production. Norway became involved in coproduction of military equipment with other European countries, frequently in licensed production of US technology, e.g. in tactical missiles such as Bullpup and Sidewinder and the anti-tank weapon M-72.

As Norway began to make major arms purchases – in particular the 'arms deal of the century', the joint purchase with Belgium, Denmark, and the Netherlands of fighter aircraft in the mid-1970s – *offset agreements* emerged as an increasingly important third pillar of Norwegian policy. In return for Norway making a major arms purchase from a foreign firm, the firm would place orders for goods and services in Norway. The nature of the offset agreements played a decisive influence in the selection of the F-16 by Norway and the other three nations (Forbord, 1976; Dörfer, 1983). In return for the purchase of the F-16 aircraft, Norway was offered a share of the production calculated to generate 4,000-5,000 person-years of employment. If we take as the cost of generating this employment the Defense Ministry's own estimate of the price increase due to the coproduction arrangement, i.e. due to a loss of economy of scale, the figure is NOK 403 million. A similar increase in public spending generally would have generated about 5,600 person-years of employment, thus well exceeding the employment effect of the F-16 coproduction arrangement. In fact, the estimated direct employment effect of the arrangement was probably too optimistic.

As a result of the official support for domestic defense production military production today is rather diversified. About 2,000 firms were registered in 1990 by the Norwegian Military Supply Agency (Forsvarets Felles Materielltjeneste, FFMT), but only 64 had joined the Norwegian Defense Industry Group (Norske Forsvarsleveranser, NFL). According to the report of the Thulin Committee, a subcommittee of the Defense Commission since 1982, 62 offset agreements have been concluded with 35 foreign firms, and offset agreements are now standard practice for any military purchase exceeding NOK 40-50 million (Thulin et al., 1991, p. 42). The average degree of compensation is said to be two-thirds of the value of the contract.

This military industry-promoting policy of successive Norwegian governments has created some problems; One is a continuing pressure from industry for increasing exports and more liberal rules for arms exports.[13] This runs counter to broad political sentiments, skeptical of delivering arms to regimes which might use them in war or in internal repression. Norwegian rules governing arms exports have generally been formulated in response to a series of scandals. In 1935 the Storting decreed that 'exports of arms and ammunition may only be permitted to countries not at war or civil war, unless the war is declared as a legal defensive war by the competent bodies of the League of Nations',[14] in the wake of a scandal involving exports to Bolivia, then in the bloody Chaco War with Paraguay.

In late 1958 the Labor Cabinet agreed to exports of small arms from Raufoss Ammunisjonsfabrikker to the Batista regime in Cuba. This became public when the arms reached Cuba after Castro's takeover, and the resulting furore nearly brought down the government. A declaration by the Prime Minister to the Storting in March 1959 to the effect that armaments were generally not to be exported 'to areas where there is war or a threat of war'[15] formed the basis of policy for years to come.

In early 1950 Norway joined CoCom, the secret Western organization formed to wage a moderate form of economic warfare on the Soviet Union and its allies (Førland, 1988, 1991). But in 1987 the publicly owned Kongsberg Våpenfabrikk was revealed to have collaborated with Japan's Toshiba in supplying technology to the Soviet Union which allegedly would enable it to build stealthier submarines, thus complicating Western tracking and antisubmarine warfare. As part of a housecleaning drive the Storting passed in late 1987 an entirely new law dealing with exports of arms and military technology, supplementing legislation from 1961 which had concerned only small arms and ammunition. While this legislation, as well as the entire CoCom procedure, was directed primarily against exports to the enemy, the political debate has been concerned just as much with exports of arms to allies and to Third World countries.

Norway has had – at least on paper – relatively strict rules regulating arms exports. In practice, the authorities frequently claim, Norwegian arms have been exported almost exclusively to NATO allies as well as the other Nordic countries. An informal rendering of this view is 'no one can buy weapons from Norway unless they can prove that they don't need them'.[16] This view is overly rosy. In fact, Norway has exported arms to a rather wide range of countries. Coproduction arrangements have increased the probability that weapons partially produced in Norway could end up in Third World conflicts. Even if Norway's CoCom membership prevented the export of strategic goods to the Communist countries, such goods have been exported to many other politically controversial countries. A particularly noteworthy case is the export of Norwegian heavy water which, apart from sales to the UK and France, has also found its way to India and to Israel. Israel used Norwegian heavy water in the Dimona reactor, at the heart of its nuclear weapons program (Hersh, 1991). Yet there are few areas which in the postwar period have qualified better than the Middle East for a shortlist of 'areas where there is a threat of war'. The Norwegian government belatedly tried to retrace its steps by invoking an inspection clause in the sales agreement with Israel, but was unable to achieve more than the return of the bulk of the original supply of heavy water after about 30 years. Several other examples of controversial Norwegian arms exports indicate a certain discrepancy between official policy and actual practice.

On many occasions the Norwegian authorities have been accused of liberalizing the rules for arms exports (e.g. Holm, 1989). Wicken (1992), the most detailed study of Norwegian arms exports to date, considers that the main trend up to the end of the 1970s was restrictive, while there has been a liberalization since then – but there are exceptions to this generalization. Most recently, in January 1992, the requirement for an end-use certificate was removed for weapons only partly produced in Norway.

The Thulin Committee found that increasing costs of development and production made large-scale production and exports desirable, yet political considerations made this difficult (1991, pp. 50-51). The Committee found that existing regulations for arms exports take insufficient account of collective security, build on a simplistic definition of 'arms', and fail to deal with the problem of international collaboration in arms production – with considerable negative consequences for industry (pp. 63-65). On this basis the Committee recommended international harmonization of arms export regulations. In particular, if Norwegian industry is to be accepted as a serious long-term partner in multinational projects, the Committee felt that Norwegian regulations would have to accept that exports from collaborating countries were governed by the regulations of those countries and not by stricter Norwegian standards. It may seem paradoxical that rules regulating arms exports should be liberalized in a period of declining world tension, but this should probably be interpreted more as a question of industrial policy than of security policy.

As the Thulin Committee argues, domestic military production in a country with a military establishment of only modest size necessarily leads to pressure for exports. In addition to the three major scandals mentioned above, new controversies have arisen regularly – regarding exports of arms or military technology to Greece (in 1967, after the military takeover), to the USA (during the Vietnam War), to Central America (during the civil wars in the 1980s), to Turkey (during the military dictatorship), to Libya, and to others. None of these exports has had much significance in macroeconomic terms.

The actual value of Norwegian arms exports is difficult to estimate, in part because of secrecy, in part because of definitional problems. In the *SIPRI Yearbook* for 1981 Norway emerged as the world's eighth largest arms exporter for the period 1977-80[17] or really the seventh largest since number seven on SIPRI's list was 'the third world'. The SIPRI statistics were for 'major weapons systems', i.e. missiles, warships, aircraft, etc. and Norway was listed as accounting for only 1.3% of the total value of world exports in this area, but this was enough to bring the country into a high position on SIPRI's ranking. The SIPRI ranking-list created a minor sensation. Peace movements and left-wing politicians demanded an end to arms exports, while the establishment questioned SIPRI's statistics. Thorvald Stoltenberg, then Minister of Defense, explained the high figure as resulting from special circumstances of that four-year period, while the economic historian Olav Wicken interpreted the figure as a result of a deliberate Norwegian policy from the early 1960s to expand military production.[18] The next year this particular table vanished from the *SIPRI Yearbook*. When the ranking-list reappeared in the late 1980s, Norway was no longer among the top exporters. For the period 1988-92 Norway is listed as number 15 in exports of major conventional weapons systems to the industrialized world, but not among the top 15 in exports to all countries.

One of the arguments against the SIPRI statistics put forward by Norwegian officials was that they did not provide a complete picture of the international arms trade. However, since the Norwegian arms industry is more involved in coproduction and offset agreements than in the production of major weapons systems, a more comprehensive accounting might just as well place Norway higher rather than lower on an international ranking list. A more realistic objection to the SIPRI statistics is that they do not build on actual sales figures, but on SIPRI's estimates of the market values of the weapons exported. SIPRI had probably put unrealistically high values on Penguin missiles exported by Norway. Because of the poor official records on Norwegian arms exports, Norwegian officials were not in a position to provide a convincing rebuttal to the SIPRI figures.

Much more comprehensive arms trade statistics, based on US intelligence sources, are provided by the US Arms Control and Disarmament Agency on an annual basis. ACDA defines arms as 'military equipment, usually referred to as «conventional», including weapons of war, parts thereof, ammunition, support equipment, and other commodities designed for military use'.[19] ACDA placed Norway in 34th place in 1989 with only 0.07% of world arms exports.[20] These data also show a peak around 1980; Norway was then in 22nd place, with 0.25% of world exports – but the peak is much lower than the one in the SIPRI statistics.

3.7 Military R&D

Prior to World War II, Norway had practically no military R&D. During the war, the Norwegian government in exile in London engaged in close military collaboration with the allied authorities in a number of areas, including military R&D. After the war, the Norwegian Defense Research Establishment was set up under the Ministry of Defense. The institute quickly obtained a central place in Norwegian defense planning, and gradually also became important in industrial policy.

In the early years, NDRE received very extensive research contracts from the Pentagon, some of which were related to various projects undertaken by the US Department of Defense in Norway because of its proximity to the Soviet Union, such as antisubmarine warfare, signals intelligence, and military communications. Other projects were of a more general military character, contracted to the NDRE because of special competence found there. From the early 1950s to the early 1970s such contracts made up a substantial proportion of the NDRE's funds, in the past 20 years these contracts have continued but at a much lower level (Christensen, 1989, p. 38).

However, data for Norway confirm what we have shown earlier for the OECD countries generally, military R&D has not kept pace with civilian R&D spending. This is shown in Figure 3.6. Both civilian and military R&D have increased in constant prices, but civilian R&D has risen much more rapidly.

3.8 International Comparisons

Norway has a military sector relatively typical of that of small industrialized countries in Western Europe. The absolute size of the military establishment is very limited in terms of the total armed forces in the East-West confrontation: in 1987 Norway's military spending[21] accounted for 0.3% of the global spending, or 0.6% of NATO spending.[22]

The dominant self-perception is that Norway is a very small country. However, in global terms it is larger than the *median* on important indicators of size such as population, national product, land area, economic zone, and central government expenditure, as shown in Table 3.1. Because of extremely skewed global distributions, Norway is lower than the *average* on all these indicators, except the size of the economic zone and central government expenditure. More important to the

Figure 3.6 Norwegian Military and Civilian R&D, 1963-87, 1975 Prices and Purchasing Power Parities

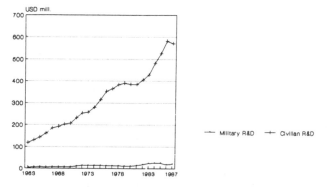

Figure prepared by Nils Petter Gleditsch and Arne Magnus Christensen and first published in Christensen (1989), p. 35 based on OECD statistics.

self-perception is probably that Norway is lower on such indicators of size than most members of its reference group, the countries with which comparisons are usually made.[23]

Table 3.1 Norway's Size in World Perspective, Absolute Measures

	Population 1989 ('000)	GDP 1989 (USD Million)	Land area 1983 ('000 km2)	Economic zone 1987 ('000 km2)	Central government expenditure 1987 (USD Million, 1988 Prices)
Norway	4,200	88,510	324	2,024	42,160
World median	2,873	8,334	84	407	2,300
World average	19,398	138,264	630	586	39,720
Norway's rank	93/212	30/144	61/215	14/188	21/144
Norway's share	0.10%	0.44%	0.24%	1.84%	0.73%

The averages are unweighted.
Sources: Gleditsch (1988), US ACDA (1991)

In military terms as well, Norway is a medium-sized country rather than a small one, as is evident from Table 3.2. For the number of personnel, Norway is slightly below the world median, but Norway's figure is lower than the one we use elsewhere in the book because civilian personnel in the armed forces are not included.

Table 3.3 gives a set of relative measures of military spending. Again, Norway is not found in an extreme position, but well above the median on all these measures. For both per capita measures, Norway· is even higher than the world average. As might be expected for a rich country, Norway's highest rank is on military expenditure per capita, where Norway is in the top decile. The rank for armed forces personnel per capita is lower than for military spending per capita; this reflects the higher cost of labor in Norway. The final column in this table compares military expenditure to the length of the country. This is a simplified version of military spending relative to the length of the boundary, for which we do not have data.

Table 3.2 Norway's Military Establishment in World Perspective, Absolute Measures, 1989

	Number of personnel in armed forces ('000)	Military spending (USD Million)	Arms exports (USD Million)
Norway	43	2,925	30
World median	47	298	0
World average	199	7,181	100
Norway's rank	77/144	35/144	34/100
Norway's share	0.13%	0.28%	0.07%

Figures in these comparative tables are not necessarily identical to the ones we use elsewhere, which are based on Norwegian sources. Figures in the first column refer to active-duty military personnel, including paramilitary forces if those forces resemble regular units in their organization, equipment, training, or mission. Civilian personnel are therefore not included, nor are reserve forces.
Source: US ACDA (1991)

3.9 Composition of the Military Establishment

Having reviewed the aggregate size of the military establishment over time, and compared it to other countries, we shall now look at some breakdowns important to the later discussion of conversion. We shall limit ourselves to three disaggregations of Norway's military manpower, by status, region, and function.

3.9.1 Military Manpower by Status

Four categories of Norway's military manpower are easily distinguishable in legal terms. Disarmament will have different economic and social consequences for the four.

Conscripts are involuntary members of the armed forces, drafted by law from the age of 19 initially, and for shorter refresher courses until the age of 44.

Table 3.3 Norway's Military Establishment in World Perspective, Relative Measures

	Armed forces per '000 population 1989	Military spending				
		Per capita (USD) 1989	As share of GNP (%) 1989	As share of CGE (%) 1989	By area (USD/km²) 1987	By length (USD/'000 km) 1987
Norway	10.2	691	3.3	6.9	3108	1236
World median	5.0	40	2.9	12.1	582	328
World average	5.7	212	5.4	18.7	3200	2316
Norway's rank	34/144	12/144	63/144	103/144	42/132	38/136

CGE = Central government expenditure. As to the figures for the absolute size of Norway's armed forces, see note to Table 3.2.
Sources: As in Table 3.1 and our own measures of length

Enlisted personnel are also generally younger people, serving in a contractual relationship in more specialized tasks for an initial three-year period, renewable for a further two or three. In countries which have abolished conscription, enlisted personnel make up the bulk of the force; in Norway enlistment is an alternative to conscription chosen by a small minority. This alternative has the advantage of offering vocational training which may prove useful in later civilian life; the disadvantage is being bound by a period considerably longer than one year or so of national service.

Officers are career military people serving permanently in one of the three branches of the armed forces. They are sometimes subdivided into officers who have graduated from the war colleges (*krigsskole*) of one of the three major services, and those who have merely completed the school for junior officers (*befalsskole*). The latter are usually restricted to lower positions. A small minority of 'civilian officers' obtain high-level positions, e.g. in the intelligence service, without having completed war college. Such distinctions are important in military trade union affairs, and will probably play a significant role in any actual shrinking of the armed forces; however, they are less important here. Officers are usually subject to transfer from one location to another. The retirement age for officers – 60, with rare exemptions – is lower than for civil servants generally. Many officers pursue a second career after retirement from the military.

Finally, many positions in the armed services are filled by *civilians*, whose status and retirement age is like that of other employees in public service.

Conscription is nearly as old in Norway as the military establishment itself. As early as the eleventh century the Gulating code, which covered most of Western Norway, prescribed that all men, even thralls, were to assemble at a specified place in the event of an attack. This *leidang* system divided the coast into small districts, each of which had to maintain a warship of a certain size. When Norway fell under the domination of Denmark, this system fell into disuse and most military matters were handled by professional soldiers in the pay of the Danish king. During the prolonged rivalry between Sweden and Denmark, King Christian IV in 1628 formed a Norwegian national army based on peasant conscription and a professional officer corps. Farms were required to cooperate in providing and outfitting soldiers, and sailors to the navy were drafted from the coastal population. The 1814 Constitution advanced egalitarian ideals in several ways and extended conscription in theory to the whole population, although in practice there were numerous exemptions. By the 1880s male conscription had become quite general in practice and has remained so until today[24].

Norway has maintained universal male conscription throughout the postwar period. The duration of national service increased drastically as the Cold War became more intense. Perhaps because it affected nearly every family, the lengthening of the national service was accompanied by a great deal of public debate; later, after the Cold War had peaked, the service was reduced once again. The present initial service is 12 months in the Air Force, Army, and Coastal Artillery, and 15 in the Navy. In addition, conscripts may be called up for refresher courses and exercises comprising in all a few months.

The rate of conscientious objection has shown a long-term increase since its first organized beginnings at the end of the nineteenth century, but the many ups-and-downs of the rate of objection have obscured the long-term trend. Today, applicants for CO status make up about 7-8% of the annual cohort, and the 'net loss' (successful applicants less those who return from CO status to the military) at 5-6%; this is enough to cause some concern in the military establishment, but hardly enough to threaten the supply of conscripts to the military establishment. A more serious loss factor for the military is rejection on medical grounds. A study from the mid-1970s showed that 25-30% of the conscripts were exempted due to medical problems (Hanoa, 1976, p. 18).

For 1989 a total of 52,793 person-years was budgeted within the armed forces, or 2.6% of the total labor force. Of these, 44% came from conscripts. Table 3.4 gives a breakdown and a comparison with figures from 1978, which indicates that the relative composition has remained relatively stable over the past decade and a half.

Table 3.4 Labor Force in the Norwegian Armed Forces, 1978 and 1989

	1978		1989	
	Budgeted person-years	Relative (%)	Budgeted person-years	Relative (%)
Conscripts			23,350	44
Enlisted personnel	24,400	49	17,365	33
Officers	13,400	27		
Civilians	11,900	24	12,078	23
Total	49,700	100	52,793	100

Absolute figures are budgeted person-years, relative figures in percent. Data for 1978 from the Norwegian defense budget (*Forsvarsbudsjettet, St.prp.* no. 1, 1978, p. 9); data for 1989 are estimated in Statistics Norway (Årethun, 1990). These figures differ from figures for military employment used elsewhere in the book, due to inconsistencies in the accounting procedures of the Ministry of Defense.

Women are not subject to conscription, but they may join the armed forces on a voluntary basis and have been doing so on an increasing scale since the end of the previous century. In 1970 7.5% of the persons in the armed forces were women; in 1988 the figure had risen to 13%. Women may attend the schools of the armed services at all levels and have the same terms of service and career opportunities as men (Ministry of Defense, 1993, pp. 48ff). Conscription for women does not require a constitutional change; a change could be introduced merely by changing the law on conscription. However, this is not on the political agenda.

3.9.2 Military Manpower by Region

A second breakdown of considerable political importance is the *regional* distribution. In absolute terms, the military labor force is concentrated in the Southeast (nearly 39%) and in the North (28%). During most of the Cold War period the prevailing war scenario has envisaged mobilizing troops and sending them to Northern Norway, where most conscripts have also served, after basic training. Like other aspects of the Cold War these war scenarios are becoming less relevant, but the peacetime deployment of the armed forces remains a strong economic reality. Relative to the total labor force, the concentration of military manpower is much higher in the sparsely populated Northern Norway than in the rest of the country. We return to the regional issues in much greater detail in Chapter 6.

3.9.3 Military Manpower by Function

In terms of employment the Army is the largest service in war as well as in peace, as shown by Table 3.5. The Navy and Air Force are roughly the same size, where as the Home Guard is minuscule in peacetime, but expands to the second largest in wartime. The defense budget cannot easily be divided by service since most of the expenditure is listed as 'common expenditure'. But for the budgetary items which can be divided about 40% is army expenditure. Apart from the military establishment proper, civil and industrial defense exceed the personnel strength of the Home Guard.

Table 3.5 The Norwegian Armed Services in Peace and War (% of the Total Combat Force), 1989

Service	Peacetime	Wartime
Army	47	52
Air Force	22	12
Navy	29	11
Home Guard	1	26
Total	99	101
(n)	42,500	310,000

Source: Calculated from data in Ministry of Defense (1993); pp. 16-34

When in 1977 Norway claimed a 200 nautical mile economic zone, this represented an enormous expansion beyond the old territorial limit of approximately 4 nautical miles.[25] This gave Norway one of the 15 largest economic zones in the world.[26] Although the Norwegian military establishment was still mainly concerned with meeting the threat from the East, there was wide agreement that Norway needed to be able to back up its exercise of sovereignty with a suitable instrument. The Norwegian Coast Guard was founded in 1978 as a separate branch of the Armed Forces specifically to maintain jurisdiction in Norway's coastal waters and vast economic zone – more than six times the land territory. Even before the end of the Cold War, the Norwegian Coast Guard played the most visible role in exercising the daily tasks of maintaining Norwegian sovereignty – against pirate fishing-vessels etc. rather than traditional military threats. After the Cold War, with less military tension and increased economic activity in Northern waters, the tasks of the Coast Guard increased in importance. Nevertheless, by 1993 expenditure for the Coast Guard amounted to only about 2% of the defense budget, although for a realistic estimate one would have to add spending for some of the resources of the Navy and Air Force on which the Coast Guard draws heavily in its work. Nevertheless, it seems reasonable to conclude that the defense of land territory (and its airspace) continues to enjoy priority over the protection of sea territory.

Notes

1. The data on Nordic wars are from an unpublished compilation made by the first author, based on standard histories of the Nordic countries and compilations of international wars such as Levy (1983), Luard (1986), Small & Singer (1982), and Wright (1965).

2. A thorough, largely chronological overview is found in Tamnes (1991). For a more functional overview, and also somewhat more critical view of Norwegian military ties with the USA, see Chapter 12 of Wilkes & Gleditsch (1987).

3. In fact, the defense budget increased by 2.4% in current value, but this was less than the expected rate of inflation (4%). The Ministry of Defense estimated that the 1991 budget implied a reduction in activity by 1.7% from the 1990 budget and 0.8% from the revised budget.

4. Cf. the Norwegian Defense Budget for 1992 (Ministry of Defense, 1991), p. 52.

5. Brief historical summaries of the length of military service are found in Ministry of Justice (1955), p. 64 and NOU (1972), pp. 32-35.

6. A thumbnail sketch of nuclear protest in the 1950s and up to 1961 is given in Ustvedt (1979). The large and quite successful nuclear protest movement in 1961 is the subject of a thesis in history (Lindstøl, 1978).

7. A pamphlet from the Ministry of Defense (1981) gives a survey of such benefits of the military establishment derived by the civilian sector, but does not provide any overall estimates of their value.

8. Holst (1978), p. 95; cf. also Holst (1967), vol. II, pp. 23f.

9. Calculated from Fiscal Accounts figures, chs 4799 and 4790.41 in the Defense budget.

10. For the Omega story, cf. Wilkes & Gleditsch (1987), particularly Chapters 7, 11, and 12. Although the budget item has retained its camouflage, the figure for the US subsidy is not secret. The figures for 1986-90 were obtained from the financial department of the Norwegian Telecommunications Agency. Yearly figures fluctuate, so we report the average for the period.

11. For a discussion of US-funded military R&D in civilian Norwegian institutions, see Gleditsch et al. (1978), chs 6-8. There are no relevant statistical sources in Norway, but the annual publication *Federal Funds for Research and Development* from the US National Science Foundation contains data for the total value of DOD grants to institutions in Norway and contract listings are available from the Pentagon.

12. The intelligence subsidy is unlikely to be included in the budget item for 'foreign contributions' because (a) this item is currently too small; (b) the size of the current budget line fits well with the activities overtly funded by the USA and NATO; (c) it would be contrary to the practice of intelligence organizations to include a trans-national subsidy in such a relatively transparent budget item.

13. Most of the relevant literature is in the Norwegian language. Wicken, in addition to several informative publications in Norwegian (1985a, 1987ab, 1988a, 1992) has three useful historical articles in English (1985b, 1988b, 1990). A comparative study by SIPRI of arms exports regulations (Anthony, 1991) contains a brief summary of Norwegian legislation and practice (Ch. 15, pp. 121-128, by Espen Gullikstad).

14. Quoted from Gleditsch & Lodgaard, 1970, p. 44.

15. For the exact wording in Norwegian see Gleditsch & Lodgaard (1970), p. 44.

16. Credited to an anonymous source in the Ministry of Trade, in Gleditsch & Lodgaard (1970), p. 44.

17. SIPRI. (1981), p. 188.

18. Cf. Wicken (1985b), which also contains references to the debate after the publication of the *SIPRI Yearbook*. Cf. also Barth (1982b).

19. US ACDA (1991), p. 31.

20. The decline continues in the 1990s (ACDA, 1994, p. 118). Norway's arms imports have also declined in real terms since 1989. Since a substantial share of Norwegian arms exports derive from compen-

sation agreements, a continuing decline in military spending will probably be accompanied by declining arms imports and exports.

21. We use *military spending* as a generic term. The precise technical terms are *budgeted military expenditure* (data found in the annual defense budgets), *military expenditure* (figures in the state accounts), and *military consumption* (from the national accounts). Military consumption excludes money transfers to other organizations, payments in advance or in arrear for goods to be consumed in other years, and includes expenditures for civilian preparedness, budgeted by other ministries as well as military expenditure at the local (municipal) level.

22. Based on data from US ACDA (1989).

23. A standard expression in Norwegian politics is to refer to 'countries with which it is natural to compare ourselves'. The only systematic empirical study of which countries this group might contain was made by Galtung (1968), based on a content analysis of 36 government white papers to Parliament *(Stortingsmeldinger)* in the period 1962-68. He found the following ranking: Sweden, UK, USA, Denmark, (West) Germany, Finland - accounting for 77% of the total references. Norway ranks below these six countries on most indicators of size, except area (cf. Galtung & Gleditsch, 1975, p. 744.)

24. For further details about the Norwegian conscription system see Gleditsch & Agøy (1993).

25. To be completely accurate: the Norwegian territorial limit is one so-called 'geographical mile' (in Norwegian: *geografisk mil*), which is 7,420 m or very close to 4 nautical miles (7,408 m).

26. The exact size of the economic zone is still unsettled, because of a continuing dispute with Russia. In 1977, Norway and the Soviet Union concluded a temporary agreement, involving a 'grey zone' with joint responsibilities.

4

National Conversion

We concluded in Chapter 2 that the main thrust of the literature on the economic effects of military spending is that the military establishment represents a diversion away from more productive activity, but that there was a lack of model-based studies which could provide more precise estimates of the peace dividend and the adjustment problems involved in disarmament. Having given a description of the Norwegian military establishment, we now turn to what is the main purpose of this book: an analysis of the effects of lower military spending in Norway. We start by analyzing the national effects, i.e. the effects on the Norwegian economy as a whole. In Chapter 5 we examine some disaggregated effects, i.e. effects on particular industries and regions. In Chapter 6 we examine some effects of global disarmament.

Our main interest is in disarmament, but we focus on conversion: the combined effect of reducing arms spending and reallocating the resources to civilian activities. This is a wider conception of conversion than frequently found in the literature, where conversion often refers to the process of change in an individual industry or even within a single firm.

4.1 Conversion Scenarios

To study the economic impact of conversion, we first need a scenario for Norwegian disarmament. This scenario could be based on specified (and perhaps quite arbitrary) *percentage cuts in military spending*, global or regional *disarmament proposals*, on alternative concepts for the future development of Norwegian defense (*transarmament scenarios*), or on *comparisons* with relevant countries.

4.1.1 Percentage Cuts

Of these, by far the simplest and most commonly used approach is to assume a percentage cut across the board. This is flexible, permitting the study of any degree of disarmament, from a modest reduction in spending (or even just reduced growth) to a drastic decision to abolish all military forces. The main disadvantage is that it is not linked to politically meaningful alternative policies, at the national or the international level, and may not make the best use of the total amount of the remaining defense resources.

The degree of reduction chosen depends on the prospects for radical change. The Thorsson committee on disarmament and development (United Nations, 1982) envisaged only a very modest degree of disarmament. For our own first conversion study (Bjerkholt et al., 1980), which will be cited frequently in the following, we used as one of our scenarios a reduction of military spending by about 15% over the period 1978-90.[1] At the time it seemed a very modest scenario. Yet, it later seemed rather radical, compared to the actual development of

Norwegian military spending, which increased by nearly 50% during the same period.

On the other hand, the end of the Cold War demonstrated that there are circumstances under which radical change is possible. The demise of the German Democratic Republic and the reunification of Germany occasioned rapid and drastic reductions in military effort. In 1989 SIPRI credited the GDR with a defense budget of about 20% that of the Federal Republic; by 1992 united Germany spent 5% less in real terms than West Germany alone in 1989. After major wars even deeper cuts have occurred in a number of countries. Drastic disarmament is feasible when the political circumstances are right.

4.1.2 Disarmament Plans

To date, global or regional arms control and disarmament proposals and agreements have had little to contribute to studies of national conversion. Many such plans have been grandiose, utopian schemes with little direct relevance to policy planning. A prime example is the joint statement by the Soviet Union and the United States (the McCloy-Zorin declaration) at the start of the Geneva disarmament negotiations in 1961 which defined the goal as general and complete disarmament. Such a goal was completely unrealistic as long as a substantive basis for the East-West conflict remained.[2] Such grand visions have their uses, but they provide little guidance for conversion studies.

Other disarmament or arms control measures concentrate on particular weapons systems or particular classes of weapons. The most important such treaties to date are probably the INF Treaty between the Soviet Union (succeeded by Russia) and the USA, scrapping a whole class of weapons systems, and the START treaties, severely curtailing their strategic nuclear weapons. These treaties involve significant conversion, largely overshadowed in the public discussion – for good reasons – by the political and military effects.[3] Production lines for missiles and warheads are closed down, bases become redundant, and large numbers of military personnel are shifted from one job to another. Yet, such treaties need not in themselves imply any overall disarmament. The parties are free to move released resources into other weapons systems. The INF Treaty, for example, directly affected the delivery vehicles of only about 10% of US nuclear warheads in Western Europe as of December 1988,[4] and this firepower could have been delivered by other vehicles, such as fighter-bombers, or eventually replaced by more modern offensive weapons, such as laser weapons. Similar arguments apply in principle to the Treaty on Conventional Forces in Europe (CFE), signed in November 1990, and to the Strategic Arms Reduction Treaty (START), signed in July 1991, although the greater scope of these treaties makes it less likely that the discarded weapons and withdrawn forces will be replaced in the short term by other weapons and forces. However, so far none of the major military powers has submitted formally to any restraint on the *overall* size of its military forces, nor committed itself to any freeze or reduction in military spending. Some reductions in overall military spending or in force levels are nevertheless likely, but this is more because of the political and military climate associated with these treaties. These disarmament agreements, as well as the overall arms reductions, have resulted from the political upheavals which started in 1989, eventually ending the East-West conflict. But the reductions in arms spending cannot be deduced directly from the treaty texts.

This is not to denigrate the military and political importance of such treaties as the INF Treaty; only to point out that while it involves a certain amount of conversion, there is not necessarily any peace dividend to be gained. Reductions in overall military spending or force levels are likely because of the overall political and military climate and the changes in threat perceptions and military doctrines following the elimination of the Soviet challenge to Western capitalism. But such overall disarmament does not follow directly from the treaty provisions, which are of little direct help in designing disarmament scenarios for any country.

Of these three treaties, only the CFE Treaty directly affects Norwegian armed forces or Norwegian territory, and then only marginally. Norway is part of the so-called 'flank zone'. NATO has negotiated a set of national limits within the overall Western force ceilings defined by the CFE Treaty. The Norwegian national limits imply a 17% cut in battle tanks and a 1% cut in artillery, while the limits for armored combat vehicles, and armed vehicle launched bridges are actually higher than current levels.[5] Of much greater significance for Norway are probably the limitations imposed on Russia, but that will not be our concern here. The main point in this connection is that current disarmament and arms control treaties do not provide precise parameters for the study of conversion.

4.1.3 Transarmament Scenarios

Norwegian public discussion on national security issues has not yet had much to offer, either. In public opinion, as well as in the Storting (the Norwegian Parliament), there is broad support for the current defense policy.[6] While there is also a strong sentiment in support of disarmament, little thought has been given to what Norway's defense might look like after substantial disarmament. The closest approach to a coherent alternative can be found in the minority view in the 1978 report from the 1974 Defense Commission, and some related writings.[7]

The type of alternative outlined in writings on alternative defense, or non-offensive defense, usually has the following main features:

- defensive military doctrine
- defensive force structure
- stronger emphasis on decentralized forces and sometimes these additional ones:
- non-alignment
- the relinquishing of weapons of mass destruction
- stronger emphasis on mobilization
- a smaller permanent officer corps and fewer full-time civilian employees in the armed forces

It is usually very difficult to translate these general ideas into precise budgetary consequences. Although non-offensive defense is usually presented as a less militaristic alternative, it is not always obvious that it will lead to lower defense spending.

A case in point is the German debate on non-offensive defense, by far the most comprehensive such debate in any European country. In the following we build on the extensive review in Møller (1991), where more detailed references can be found. Horst Afheldt has outlined a defense structure built on so-called 'techno-commandos', consisting of light infantry troops, which would saturate the entire territory to be defended. Lucrative targets, like airfields, would be avoided as much as possible, and Afheldt recommends doing without long-range missiles, heavy armor, and military aircraft. Although the fighting units would be small, they would also be numerous, so this would presumably be a personnel-intensive form of defense in wartime. Less certain is whether it would also involve more personnel in peacetime. Expenditure for weapons procurement would presumably decline, although Afheldt advocates modern short-range missiles and precision-guided munitions, particularly to combat Soviet tank troops. Norbert Hannig, on the other hand, emphasizes forward defense, more specifically a linear border defense with fire barriers. This defense scheme would have modest manpower requirements and would be very capital-intensive. The so-called SAS model, developed by Lutz Unterseher and associates, draws heavily on Afheldt's thinking, but adds a stronger mobile element. The SAS scenario is said to involve 'substantially lower troop numbers than the present structure without at the same time necessitating unaffordable investment costs' (Møller, 1991, p. 102). As an intermediate position it is not clearly more capital-intensive or more labor-intensive than the existing defense structure.

The situation is different in the USA where several economists have outlined alternative defense structures and calculated their costs.[8] However, most of this debate concerns the international role of the US armed forces and is not very useful as a model for transarmament scenarios for smaller countries.

Such proposals are not inherently more or less costly than the existing military establishment. Whether priority is given to territorial techno-commandos or to fire barriers, the seriousness of the perceived threat (and thus the *level* of defense) is more decisive for the cost than is the *structure* of the defense establishment. Thus, at this stage the debate about non-offensive defense is very difficult to use in order to outline specific transarmament scenarios.

Applying these general principles would – in the context of the debate follow-ing the 1978 report – mean that Norway resigned from NATO (and in particular from the integrated command structure), followed by a close-down or reorganiz-ation of the facilities used by allied forces (such as airfields and installations for the command and control of allied forces), cancellation of the order for F-16 fighter aircraft, increased emphasis on coastal defense, territorial defense along the lines of the Home Guard, civil defense, non-violent defense against occupa-tion, etc. Today, this list can be repeated except that the F-16 fighter aircraft purchase is complete and, apart from supplementary aircraft to compensate partly for depletion, the purchase of the next generation of aircraft is not on the immediate agenda.

A minority on the 1978 Defense Commission suggested that military spending should be cut to about half of the level at the time. The number of employees of the defense establishment (civilian and military) would be cut to about 20% Conscription would be retained, but the duration of military service would be reduced to about 3-4 months, i.e. the number of person-years of conscripted personnel would be cut to about 25%. In wartime, the existing mobilization army would perform Home Guard-type functions, and a new mobilization force for civil defense and civilian resistance to occcupation would be added. Thus, this type of military organization would be much *more* labor-intensive in wartime (in the case of full mobilization), but a great deal *less* labor-intensive in peacetime.[9]

Implicit in most proposals for non-offensive defense is a more intensive use of the potential for mobilization. Norway can mobilize a higher percentage of the population (about 8%) in wartime than most NATO allies, although not as high as Finland (about 15%). An even greater degree of mobilization might be achieved by extending military service to the over 25% of each male cohort who currently escape conscription for medical reasons and possibly to some of the 8-9% who refuse military service as conscientious objectors. Conscripts might also be retained in the mobilization force beyond the present age limits (19-44), which would engage a larger share of the labor force in refresher courses. The conscription of women would by itself double the number of conscripts, assuming no general exemption was granted to young mothers. Thus, it is quite possible that this type of defense would be more labor-intensive in peacetime as well as in wartime, but numerical estimates would be guesswork. Other aspects of such alternative conceptions of defense also remain too vague to permit specification in terms of the national accounts.

In early 1990 the Norwegian Cabinet appointed a new Defense Commission, whose main stated objective was 'to review the security, technological, and strategic developments which are assumed to be of significance for our country in the time ahead' (*NOU*, 1992: 12, p. 11). The Cold War died rather more rapidly than anticipated and this made relevant a wider range of possible changes. The report of the new Defense Commission was published too late to influence our choice of scenarios in this book. Not unexpectedly, the pattern from 1978 repeated itself: neither the majority report nor the minority views were specific enough to provide precise transarmament scenarios for a conversion study. The Commission did initiate various conversion studies, but not linked to alternative models of defense.[10]

In conclusion, transarmament scenarios – which have important military and political consequences – have not as yet given any firm basis for conversion studies. Rather than starting from the structure of the military establishment and calculating its future cost, we must derive our scenarios for future military spending in some other manner. In fact, it is not unlikely that the question of the structure will be settled more as a function of the level of spending than the other way around.

4.1.4 Comparison-Based Scenarios

A fourth alternative is to base the conversion scenarios on comparisons with other countries. The neutral countries in Europe appear as possible role models. Among these, Yugoslavia ruled itself out, even before the wars between Serbia and the other republics, because of a very high level of military spending. Iceland has no domestic military forces, but hosts a major US base – a policy combining two extremes, both of which would be politically unacceptable in Norway. Ireland has low military spending (around 1.5% of the national product in the 1980s) and is neutral, but has too peripheral a location to be of high relevance to Norwegian policy planning.

This leaves Austria, Finland, Sweden, and Switzerland, all industrialized countries roughly Norway's size: in terms of population they range from slightly larger (Finland) to about twice the size of Norway (Sweden). Like Norway, they are geographically located between East and West, although Switzerland does not border directly on Eastern Europe. All are non-aligned, and might be expected to be less attached to the arms race. Sweden actually had higher relative military spending than Norway until the early 1980s and has therefore been less suitable as an example of disarmament. Switzerland, Finland, and Austria have all had significantly lower relative military spending (between 1% and 2% of GDP throughout the 1980s) and are therefore more suitable. Denmark, with military spending as a share of GDP declining since the early 1960s and in the range 2-2.5% throughout the 1980s, is a possible disarmament model among the NATO allies.[11]

Although the three neutral countries have lower military forces in peacetime measured as a share of the population, all of them have a high mobilization potential – up to 15% in the case of Finland, 13% in Austria, and 9% in Switzerland. Denmark, on the other hand, can mobilize only 2% of its population in wartime. The three neutral countries also share some aspects of geography which slow down an invading force: mountains in the case of Austria and Switzerland, water (lakes and a coastline littered with islands) in the case of Finland – and both of these in the case of Norway. Population density is also low in all the four countries. Denmark on the other hand is densely populated, flat and very hard to defend, although about three-fifths of the population live on islands which are somewhat more resistant to occupation than Jutland. On the whole, the three neutrals seem to offer more of an alternative. Choosing one or more of these as a role model involves to some extent a simple 'percentage cut' – lowering Norway's military spending to their level – but also opens up the opportunity to study their defense organization as a model in other ways, too.

4.1.5 Specific Scenarios

Most of the empirical results in this book will be reported from calculations based on four sets of scenarios. Our 1980 study was based on three disarmament scenarios, as outlined in Table 4.1. These scenarios took 1978 as the base year and looked at the developments for the decade following the year of publication. The scenarios ranged from a very modest scaling down of military expenditure to complete disarmament. Since the baseline implied continued 3% growth, the difference between the baseline scenario and even the most modest disarmament scenario becomes quite drastic after a decade.

The 1980 study made use of a comprehensive but essentially static model (MODIS IV), whose main features are explained in Section 4.3 and in greater detail in Appendix B. Stretching out the conversion over time would not result in any self-adjustment in the economy. Hence, we chose to concentrate on the analysis of the effects of disarmament in a single year. The effects of a few percentage points of reduction in military consumption as indicated in Table 4.1 for the first year of the disarmament period would, of course, be negligible. In fact, the analysis showed that national adjustment problems would be manageable, even in the face of complete disarmament within a single year. We therefore chose to focus on the most drastic alternative: complete disarmament in a single year. Regardless of the political realism of this alternative, it was the most suitable scenario for bringing out the potential problems of the conversion process. It could also function as a worst case: if that could be handled, then any lesser degree of disarmament should also be manageable.

Table 4.1 Disarmament Scenarios for Norway 1978-1990, Absolute Figures, NOK Million, 1978 Prices

Scenario	Hypothetical military expenditure 1990	Difference 1990-1978	Annual change in military spending	
			Absolute difference	% Reduction in the first year
Baseline	9,763	+ 2,915	+ 224.2	+ 3.0
Expert group	5,821	− 1,027	− 79.0	- 1.2
Two neutrals	2,050	− 4,798	− 369.1	- 5.4
Complete	0	− 6,848	− 526.8	- 7.7

Budgeted military expenditure in 1978 was NOK 6,848 million.

The *Baseline* scenario corresponds to the 1978 decision of the NATO Council to increase military spending in real terms by 3% per annum.

The *Expert Group* scenario corresponds to a 15% reduction of military spending from 1978 to 1990, as suggested by the Norwegian member of the Thorsson committee on disarmament and development. The *Two Neutrals* scenario involves reducing Norwegian military spending to the level of the average of Austria and Finland in the period 1978-1990, i.e. to about one-third.

The absolute changes given in the second to last column are the arithmetic means of the absolute changes during the 13 years – assuming changes start in 1978. With constant per annum percentage changes, the absolute reduction would be larger in 1978 and grow progressively smaller as the level decreased. The opposite would be the case with the increases under the *Baseline*. The actual increases would grow from NOK 205 million in the first year to NOK 285 million in the final year (in 1978 prices).

These scenarios are calculated in terms of budgeted military expenditure. In the analysis of the economic effects we have actually looked at a reduction in military consumption of the same magnitude. Military expenditure and military consumption differ somewhat, as explained in Appendix A, but with negligible consequences for the disarmament scenarios.

In our more recent work, we have used models better suited for analyzing gradual changes in the economy. In the first such study we used the Norwegian MSG-4 model, in conjunction with the World Model, an input-output model of the world economy. (Both are described briefly in Appendix B; the results of the international study are reported in Chapter 5.) The baseline scenario for the World Model assumed continued 3.7% annual growth in military spending world wide for the period 1970-2000, with important regional variations, while our application of the MSG model used 2.5% real growth of Norwegian military spending. Two disarmament scenarios were used: one reducing military spending by 15% for each decade over the two decades following the base year (1980); the other based on twice that rate of disarmament.

In a 1990 study (Cappelen et al., 1992) we retained the baseline scenario of 3% real growth, comparing it with two conversion scenarios, based on different alternatives for spending the peace dividend but with the same degree of disarmament: 1.2% per annum for the period 1990-2007. Military spending in the baseline and conversion scenarios move in different directions, and the level of military spending in the conversion scenarios by 2007 is only 50% relative to the baseline scenario. The baseline and conversion scenarios assume the same military employment over the entire period. Hence, there is also an implied change in the structure of military expenditure.

Finally, in our most recent study (performed in 1992 and reported for the first time in Section 4.9 below), we have once again assumed continued growth in defense spending in the baseline scenario. However, instead of retaining the 3% real growth target, which now seems to have lost any credibility or legitimacy, we simply let the defense budget expand in the baseline scenario in proportion to the expected growth in GDP, i.e. 2.3% annual growth until 2005. The disarmament scenario in this study involves a 10% per annum cut in real military expenditure from 1991 to 1999; the remaining 20% are phased out gradually until complete disarmament is reached in 2005. Military employment was held constant in the baseline scenario, while in the disarmament scenarios it was reduced proportionally with military spending. The scenarios of the 1990 and 1992 studies are described in greater detail in Section 4.9.1

During the 15-year period when these various scenarios were being developed, the structure of the Norwegian economy underwent considerable changes. Dependence on oil revenues increased from 1980 to 1992, as Norway became the largest oil-exporting country outside OPEC; full employment gave way to unemployment at unprecedented levels, and the industrial structure shifted from manufacturing to services. The modeling framework also changed considerably. Nevertheless, the broad features of the results are comparable between the various studies. When comparing below we will attempt to point out what differences may be due to changes in the models rather than to structural changes in the economy.

In retrospect, the most important distinction between the models is how they deal with long-term changes. As noted, the static model MODIS IV, used in our first study, was not very helpful in analyzing anything but short-term changes. The results which we quote from the 1980 study therefore generally assume that all the disarmament scenarios – including total disarmament – take effect in a single year. In reporting the essence of the various studies here, we have grouped the results into short-term effects (in Sections 4.4-4.6) and extended conversion (in Sections 4.7-4.9).

We have also studied different *countermeasures*, by which we mean economic policies designed to counteract the negative economic impact of disarmament measures. Some general principles for selecting countermeasures are discussed at the beginning of Section 4.5, and specific countermeasures are included in the discussion of short-term as well as long-term conversion.

Our first study – part of a larger international study of disarmament and development – involved an analysis of the effects of earmarking for development aid a substantial portion of the resources released. This is not a countermeasure in the usual sense, although it may have some of the same effects, such as increasing public expenditure. However, it seems more appropriate to interpret increased development aid as a restriction on the freedom to choose domestic countermeasures. Results of such policies are also discussed in Section 4.6.

4.2 Conversion Indicators

The *economic* consequences of disarmament are not the only effects or, indeed, even the most interesting ones. The main rationale for implementing disarmament measures is usually found in *non-economic effects* – such as increasing confidence building, decreasing the probability of escalating arms races, reducing the probability of war, and diminishing the destructive potential of war should it nevertheless break out. However, given the considerable resources expended in the arms race, the economic content is also of importance. In a stable relationship between peaceful neighbors with no outside enemies, it can even be argued that the economic factors are decisive. Between, say, the Nordic countries, the overall relationship is completely dominated by non-military factors. Thus, it would hardly affect their relations if military expenditure were much higher than it is today. The probability of escalating a dispute to war would remain close to zero almost regardless of the level of armaments. In such a relationship, and ignoring relations to potentially less peaceful neighbors, the dominant motivation for disarmament will indeed be economic.

As noted in Chapter 2, *beliefs* about the effects of changes in economic spending may be exaggerated, not coinciding at all with the findings of economists. Thus, economic considerations may play a greater role in decision-making about defense than is warranted. Seen from this perspective, the continued study of economic effects of disarmament may be seen as a pedagogical exercise to reduce the economic effects to their proper status.

The economic indicators used in studies of the effects of disarmament are not radically different from those of other studies of economic policy. We have chosen to concentrate on the rather conventional measures of *employment* and *economic growth*. We might have added others, such as fiscal balance, balance of payments, imports, income distribution, or male/female employment. The first three are measurable effects within the models we have used, and will be commented on from time to time. We nevertheless consider them lesser political priorities than employment and economic growth. The effect on income distribution is not given directly by the models, but could be found by additional calculations. The balance between male and female employment is given by the model, and we do comment briefly on it in Section 4.8. But these features of conversion are hardly distinctive enough to warrant major consideration.

More recently the question of the effects of conversion on the environment has generated considerable interest (Gleditsch, 1992b). The environmental impact of military spending is a complex issue; in this book we look only at what effect disarmament is likely to have on the emission of greenhouse gases and a few other forms of pollution (Section 4.10).

4.3 Modeling Framework

Our analysis is conducted within a national accounting framework, using the macroeconomic models MODIS IV (for the 1980 results) and MODAG (for more recent calculations). Both are general-purpose input-output models developed by Statistics Norway. 'Macroeconomic' in this context does not mean 'aggregate'. The analysis is based on a detailed industry-level analysis. The main results reported are in macroeconomic aggregates, but the basis for arriving at them is an elaborate model with a detailed description of many aspects of the economy.

The two models contain highly detailed descriptions of the Norwegian economy: the MODIS model, now obsolete, was primarily a very detailed static input-output model with some 150 sectors and 200 commodities, while the MODAG model has an input-out core of some 25 sectors and 40 commodities, with more behavioral relations and dynamic elements than its predecessor. The number of variables runs into 4,000-5,000 for MODIS IV, while the MODAG model has 1700 variables. Both models are based on a comprehensive and reliable data base provided by the national accounts, including annual input-output tables and additional data. A fuller presentation of these and other models is given in Appendix B.

The limitation to an industry-level analysis bars us from addressing the conversion problem of the individual firm or local labor union, or the question of how to turn tanks into tractors. Norwegian military production consists largely of general goods rather than specialized military equipment. Aircraft, tanks, communications systems, and other types of technologically advanced, specialized military equipment are mostly imported. The comparatively few major enterprises heavily involved in military production and in military R&D also maintain civilian lines of production of tools, electronic components, computers, etc.

In using these models we thus assume that the main effects of conversion in Norway can be dealt with as a general problem of reallocation of resources between industries, with no particular focus on technological readjustment at a lower level. On the other hand, our industrial analysis is rather disaggregate.

The economic effects are dated in the sense that they are related to realized or prognosticated figures for given years. Large changes over a brief time-span may not be completely realistic for microeconomic reasons ignored in the model calculations. Our calculated changes are sufficiently small to be implemented fairly easily over a time-span of a few years, taking into account such factors as the existing capital structure and the qualifications of the labor force.

Statistics Norway also has a multiregional model based on regional input-output tables that can be run in a top-down fashion linked to the national models. This model system can be used to analyze the regional impact at the level of the 19 districts (*fylker*) of changes in military expenditure, although the military sector is incompletely regionalized. The results of our regional analyses are reported in Chapter 6.

4.4 Short-Term Effects of Disarmament

We start with the short-term effects on employment of pure conversion in the most naive form: complete disarmament in a single year with no countermeasures. In reporting this, we compare our own results with those of previous studies. In Table 4.2 we first look at the effects on employment. It is assumed that immediate complete disarmament leads to a loss of all direct military employment. Even more drastically, it is assumed that all *indirect* military employment is lost immediately and that the economy has had no time to adjust to the sudden availability of a large labor force. This is, of course, a 'worst case' rather than a realistic scenario. Even if such an unlikely policy as complete and immediate disarmament with no countermeasures were to be decided upon, it would still take time before all the indirect employment generated by the defense sector was lost. Industries catering to the needs of military personnel would not cut back their employment immediately. On the other hand, this naive calculation provides an upper limit to the national conversion problem in the case of a radical disarmament policy.

Table 4.2 Impact on Employment of Immediate Complete Disarmament with No Countermeasures (% of Total Employment, Except Where Noted)

	OB 1964	TA 1969	OB et al. 1978	New results 1992
Direct effect	-3.9	-3.6	-3.4	-2.7
Indirect effect	-2.2	-1.2	-1.8	-0.9
Total effect	-6.1	-4.8	-5.6	-3.6
Multiplier	1.6	1.3	1.6	1.3
Existing unemployment	1.8	1.6	1.8	5.9
Total effect/unemployment	3.4	3.0	3.1	0.6

Multiplier is *Total effect* divided by *Direct effect*. The final line is the absolute value of *Total effect* divided by *Existing unemployment* at the time of the study.
For results from the study labeled *OB 1964*, see Bjerkholt (1965, 1967); *TA 1969*, see Andreassen (1972); *OB et al. 1978*, see Bjerkholt et al. (1980); *New results*, 1992, see Section 4.9 below. Note that direct military employment from an older study will not necessarily coincide with the figures in Appendix A, which builds on revised national accounts.

The multiplier varies somewhat and tends to decrease over time. Most of the variation in total employment loss caused by disarmament is due to differences in the direct military employment.

The major new factor in 1992 is the high level of actual unemployment. In 1964 – and well into the 1970s – immediate and complete disarmament would have more than tripled the level of unemployment immediately, and even much less drastic forms of disarmament would have made themselves felt in the overall level of unemployment. By the early 1990s, unemployment had risen to unprecedented levels; it now exceeds by far the total employment, direct and indirect, generated by military spending. Clearly this creates a very different context for studying conversion. Even the most ardent enthusiasts on opposite sides of the defense debate can no longer argue that the unemployment problem can be solved by higher, or lower, defense spending. The net political effects are neither simple nor obvious. Unemployment has become a very sensitive political issue, and faith in society's ability to accommodate additional unemployment is probably lower. At the same time, society is 'learning' to live with unemployment, and the adjustment effects of disarmament may appear less drastic than in the long period when virtually full employment seemed a permanent feature of the Norwegian economy.

In Table 4.3 we perform a similar calculation for the loss of GDP occasioned by an immediate close-down of the military sector. Again we assume unrealistically that the entire effect deriving from the loss of the military sector occurs at once and with no time for compensatory economic processes to take root. The multiplier for defense spending in relation to GDP has been lower than that for employment, but for the most recent study they come out about the same. The total decline in GDP in the case of disarmament is rather similar in all the studies and is relatively modest – between 3% and 4%.

Table 4.3 Impact on GDP (at Constant Prices) of Immediate Complete Disarmament with No Countermeasures (%, Except Where Noted)

	OB 1964	TA 1969	OB et al. 1978	New results 1992
Direct effect	-3.4	-3.5	-3.0	-2.2
Indirect effect	-0.4	-0.2	-0.8	-1.1
Total effect	-3.8	-3.7	-3.8	-3.3
Multiplier	1.1	1.1	1.3	1.5
GDP growth rate	5.0	4.5	4.5	3.3
Total effect/growth	0.8	0.8	0.8	1.0

Direct, Indirect and *Total* effects on GDP in the case of complete and immediate disarmament with no countermeasures are measured in percent of total GDP for that year. The multiplier is the total loss of GDP divided by the product consumed directly by the military sector. *GDP growth rate* refers to the average growth in GDP in the preceding three-year period. The final row shows the calculated loss of GDP due to immediate complete disarmament, divided by the actual level of current growth. For full references to the various studies, see note to Table 4.2.

Once again, the question arises: what is a reasonable baseline for measuring the decline in GDP resulting from disarmament without countermeasures? The actual growth in GDP may be a reasonable basis for comparison. In 1964 Norway was still in the long postwar growth period. The total effect of the removal of the military sector with no countermeasures corresponded to less than one year of growth in national product. By the early 1990s, growth had become more haphazard. Recouping the GDP loss from sudden disarmament would be a longer process, and the end result might appear less predictable.

Table 4.4 gives some results for two other economic indicators – imports and balance of payments – for the studies in which they are available. Contrary to the case with the previous two indicators, sudden disarmament with no countermeasures has a *positive* impact as far as these two are concerned: imports go down and the balance of payments is improved. Table 4.4 shows that the effect on imports is particularly high in the most recent study. This may help to explain why the direct effects of disarmament on employment as well as GDP were found to be somewhat lower in the 1992 study. Import leakage is now higher – Norwegian defense

Table 4.4 Impact on Imports and Balance of Payments of Immediate Complete Disarmament with No Countermeasures (%)

	OB 1964	TA 1969	OB et al. 1978	New results 1992
Imports (% change)	-2.5	-3.1	-3.1	-4.7
Balance of payments (In % of GDP)	-	-	2.0	1.8

For full references to the various studies, see note to Table 4.2.

spending generates relatively more employment and growth outside the country than domestically, compared with previous years.

We may conclude that sudden disarmament without countermeasures would create an immediate problem in terms of employment and GDP. Whether or not these problems should be called 'large' is a matter of political taste. In the case of employment, the degree of conversion necesssary for total disarmament was until recently much higher than the current level of unemployment, but this is no longer true. It can be debated whether this means that the problem has become worse. In real economic terms, it is probably more serious to have 5% percent unemployment added to an already high level. In psychological terms this may work differently: long-term high unemployment may erode the political stigma attached to unemployment.

With regard to GDP, the degree of conversion used to be a little less than the annual growth rate. Now, however, the total effect of disarmament well exceeds annual growth. Thus, while the immediate loss from conversion could be recouped in less than a year's growth in the mid-to-late 1960s, today it may take at least a year. For imports and balance of payments, however, disarmament without countermeasures would not appear to present any problem – quite the contrary.

4.5 Conversion with Countermeasures

So far our discussion has concerned short-term effects resulting from very rapid disarmament with no countermeasures. Selecting a set of countermeasures is a question of determining a set of economic policies which will counteract the reduction in military spending and create benefits from shifting resources from the military to the civilian sector. We may interpret the former as *the conversion problem* and the second as *the long-term peace dividend*. One is not necessarily the negation of the other, since there is a difference in the time perspective. The economic policies suitable for overcoming short-term adjustment problems may not be conducive to increasing employment and economic growth in the longer run. Also, in the long run, on-going economic processes will deal with some of the conversion problems without explicit government intervention. Theoretically, short-term countermeasures may even be counter-productive if they impede the adjustment processes in the economy.

In the following subsection we discuss possible countermeasures for the short term and the long term. Then (Section 4.5.2) we give some results for short-term effects of one particular set of domestic countermeasures. Finally (in Sections 4.7-4.9) we discuss conversion extended over a longer time period, reporting on the adjustment of the economy to the dismantling of the military sector, as well as results for several alternative countermeasures.

4.5.1 Choice of Countermeasures

When military expenditure is reduced sharply, the political authorities have considerable latitude in deciding how to channel the resources that formerly went into the military sector. In an actual disarmament process, the latitude may not in fact be all that wide, because rising demands outpace the availability of the resources. In fact, in some Western countries, it can be argued that the expectations of a large peace dividend at the demise of the East-West conflict caused public funds to be spent before they had even become available.

Among the most frequently mentioned options for the government are

- tax reduction
- reducing the fiscal deficit (or increasing the surplus)
- increased public investment
- increased public consumption
  - for education
  - for health
  - for social services
  - for environmental improvement
  - for development aid

One's view on the wisdom of these various options is likely to be colored as much by general political priorities and views on economic policy as by the particular question of selecting countermeasures for conversion. In the following we shall give some examples of how countermeasures may work, but with no claim that these are the only or even the best countermeasures when seen in a wider perspective.

Since continued high employment has been a high political priority in Norway throughout the postwar period, we have primarily looked for countermeasures which can generate much alternative employment, distribute the work satisfactorily on a number of variables, and fulfill certain other criteria. Ideally, a good countermeasure should

- be highly labor-intensive
- provide a regional matching of new jobs with the released labor power
- have a positive (or at least not a negative) effect on female employment
- be relatively independent of other scarce or slowly developing resources (such as urban land or trained manpower)
- tap a partially unused labor reserve
- fill an unmet demand
- be popular and visible as a peace dividend
- have few other known negative effects

Increased public spending for social programs and in regional policy is generally labor-intensive and gives a good regional distribution. Some of these programs, however, have obvious weaknesses in relation to the criteria mentioned above. For instance, reliever and stand-in arrangements in agriculture and support for local grocery stores both provide additional employment in the geographical periphery, but neither has very high additional employment-generating potential overall. The expansion of professional day care, while popular and in great demand, is highly dependent on the availability of suitable sites, buildings, and trained personnel.

A promising example in the social sector is provided by social home-help services. Essentially, this program functions as an alternative to the institutionalization of the old and the sick in hospitals, nursing homes, or retirement homes. It is highly labor-intensive: about 80% of all costs are labor costs. It gives a good geographical spread: since 1974 all Norwegian municipalities have been administering such programs. It taps to some extent an unused labor reserve: experienced housewives, although others may be trained for the job without any extensive educational program. The potential demand is enormous, as evidenced by the rapid expansion of the program in the 1970s, although more restrictive fiscal policies curtailed the program in the 1980s. The eventual demand is hard to estimate, but the number of aged and disabled persons will continue to rise towards the end of this century and well into the next. Unless some form of home-help service is provided, about one-third of the population may at some point in their lives require institutionalization,[12] which will be much more expensive. Social home-help programs have a potential for affecting every family and are in that sense an ideal candidate for a visible and popular expression of the peace dividend. The program is already 90% publicly financed, with the funding shared by the state and local councils; if a regional twist is desired, the percentage of state refunds to local councils can be increased in certain regions. Finally, the program has a favorable effect on female employment. Indeed, a counter-argument may be that the program leans *too* heavily towards female employment and that conversion of the military sector might require a conversion at the family level, where underemployed women would find work and employed men in the military sector would become unemployed. However, as home-help programs expand, more emphasis can be put on such things as janitor services, repairs in the home, etc., creating a demand for technical skills which would be found in the military, and frequently among men.

4.5.2 Results

Table 4.5 sums up the economic effects of complete disarmament and various countermeasures in 1978. The effects have been calculated for employment, GDP, imports, and balance of payments. We assume that *all* the savings from the defense budget are put into a single countermeasure. We further assume that as the countermeasures are expanded, they use the same mix of resource inputs as the current programs. In expanding *development aid* we have selected the most favorable development policy from a conversion perspective. (See Section 4.6 for further discussion of alternative development policies and their implications for conversion.)

Table 4.5 Economic Effects of Immediate Complete Disarmament and Reliance on a Single Countermeasure, 1978 (%)

Countermeasure	Employment	GDP	Imports	Balance of payments (in % of GDP)
Tax reduction	-3.7	-1.5	0.1	0.0
Government investment	-2.3	-0.5	0.1	-0.1
Private investment	-2.9	-1.2	0.7	-0.3
Central government expenditure	-0.7	0.3	-0.5	0.2
Social home-help services	1.6	0.5	-0.6	0.2
Development aid	-1.8	-0.8	1.2	-0.5

* A negative Balance of payments means a reduced surplus or an increased deficit.
Source: Recalculated from MODIS IV calculations, 1980. Effects of the countermeasures are reported in Bjerkholt et al. (1980), p. 81. *Development aid* refers to policy alternative 3 in Section 4.6 below

Table 4.5 indicates that in 1978 a policy of immediate complete disarmament could be implemented with minimum macroeconomic dislocation using a single countermeasure: expanding social home-help services. Using increased central government expenditure as the countermeasure would also ease the transition. Most of the other countermeasures would involve some problem or other in the short term. Cutting taxes or increasing investments – public or private – would lead to a drop in employment. Increasing development aid would have the same effect, although to a more limited extent, while also increasing imports and worsening the balance of payments. All of these programs would also have a negative short-term effect on GDP, although if increased public investment were chosen as the countermeasure, the effect on GDP would be small. Increasing central government expenditure would yield net effects close to zero, while increasing social home-help services would have positive effects on all counts: employment and GDP up, imports down, and balance of payments unaffected. Of course, this example is politically unrealistic in the sense that all the resources released from disarmament would hardly be put into a single program. The value of this calculation is that it shows that even such a simple strategy can quickly overcome the short-term adjustment problems at the national level.

In a later study Cappelen (1986) calculated the effects of three countermeasures in a disarmament scenario, showing clearly that increased local government funding has better short-term effects on employment, GDP, and imports than does increased public investment or lower taxes (Table 4.6). This is in line with our previous findings, since social home-help services is basically a municipal pro-

Table 4.6 Economic Effects of Immediate Complete Disarmament and Reliance on a Single Countermeasure, 1983 (%)

Countermeasure	Percentage change in			Change in Balance of payments (in % of GDP)*
	Employment	GDP	Imports	
Tax reduction	-3.0	-1.2	-1.3	0.5
Government investment	-1.3	0.2	0.0	0.0
Local government expenditure	3.0	2.5	-0.7	0.2

* A negative Balance of payments means a reduced surplus or an increased deficit.
Source: Recalculated from MODIS IV calculations reported in Cappelen (1986), Table 4, p. 36

gram, although funded about half by central government funds. If the savings in military expenditure were put into increased central government funding for various local government programs, this would clearly have a beneficial effect on employment and growth, with only a minor effect on imports.

Finally, we have calculated the effects of disarmament and a set of counter-measures in 1992. The results, given in Table 4.7, point in the same direction: increased local government expenditure is a very effective countermeasure in the short run, certainly more effective than tax reduction.

Table 4.7 Economic Effects of Immediate Complete Disarmament and Reliance on a Single Countermeasure, 1992

| Countermeasure | Percentage change in | | | Change in Balance of payments (in % of GDP)* |
	Employment	GDP	Imports	
Tax reduction	-2.7	-2.7	-4.5	1.8
Local government expenditure	2.7	0.9	-1.8	0.9

*A negative Balance of payments means a reduced surplus or an increased deficit.
Source: MODAG calculations, 1992

In conclusion, then, three sets of calculations over a 15-year period yield a robust finding: The short-term national effects of even an extremely rapid and drastic form of disarmament can be overcome with the right set of countermeas-ures. In fact, even in the short run, there is a double peace dividend: local government programs which heighten the life-quality of the Norwegian popula-tion can be expanded, and employment and economic growth increase in the process.

This is indeed a rosy picture – but so far the analysis has been limited to a short-term perspective at the national level. In Section 4.7 we turn to the medium-to-long-term effects of conversion and in Chapter 6 we look at disaggregate effects. In Chapter 5 we shall look at the international effects of conversion and show that conversion at the global level is likely to have particularly beneficial effects for Norway. But first let us briefly return to a theme popular in conversion research in the late 1970s and the early 1980s, and see how the adjustment problems may be tackled at the national level if a major portion of the savings from cuts in military expenditure is reserved for increased development assistance.

4.6 Disarmament and Development

The Charter of the United Nations defines as two main goals of the organization to maintain international peace and security and to promote social and economic development. In several ways the organization has tried to link these two goals. The enormous resources invested in the arms race have been seen as a source of potential development, particularly in the Third World. Various UN studies have described the negative social and economic effects of the arms race (United Nations, 1962, 1972, 1978, 1983, 1989). The first of these reports struck an optimistic note: a 'much larger volume of resources could be allocated to investment for productive development in [the developing] countries even if only a fraction of the resources currently devoted to military purposes were used in this way. Disarmament could thus bring about a marked increase of real income in the poorer parts of the world' (United Nations, 1962, p. 51). Other reports have discussed the relationship between disarmament and development (United Nations, 1973, 1982, 1985, 1986). The 1973 report, for instance, concluded that 'most of the resources released by disarmament, total and partial, would be readily transferable to other uses' and that 'disarmament would contribute to economic and social development through the promotion of peace and the relaxation of international tension, as well as through the release of resources for peaceful uses' (p. 23).[13]

Development assistance is not an ordinary countermeasure designed to alleviate short-term domestic conversion problems. Rather, it aims at solving problems in other countries, by increasing transfers. It would be somewhat naive to think that the defense budget could simply be transferred to the budget for development aid, with no regard for the adjustment problems of the donor. We conducted such an analysis as part of our Norwegian study for the United Nations Group of Governmental Experts on Disarmament and Development (the Thorsson Committee) in 1980. A few of the key findings will be reported here.

In the industrialized world the Scandinavian countries have been leaders in terms of the relative size of their development aid. The target of 0.7% of GDP in official development assistance (ODA) by 1975 which the UN General Assembly set in the fall of 1970 was reached by Norway in 1976; its aid peaked at 1.17% of GNP in the 1990 budget, subsequently reduced to 1.02% in 1993, amidst considerably controversy. Among the OECD countries, only Denmark, the Netherlands, Norway and Sweden have reached the 1970 UN target; as of 1990 only Norway had reached the more ambitious 1980 UN target of 1% of GDP in official development assistance. Norwegian ODA has been relatively altruistic, in that most assistance has been provided as gifts, rather than loans, and without political or economic strings attached. About half of the aid is provided multilaterally, through the UN family and other international organizations.[14]

Different kinds of aid have different economic consequences in the donor country. 'Egoistic' forms of development assistance which tie the aid to purchases in the donor country are, of course, more likely to generate employment and income there. Thus, they are better suited as countermeasures in a conversion process. In the 1980 study we developed five policy alternatives for increased Norwegian ODA:

1. *Financial transfers.* The increased funds are given as *gifts*, either bilaterally or through the UN. We assumed that such gifts would have no effect on domestic production or employment. Thus, we ignored domestic administration of the ODA, on the assumption that financial transfers involve a minimum of administration and could be handled by the existing administration. We also ignored any 'recycling' of the increased transfers back to the donor, due to increased import capacity of the recipient countries. This seems justified since Norway represents a very small part of the world economy – less than 1% of world trade during the period we have studied.

2. *Egoistic commodity exports* (commodities that Norway would like to get rid of). This policy has not played a major role in Norwegian ODA so far, although various interest groups have called for the use of Norwegian aid funds to reduce excess capacity of consumer or investment goods in the Norwegian market. We operationalized this policy by calculating the effect of heavily subsidized exports of ships (e.g. fishing vessels) from the crisis-ridden Norwegian shipping industry.

3. *Altruistic commodity exports* (commodities which the developing countries want). We have made no attempt to measure objectively the needs of the developing countries; this policy simply aims to mirror the subjective needs of these countries by subsidizing exports from Norway of commodities that the developing countries are already buying. Because they were purchasing ships from Norway, there is a degree of overlap between this alternative and the previous one, although the underlying rationale is different.

4. *Benevolent commodity exports* (commodities which we think they need). This policy is also based on subjective needs, but seen from the opposite end. What Norway thinks the developing countries need cannot be adequately reflected in any existing pattern of exports or gifts; we therefore looked to policy statements. One main principle in Norwegian ODA in the late 1970s was 'aid for self-reliance'. Traditionally, this has been interpreted as assistance to build infrastructure, hospitals, schools, etc. in addition to increasing capital formation especially in agriculture and fisheries. Specifically, we looked at machinery for agriculture, for mining, manufacturing, and construction, for hydro-electric power plants, fishing technology, and equipment and experts for education and health services. These correspond to specific investment activities in the national budget; we have simulated the effects of this policy by increasing exports of the commodity composition of these investment activities.

5. *Unchanged composition* The final policy we studied was simply an expansion of the current ODA package, with the same proportions going to multilateral aid, to financial transfers, etc. The proportion of Norwegian ODA given in the form of financial transfers in the mid-1970s was estimated as 63%.[15] Thus, policy 5 and policy 1 overlap to a great extent and will have very similar impact.

As was evident from Table 4.5, complete disarmament combined with increased development aid is not a happy choice from a domestic point of view. Even on the assumption that we follow the ODA policy most favorable from a conversion perspective (policy 4), employment and GDP are down, imports are up, and the balance of payments deteriorates. Although none of these effects is very large, the combination is not one likely to enjoy much domestic acceptance.

Table 4.8 looks at this in greater detail by comparing the effects of the five transfer policies on our four economic indicators. As expected, the commodity export policies turn out to be more favorable economically for Norway. Less expected is the finding that Benevolent Exports (export of products which we think they need) proves more favorable than the other two, including the one that is most egoistically formulated (give them what we no longer want). It can be concluded from Table 4.8 that a policy of mere financial transfers (or even expanding current ODA) would not be a successful part of a conversion policy. While the simple notion of scrapping the defense establishment and giving the money to the UN may have other virtues, it would hardly be an economically viable policy for Norway.

Table 4.8 Economic Effects of Immediate Complete Disarmament and Transfer of the Entire Peace Dividend to Increased Development Assistance, 1978 (%)

Development aid policy	Percentage change in			Change in Balance of payments (in % of GDP)*
	Employment	GDP	Imports	
(1) Financial transfers	-5.6	-3.8	-3.1	-2.0
(2) Egoistical exports	-2.1	-1.0	1.1	-0.5
(3) Altruistic exports	-2.3	-1.0	1.0	-0.4
(4) Benevolent exports	-1.8	-0.8	1.2	-0.5
(5) Current composition	-4.2	-2.7	-1.8	-1.3

* A negative Balance of payments means a reduced surplus or an increased deficit.
Source: Recalculated from MODIS IV calculations reported in Bjerkholt et al. (1980), Table 3.9, p. 57

By settling for a lower level of disarmament, the adjustment problems can, of course, be correspondingly reduced. We do not report such results here. But since the effects are proportional to the degree of disarmament, the results for a different degree of disarmament can easily be worked out from the tables above. Even so, the economic indicators generally point in the wrong direction, and the conclusion remains: disarmament plus altruistic aid is a poor conversion policy at any level of disarmament. The combination of disarmament and development is therefore dependent on either tying some ODA to purchases in Norway or assembling a package where part of the money is spent on domestic projects that provide employment and income for Norway. Such a package can be put together in a number of ways. We asked ourselves: how much of the peace dividend must be spent on a domestic employment-generating program in order to keep employment constant? The rest could then be spent on the most altruistic form of development aid, financial transfers, and the net employment effect would be zero. The answer proved to be that if about three-quarters of the defense budget is spent on social home-help programs, about one-quarter can be spent on increased financial transfers to developing countries. If a less altruistic form of ODA is chosen, a larger share can be allotted to development, and social home-help programs can still make up for employment lost from closure of the defense establishment. Table 4.9 gives the effects on GDP, imports, and balance of payments under the condition of no change in the level of employment. The 'conversion index' measures the share of the defense budget allotted to development aid.

The combination of disarmament and development is therefore dependent on either tying some of the development aid in order to make up for employment lost in the defense sector, or allotting a portion of the defense budget to a domestic

Table 4.9 Economic Effects of Immediate Complete Disarmament, Increased Development Aid, and Social Home-Help Programs, 1978 (%)

Development aid policy	Effect on			Balance of payments*	Conversion index
	Employment	GDP	Imports		
(1)Financial transfers	0	-0.05	-0.14	-0.03	23
(2)Egoistical exports	0	-0.02	0.01	-0.01	45
(3)Altruistic exports	0	-0.01	0.01	-0.00	42
(4)Benevolent exports	0	-0.02	0.03	-0.01	48
(5)Current composition	0	-0.05	-0.11	-0.02	28

* A negative Balance of payments means a reduced surplus or an increased deficit.

The *Conversion index* is the proportion of the defense budget allotted to ODA in the conversion package. This index is fixed so that the net effect on employment is zero. Whatever is left of the defense budget is allotted to social home-help programs.

Source: MODIS IV calculations reported in Bjerkholt et al. (1980), Tables 4.12-4.14, pp. 83-84

employment-generating program, such as home-help. With the most egoistical form of ODA, almost half the defense budget can be given away, without additional unemployment. With the most altruistic form of aid, only about a quarter of the defense budget can be assigned to aid. Regardless of what development policy is chosen, once employment has been kept level, the consequences for the other economic indicators are extremely minor. The only effect exceeding 0.1% is for imports in the case of the altruistic development policies, and that change is in the direction of lower exports.

We can conclude that, as of the late 1970s, a policy of disarmament and development was possible: a substantial proportion of the defense budget could have been allotted to development aid, without any adverse consequences for Norway's domestic economy, as long as a portion of the defense savings was assigned to a domestic employment-generating program. We have not carried out a similar analysis for the early 1990s, but there is no reason to expect fundamental changes in this conclusion, although the state of the domestic economy is considerably altered. The average Norwegian citizen is substantially wealthier – GDP per capita rose by one-third from 1978 to 1990, but the structural problems of the economy are more pronounced, and above all unemployment is much higher. Even in the absence of disarmament, ODA is higher in relative terms – 1.2% in 1990 vs. 0.8% of GDP in 1978. On the whole, it seems less likely that an extremely altruistic policy would be chosen in the case of disarmament. We return to these questions of public acceptance in Chapter 7.

4.7 Extended Conversion

4.7.1 A Static Approach

The short-term adjustment problems may be analyzed by assuming that the disarmament takes place in a single year. It is more realistic, however, to assume disarmament occurring over a number of years. This may be the result of a decision to scale down the military establishment, but may also result from a situation in which the visible threat has withered away. This will considerably diminish the short-term problems to be dealt with. Conversion extended over time raises another issue: the longer-term effects of disarmament. In this section we look at those effects.

For a realistic estimate of the impact of a gradual and long-lasting process of disarmament, we need to take into account how other processes of economic change affect the economy. Thus when in our 1980 study we tried to model a disarmament process extended over 12 years (1978-90), we were faced with the problem that military expenditure in the baseline scenario increased by over 40% during that period. However, other economic entities will increase as well. We assumed – in line with policy statements made at the time[16] – that military expenditure and GDP would both grow by 3%, imports by 5%, employment by 0.5%, and productivity by 2.5%. For ODA we assumed that the rate of growth would continue along the trend line (16% growth) until reaching the target of 1% of GDP, and from then it would follow the growth in GDP.

We then calculated (using a simplified version of MODIS)[17] the effects of extended disarmament on employment and GDP in 1990. In Table 4.10 we show the new results next to the results for immediate disarmament in 1978. The Table includes only the most drastic case, complete disarmament with no domestic countermeasures, and only one development aid policy (the one most favorable from a conversion perspective, Benevolent exports).

Table 4.10 Effects of Complete Disarmament on Employment and GDP, Immediate and Extended Disarmament (%)

| | Effect on | | | |
| | Employment | | GDP | |
Disarmament type	Instant (1978)	Extended (1978-1990)	Instant (1978)	Extended (1978-1990)
Disarmament, no countermeasures	-5.6	-6.1	-3.7	-3.5
Disarmament and development aid (Benevolent exports)	-1.8	-2.2	-0.8	-0.9

Source: Own calculations on a simplified version of MODIS IV, cf. Bjerkholt et al. (1980), Section 4.2.2

Somewhat disappointingly, it seems as if nothing is gained by extended conversion! By stretching out the process of disarmament, the loss of employment is *increased* and the drop in GDP is about the same. However, this conclusion is in fact unrealistic. We have to expect changes in the industrial composition of the economy, including the military sector, along with the growth of the economy or as a result of government actions other than conversion. If we assume that such changes are independent of conversion, we might still say that Table 4.10 indicates the direction of the effects of conversion, although not its magnitude.

Gradual conversion is likely to trigger off adjustment reactions in the economy, compensating for the negative effects. While such reactions cannot be planned or predicted with any certainty, they should be included in any realistic model of the long-term effects of conversion. To this end we must turn to models which incorporate theoretical assumptions about economic growth.

4.7.2 The 1972 Study

The first analysis of this kind in Norway, to our knowledge, was undertaken by Andreassen (1972, pp. 80-94). His analysis consisted of two parts. The first was a simple macroeconomic exercise using a Cobb-Douglas value-added production function with labor and capital as inputs. Assuming that military expenditure and employment are reduced by 50%, and reduced expenditures are channeled into increased capital stock, Andreassen concluded that the net domestic product (NDP) would have increased by only 3% in 20 years, or that the annual growth rate would have been 0.15% higher during this period. If, however, the expenditures were used by the public sector as civilian consumption and public investment, then the level of NDP would have increased by only 0.84% in 20 years. In the second part of his study Andreassen used an earlier version of the MSG model, which we used in a later study, discussed in the next section. He assumed that military spending was halved in three years and again that these expenditures were channeled into public investment. At the end of a 20-year period the results for NDP were very similar to those found in the first part of the study, with the effect on GDP slightly larger. Andreassen concluded that lower military spending has little overall impact on economic growth.

4.7.3 Using A Growth Model – The 1982 Study

In our 1982 study (Cappelen et al., 1982) we made a more extensive analysis using the computable general equilibrium model MSG-4. This model assumes full capacity utilization of available resources and hence no unemployment. The baseline scenario for this study mirrored the latest official government Long-Term Program (LTP), published in 1981.[18] We compared this with a disarmament scenario (DIS) in which military consumption was reduced to 85% of the LTP in 1990 and 70% by 2000. Civilian government consumption was assumed to be unaffected by disarmament.

Table 4.11 gives the main results from this study, in percentage deviations from the baseline. The main finding is that the long-run macroeconomic consequences of national conversion starting in 1980 would have been very small compared to the overall changes that were likely to occur in the Norwegian economy over the period 1980-2000, according to the official government scenario. What little differences there are, however, are generally in a favorable direction. We have assumed that civilian government consumption will not change as a result of disarmament. (The LTP assumes a major increase in civilian government consumption, for other reasons.) Thus, we may interpret the disarmament scenario in this general equilibrium model as one in which the government reduces taxes as military spending declines.[19] In fact, our implicit countermeasure is tax reduction. Thus, demand from private consumers increases, and labor is reallocated from the military sector to industries producing consumer goods and services. Investment increases to enlarge the production capacity of these industries; industries producing capital goods must also increase their employment. The reallocation of the labor force and the increase in investment – and thus capital stock – results in a somewhat larger GDP than in the LTP scenario. Compared with the 60% growth

Table 4.11 Long-Term Macroeconomic Effects in Norway of Partial Disarmament, 1980-2000

Effect on	Baseline 1980 (NOK '000 mill., 1980 prices)	Deviations from Baseline 1980 (%) 1990 LTP	DIS	2000 LTP	DIS	Relative change (%) LTP to DIS 1990	2000
Military consumption	7	29	-15	57	-30	-33	-55
GDP	241	28	29	58	60	0.3	1.0
Imports	103	38	39	77	80	0.3	1.6
Exports	108	24	24	47	47	0.0	0.0
Private consumption	118	28	32	71	80	2.6	5.0
Investment*	70	39	41	64	69	-4.7	-8.0
Employment (in '000)	1691	4	4	4	4	0	0

* Excluding additions to stocks.
LTP = Norwegian Government Long-Term Program 1982-1985.
DIS = Disarmament scenario (as defined in the first row).
Source: Recalculated from the MSG-4 calculations reported in Cappelen et al. (1982), Table 5.3, p. 31

in GDP over the 20-year period this is a very minor difference, although a scenario involving 60% growth has later proven overly optimistic. Nevertheless, the results are inconsistent with the notion that lower military spending will necessarily slow down growth.

In the 1982 study we did not look at any other countermeasures than tax reduction. The studies of immediate disarmament reported above indicated that disarmament plus increased civilian public spending produced better results than disarmament and tax reduction; it is not unlikely that the same might be the case in the context of extended conversion. We return to this in the next two sections.

Today, it may be considered a weakness of the 1982 study that the MSG-4 model assumed full employment. Since Norway had experienced virtually full employment throughout the postwar period, it was not an unreasonable assumption that labor resources released by the military would be absorbed into the economy. But it was definitely an assumption and not an empirical finding.

4.8 MODAG: The 1990 Study

Our two most recent studies have used MODAG, an input-output model with more dynamic elements than MODIS.

In our work on MODIS IV, as well as MSG, we have assumed that disarmament involves proportional reductions of all the inputs to the military sector. In the 1990 study we specified that the continued arming in the baseline scenario would not involve any increase in military employment. This was not based on any special assumption about military strategy, but simply on the observation that for a long time military spending had been increasing without any corresponding increase in military employment. In the preceding ten-year period, for instance, military consumption had increased by more than 25%, with only a 0.6% increase in the total military use of manpower. In the disarmament scenarios of the 1990 study we also kept peacetime military employment constant.

The baseline scenario used in the 1990 study assumed continued growth in GDP between 2 and 3%, and a gradual lowering of unemployment from the then record high level of 5.2% through 2.7% in 2001 to 2.0 (which corresponds to the average for the period 1970-90) in 2007.[20]

In the first disarmament scenario all the resources freed are put into local government health expenditure. We call this scenario *Health*. We have retained the level of investment in the baseline scenario, increasing only the consumption of health services. One interpretation of this is that this represents a strengthening primarily of the home-based health care system. This is a deliberate attempt to generate more employment. It has also been selected in recognition of the considerable investments which have been made in the health sector and which are not fully utilized because of lack of funds. Table 4.12 presents the main findings for the *Health* scenario.

Table 4.12 The Health Scenario: Macroeconomic Effects, 1990-2007 (Deviations from Baseline)

Effect on	Baseline 1990 (NOK '000 1990 prices)	Deviations from Baseline (%)			
		1992	1995	2001	2007
Military consumption	22	-11	-22	-39	-53
Civilian public consumption	116	2.2	4.3	7.2	10.3
Private consumption	363	0.2	0.4	0.8	1.3
GDP	565	0.3	0.5	0.5	0.3
*Imports	212	-0.5	-0.8	-1.4	-1.5
*Exports	150	0.0	-0.1	-0.7	-1.7
*Gross Investment	108	0.1	-0.1	-0.7	-1.7
Current account	13	0.1	0.2	0.6	0.7
PSBR	8	-0.1	-0.3	-0.7	-1.0
Consumer prices	-	0.0	0.2	1.0	3.0
Wage rate	-	0.0	0.5	3.3	7.0
Employment	-	0.4	0.7	0.6	0.1
Unemployment rate	5.2%	-0.2	-0.4	-0.4	-0.2

* Excluding Oil, gas, and shipping.
The Unemployment rate under the *Health* scenario is measured as a difference in percentage points. A negative number means lower unemployment under disarmament than in the baseline scenario.
PSBR = Public sector borrowing requirement, i.e. the deficit.
Source: MODAG calculations reported in greater detail in Cappelen et al. (1992), Table 4.2, p. 72

In this scenario both employment and purchases of goods and services increase, so there is a direct positive impact on labor demand; this in turn reduces unemployment. At the same time the increase in demand increases female labor supply, which in the model partly depends on the sectoral composition of labor demand, an indicator of female job opportunities. Increased employment increases household income and thereby private consumption and housing investment. As unemployment is further reduced (in addition to lower unemployment in the reference scenario), wage rates increase. This leads to increased prices but less than the increase in wages – so the real wage continues to rise and consumption increases further. However, the loss in competitiveness due to increased costs leads to reduced manufacturing output and exports, as well as a reduction in investment due to lower profitability. All the same, the current account improves due to lower imports. Norway's imports are much higher than its exports excluding oil, gas, and shipping (which are exogenous to the model). The substantial strengthening of the budget balance as measured by the reduction in the Public sector borrowing requirement (PSBR) (i.e. the deficit) is mainly due to the increase in employment and wage rates, as most tax revenue derives from wage income. Thus, while a cut in public spending results in a moderate loss in taxes, an increase in other public spending increases tax revenue due to the tax on labor costs, income taxes, and Value Added Tax. Thus, it seems reasonable to conclude that not only would a cut in military spending make possible a corresponding increase in other public spending, it might also reduce budget deficits, at least in the short and medium term.

Although differently defined, the *Health* scenario used here is very similar to the local government countermeasure which we used in the static analysis (cf. Table 4.7) since we have put the whole peace dividend into local government health spending. Typically, 80% of Norwegian spending for health is channeled through local authorities, but health spending and local government spending also have a similar structure, with comparable effects. However, separate calculations (not reported in detail here) reveal that the *Health* scenario yields slightly more employment than increasing local government spending.

In the second scenario, direct taxes on personal income are reduced by an amount which – prior to income changes as a result of conversion – equals the reduction in military spending in inflation-adjusted terms. The average income tax rate for households is reduced from 34% in 2007 in the baseline scenario to 31% in the *Tax* scenario, i.e. 3 percentage points as against an average tax reduction of 2 percentage points in the year 2000. Table 4.13 gives the main results for the *Tax* scenario.

In the *Tax* scenario, the size of the public sector is reduced in line with military spending. Since the tax cut is implemented as a cut in personal taxes, the result is an increase in private consumption. This increase, measured in constant prices, is somewhat smaller than the increase in public and private consumption in the *Health* scenario, because part of the tax reduction results in an increase in household savings. In MODAG a tax cut leads to a reduction in pretax real wages that is smaller than the tax cut. Thus, real wages after taxes increase. This effect has repercussions in the labor market: labor supply increases, so that the increase in employment is greater than the reduction in unemployment. Thus the *Tax* scenario produces positive supply-side effects due to lower tax rates. But the budget balance deteriorates even when there is a cut in (military) spending along with tax cuts. Moreover, the pretax relative wage decrease is reduced in the long run as lower unemployment increases wage rates. This also reduces the positive effect on exports. In the *Tax* scenario, investment and GDP increase gradually. Thus, our model confirms one of the frequently reported effects of military spending: depressed investment and growth. However, the effect on investment is far less than in other studies. While it is common to conclude that military spending crowds out investment dollar for dollar,[21] the MODAG estimate according to the *Tax* scenario is closer to a 10% effect.

Table 4.13 The Tax Scenario: Macroeconomic Effects, 1990-2007 (Deviations from Baseline)

Effect on	Baseline 1990 (NOK '000 1990 prices)	Deviations from Baseline (%)			
		1992	1995	2001	2007
Military consumption	22	-11	-22	-39	-53
Civilian public consumption	116	0.0	0.0	0.0	0.0
Private consumption	363	0.5	1.2	2.6	4.1
GDP	565	0.0	0.2	0.5	0.7
*Imports	212	-0.3	0.5	-0.7	-0.8
*Exports	150	0.1	0.4	0.6	0.5
*Gross Investment	108	0.1	0.4	0.8	1.0
Current account	13	0.1	0.1	0.3	0.4
PSBR	8	0.1	0.1	0.3	0.4
Consumer prices	-	-0.2	-0.5	-0.8	-0.7
Wage rate	-	-0.7	-1.5	-2.3	-1.6
Employment	-	0.0	0.2	0.5	0.4
Unemployment rate	5.2%	0.0	-0.1	-0.2	-0.1

* Excluding Oil, gas, and shipping.
The Unemployment rate under the *Tax* scenario is measured as a difference in percentage points. A negative number means lower unemployment under disarmament than in the baseline scenario.
PSBR = Public sector borrowing requirement, i.e. the deficit.
Source: MODAG calculations reported in greater detail in Cappelen et al. (1992), Table 4.2, p. 72

As is apparent from Tables 4.12 and 4.13, both scenarios improve the current account. In our version of the model, nominal interest rates are constant as well as the exchange rate. At the time, the exchange rate assumption seemed fairly realistic. However, the turmoil in European exchange rates markets in late 1992 led the Norwegian government to adopt a floating exchange rate in December. Then, as of early 1993 it seemed that the Central Bank of Norway was pegging the exchange rate to a basket of currencies, although its exchange rate policy had not been made official. Assuming unchanged nominal interest rates is also dubious but not completely unrealistic, since the current account improves in both scenarios and the inflation rate is not very different from the baseline scenario. However, in the *Tax* scenario when both the current account improves and inflation decreases, one might assume additional positive effects in the economy from a reduction in interest rates.

Figure 4.1 compares the annual changes in GDP for the *Tax* and *Health* scenarios over the entire simulation period, relative to the baseline scenario. Most of the changes are quite small. The reduction in military spending in both scenarios is more than 50% by 2007, relative to the baseline. However, the share of military spending in GDP is only 3.7% in the baseline scenario, so that even at the end of the simulation period the shift in demand involves only about 2% of GDP. The main reason why tax reductions are more expansionary than increased

Figure 4.1 Annual Changes in GDP Under Moderate Disarmament 1990-2007 (Deviations from the Baseline Scenario, %)

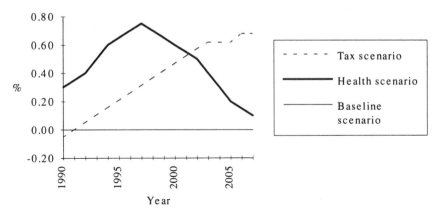

Source: Our own calculations using MODAG. Cf. Cappelen et al. (1992), p. 73.

civilian government consumption in the long run is that terminal wage rates are lower, due to a tax effect in the wage equation in the model. Given the same exchange rate, this improves competitiveness and thereby output. Thus, employment is channeled into manufacturing as opposed to remaining in the public sector in *Health*. As both the level of productivity and the growth of productivity are higher in manufacturing, the workforce – roughly the same in the two alternatives – gives higher output in *Tax*.

Another study performed for the Defense Commission (Bowitz & Cappelen, 1990) used slightly different scenarios. The baseline scenario was approximately the same, although the starting year was adjusted to 1991 and a slightly revised version of the model was used. The disarmament scenario in this study assumed zero growth rather than a slight decrease in military spending, in line with political consensus at the time. The reduction relative to the baseline scenario was assumed to occur only in the purchases of goods and services. In two alternative scenarios the resources freed were used (a) to reduce household income taxes as in the present analysis; (b) to increase public spending for educational purposes rather than health. Figure 4.2 presents the annual changes in GDP under the baseline and freeze scenarios. The Figure looks quite similar to the previous one, except that the absolute value of the changes is smaller. Overall, the results of the study by Bowitz & Cappelen are very similar to ours, as long as we keep in mind that the present study assumes larger cuts in military spending.

4.9 MODAG: The 1992 Study

In a 1992 study (reported here for the first time) we have once again assumed continued growth in defense spending in the baseline scenario. Both political changes in Europe and lowered expectations for economic growth make the old target of 3% real growth unrealistic. Instead, we have let military consumption expand in proportion to GDP in the baseline scenario. In fact, even this turns out

*Figure 4.2 Annual Changes in GDP Under Military Spending Freeze 1991-2008
(Deviations from the Baseline Scenario, %)*

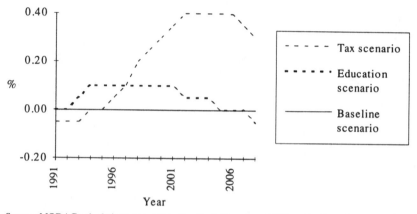

Source: MODAG calculations reported in Bowitz & Cappelen (1990) and in Cappelen et al. (1992), p.
75

to be too high. We return to the present and future development of Norwegian
defense spending in Chapter 7.

As in the previous study we have assumed that the absolute level of military
employment is unchanged in the baseline scenario. (In the previous decade,
military employment increased on the average by only 0.4% per year.) Large
military purchases (submarines, combat aircraft, etc.) are exclusively made abroad,
and we assume that in constant prices they remain at the level budgeted for 1992.
Other military purchases of goods and services are divided roughly 50/50 between
domestic production and imports. These purchases are assumed to grow just
enough to fulfill the overall target for the expansion in military consumption.

The baseline scenario is more optimistic in terms of economic growth and fiscal
balances than the most recent government long-term program for the period 1990-
2010. After the year 2010 the estimates are fairly similar.

4.9.1 The Scenarios

Apart from the baseline there are three scenarios in the 1992 study: a *Disarmament* scenario, a *Health* scenario and a *Tax* scenario, defined in relation to the
baseline scenario. The non-military aspects of the baseline scenario are described
in Table 4.14, which gives average growth rates for a number of key variables for
six sub-periods over a 38-year horizon.

The GDP of Norway's major trading partners is assumed to grow approximately 2% during the simulation period: higher in the beginning, lower towards
the end of the period. Norwegian investments in the oil and gas industry – in 1992
roughly 50% of total investments – are assumed to grow only for a few years and
then to decline. We have assumed continued growth in overall public consumption. The long-run development of GDP is highly dependent on the population
structure. Some time after 2000 the aging of the Norwegian population will lower
labor supply and the potential growth in GDP. This will reduce unemployment

Table 4.14 The Baseline Scenario 1992-2030 (Average Annual Growth in %, Except Where Noted)

Variable	1990-1992*	1993-1995	1996-2000	2001-2010	2011-2020	2021-2030
Military consumption	1.2	3.1	2.5	1.6	1.4	0.7
Civilian public consumption	3.4	2.4	2.4	2.3	1.1	1.2
Private consumption	1.5	3.6	2.7	2.2	2.0	1.4
Gross investment	-6.4	8.8	4.7	2.1	1.8	0.3
Exports	6.8	3.8	2.9	1.2	2.0	1.0
Imports	2.0	5.7	3.4	2.4	2.2	1.4
GDP	2.2	3.7	2.6	1.4	1.5	0.8
Current account (in % of GDP)	3.7	2.9	4.9	7.5	8.4	12.4
Fiscal surplus** (in % of GDP)	-0.1	-2.0	1.6	0.7	0.0	-0.1
Consumer prices	3.3	2.8	3.0	2.7	2.8	2.9
Wage rate	4.5	4.3	4.0	4.0	4.1	4.2
Employment	0.8	1.4	1.1	0.7	0.4	0.2
Unemployment rate (end of period)	5.9	5.1	3.8	3.4	3.3	2.5

* Growth rates for 1990-92 are observed, others are projected.
** A positive Fiscal surplus means an increased surplus or a lower deficit relative to the Baseline.
Source: Our own calculations using MODAG, September/October, 1992

and increase real wage growth in spite of lower productivity growth (which is due to the assumption of increasing returns to scale in the model). Thus, there is a shift in income distribution in favour of labor, and this promotes growth in private consumption, particularly after the year 2000.

The rate of unemployment slowly declines from the 1992 level close to 6% via 3.8% at the turn of the century to less than 3% at the end of the period. Fairly high growth in demand from the mainland economy contributes to the lower unemployment.

Moderate growth in the international economy and increased domestic demand will cause the balance of trade (as a share of GDP) to decline. The net interest income from abroad will increase and the current account surplus will increase. The public sector borrowing requirement will turn into a fiscal surplus by 1997. After 2010 the central government finances will be roughly in balance.

The *Disarmament* scenario involves complete disarmament put into effect by a 10% annual cut in real military expenditure from 1992 to 1999 and the remaining 20% removed gradually until complete disarmament is reached in 2005. There are no countermeasures in this scenario. Apart from domestic military expenditure we have also phased out foreign military contributions to the Norwegian defense establishment. Military expenditure remains at zero from 2006. In this study we chose to look only at a drastic disarmament scenario. From a policy perspective, if it is feasible to adjust to a major degree of disarmament, then the adjustment problems in any less drastic scenario can be managed more easily.

The *Health* scenario is complete disarmament with all the freed resources put into local government health expenditure. This is a scenario explicitly designed to generate employment, and identical to *Health* in the 1990 study.

The *Tax* scenario also involves complete disarmament, but with direct personal taxes reduced each year corresponding to the nominal reduction in military consumption. The tax reduction is divided between salary and wage earners, self-employed, and pensioners corresponding to their taxes paid in 1991. Table 4.15 compares the assumptions made in the four scenarios.

Table 4.15 The Four Scenarios of the 1992 Study

Scenario	Military consumption	Civilian public consumption	Personal taxation
Baseline	Constant share of GDP	Increases by 1.7% per year	Constant real tax rates from 1992
Disarmament	Complete disarmament in 14 years	As above	As above
Health	As above	Increased local government health expenditure	As above
Tax	As above	As in baseline	Reduced

4.9.2 The Disarmament Scenario

Results for the *Disarmament* scenario are presented in Table 4.16. In order to keep track of the long-term effects we have let the simulation run until 2030, i.e. 25 years after the end of the disarmament process.

The decrease in military demand leads to reduced GDP and imports relative to the baseline scenario. As the military demand is directed largely towards the construction and machine-building industries, these are hit first, but the effects spread quickly to other parts of the economy. The general decline in production

Table 4.16 The Disarmament Scenario 1992-2030 (Deviations from the Baseline, %)

Variable	1992*	1995	2000	2010	2020	2030
Military consumption	-11.3	-45.7	-89.1	-100.0	-100.0	-100.0
Civilian public consumption	0.0	-0.1	-0.2	-0.0	-0.0	-0.1
Private consumption	-0.2	-0.6	-0.8	-1.3	-2.3	-3.1
Gross investment	-0.3	-2.0	-1.4	-1.2	-1.5	-1.6
Exports	-0.0	-0.1	-0.1	0.2	0.7	1.6
Imports	-0.5	-1.9	-3.2	-4.0	-4.6	-5.1
GDP	-0.3	-1.3	-2.1	-2.1	-2.0	-1.7
Current account (in % of GDP)	0.2	0.9	2.0	3.8	6.7	11.1
Fiscal surplus* (in % of GDP)	0.1	0.5	1.5	3.6	6.5	11.8
Consumer prices	0.0	0.0	-0.2	-1.2	-2.4	-4.3
Wage rate**	0.0	-0.3	-1.0	-3.7	-6.1	-10.0
Employment	-0.4	-1.6	-3.0	-2.9	-2.7	-2.4
Unemployment Rate	0.2	1.0	1.7	1.5	1.3	1.0

* A positive Fiscal surplus means an increased surplus or a lower deficit relative to the baseline.
** Excluding defense.
Source: Our own calculations using MODAG, September-October, 1992

thus gives lower employment in the private sector. Nevertheless, the removal of 55,000 employees in the military establishment dominates any other change in employment in the short as well as the long run. Increased unemployment hampers wage growth. As unemployment is high anyway in the first years of the baseline scenario, the additional unemployment resulting from disarmament has only a moderate restraining effect on wage increases. The productivity declines somewhat because of lower growth in production, but the cost per produced unit nevertheless decreases. Because of the lower costs, Norwegian firms gain market shares at home as well as abroad.

The overall reduction in production also leads to declining investment and lower production in industries producing investment goods. The effect on investments is counteracted by the lower costs and increased profits. The lower wages also stimulate the substitution of capital and commodities by labor and counteracts the tendency to reduced employment. Increased unemployment also contributes to lower labor-supply, due to a 'discouraged worker' effect in some of the labor-supply equations. Unemployment therefore increases by only about half of the reduction in the number of employed.

The calculated effects vary over time. Private consumption is reduced mainly as a consequence of lower real wages and employment. Gross investment has a slightly cyclical movement. The lower growth of production leads to an intermediate period of particularly low gross investment because the firms wish to adjust to a lower capital stock. Subsequently, gross investment again follows the changes in production. The positive effects on exports appear only after approximately ten years, as competitiveness (due to lower real wages) increases only marginally for the first few years. The effect on GDP growth is at its strongest during the disarmament process itself; later on the growth rate is about the same as in the baseline scenario. In the long term, unemployment moves towards the level in the baseline scenario. In 2030 the difference in unemployment is reduced to about half of what it was when the disarmament ended. Even if the wage equations in this model are based on an equilibrium rate of unemployment of about 2.5%, it takes a very long time before the economy re-attains this level, after a 'shock' like complete disarmament.

By 2030 GDP has been reduced by about two-thirds of the change in the military demand for goods. Much of the reduction in GDP is a direct effect of the reduced value-added in the public sector as employment shrinks. For the private sector we find a 60% reduction of previous military demand; in 2030 the reduction is about one-third. In the long run the reduction in imports is about the same as the reduction in the military demand for goods – due to the large import share in the military demand for goods, and also multiplier effects from lower production in the private sector and lower consumer demand. Thus, demand effects dominate in the long run, too. This is not surprising, since this scenario involves a lasting and growing change in public demand.

The decreased wages resulting from increased unemployment imply lower costs for private firms; thus, the growth in consumer prices and in export prices becomes lower than in the baseline scenario. However, those employed in the military sector have a lower than average hourly wage rate (mainly due to the large share of conscripts). The lower growth in export prices leads to improved competitiveness for Norwegian firms.

During the disarmament period, output in manufacturing is reduced, but less than other private industries. In the long run, however, manufacturing output is higher than in the baseline scenario. The initial decline in industrial production is due primarily to the direct effect of the decline in demand from the military establishment. In the long run this is counteracted by improved competitiveness and increased exports from industry. The improved competitiveness is mainly a result of the effect of unemployment on wage growth. Other sectors face less competition from abroad; so few signs of improvement can be spotted after the turn of the century. Within the manufacturing sector, the machine-building industry and other industries producing investment goods are the ones to be hit most severely by declining military demand.

The gradual improvement in the competitiveness of industry gives increased exports and lower import shares. Heavy industry – and machine-building industry in particular – gain from this. The construction industry is also heavily affected by the loss of military demand. Reduced investment in industrial construction and in housing intensifies this effect. The service sectors, too, experience a clear and lasting reduction of production.

The main difference between the effects in industry and in other sectors lies in the estimated effect of lower cost per unit produced. For the industrial sector this leads to larger market shares; in the long run, the positive effects of this outweigh the negative effect of declining domestic demand. Private services and the construction industry are not as affected by foreign competition and are thus more severely hit by the loss of domestic demand.

The balance of trade is improved through disarmament, which results in lower imports as well as higher exports. Much of the reduction in imports is a direct result of the loss of military demand for goods. The decline in private consumption will also result in lower imports. The volume of exports increases as a result of the reduction of export prices. Disarmament leads to a reduction in exports from the military sector. As a share of GDP the balance of trade is improved by 1.5% at the end of the disarmament period and about 3% at the end of the simulation period. The improved balance of trade reduces Norway's foreign debt and gains additional net interest income. However, by 1995 Norway is expected to be a net creditor in the baseline scenario. This is accumulated over the entire simulation period and explains the increasingly favorable fiscal surplus.

The fiscal surplus is, of course, improved by reducing military expenditure. The overall effect is greater than this initial effect, since the net assets increase and net interest incomes increase later. This effect is partly counteracted by a lower level of activity which gives lower tax income as well as reduced income from VAT. In the long run, higher net assets lead to higher capital income.

4.9.3 The Health Scenario

The results for the *Health* scenario are presented in Table 4.17. We have assumed that the increase in health expenditure is divided proportionally between employment and purchases of goods and services. Health care is a typical labor-intensive activity, so any increase in activity here will have a pronounced impact on employment. The number of part-time employees is high – the average working-hours are 60% of those in the military. We have assumed that the average work-week of the employees in the health service is not altered relative to the baseline scenario. This yields a large number of employees for a given amount of expenditure.

Table 4.17 The Health Scenario 1992-2030 (Deviations from the Baseline, %)

Variable	1992	1995	2000	2010	2020	2030
Military consumption	-11.3	-45.7	-89.1	-100.0	-100.0	-100.0
Civilian public consumption	1.9	8.0	15.4	16.5	17.1	16.2
Private consumption	0.0	0.7	1.8	2.9	3.7	4.3
Gross investment	-0.1	0.3	1.1	0.6	0.1	-0.1
Exports	0.0	-0.2	-0.4	-0.9	-1.4	-2.0
Imports	-0.2	-0.7	-1.0	-0.5	0.0	0.5
GDP	0.1	0.6	1.2	0.9	0.6	0.1
Current account (in % of GDP)	0.1	0.2	0.3	0.2	-0.2	-0.7
Fiscal surplus* (in % of GDP)	0.0	0.2	0.5	0.6	0.7	0.4
Consumer prices	0.0	-0.1	0.2	1.7	2.3	4.3
Wage rate**	0.0	-0.2	0.4	3.5	5.5	7.9
Employment	0.3	1.5	3.1	2.8	2.4	1.4
Unemployment Rate	0.0	-0.4	-0.9	-0.6	-0.5	-0.2

* A positive Fiscal surplus means an increased surplus or a lower deficit relative to the Baseline.
** Excluding defense.
Source: Our own calculations using MODAG, September/October, 1992

Employment in the health service continues to increase as the military establishment is scaled down. By 2010 the number of public employees in the health service has grown by 60,000, but this increase falls to 50,000 towards the end of the simulation period. The reason for the decline is that the low rate of unemployment will exert pressure on wage levels in the economy generally and in the public sector specifically. Thus, a given increase in wage and salary costs will yield a lower increase in employment. The increased salaries as a result of increased employment in the public sector also contributes to higher salaries in the private sector. As a result, total employment in the private sector declines somewhat.

Unemployment declines less than the increase in employment – about one-quarter in the short and medium term. The main reason is that the sharp expansion of employment in the public sector leads to an increase in the supply of labor. This effect is particularly noticeable when the expansion occurs in the health service and women who have not previously entered the labor market become aware of employment opportunities close to the type of work they have been carrying out at home. In the long run, salary levels adjust so that unemployment approaches that in the baseline scenario.

The effects on GDP are clearly positive in the short run. The gross product for the civilian public sector increases more than the gross product for the military sector declines. The overall effects in the private sector are small in the short to intermediate term, while the tight labor market increases the salary level and causes deteriorating competitiveness. Thus, the gross product in the private sector is about the same as in the baseline scenario in the long run. The construction and machine-building industries are also affected by the loss of military orders, and this is only partly compensated for by the increased orders from civilian public purchases. Public purchases from the private sector are mostly for services. Gross investment in the private sector increases, which partly compensates for the decline in the construction and machine-building industries. On the whole, however, the *Health* scenario stimulates activity in the public and private service sectors, and shifts activity away from industry.

In the short term the balance of trade improves under the *Health* scenario, mainly due to the reduction in imports resulting from lower military activity. Some time after 2010 this changes, mostly because the increased salaries worsen Norway's competitiveness. The current account and the fiscal surplus do not deviate much from the baseline scenario.

4.9.4 The Tax Scenario

The results for the *Tax* scenario are presented in Table 4.18. There are two primary expansionary effects of tax reductions. First, a permanent tax reduction increases disposable income of the households and yields higher private consumption and housing investment. Second, a tax reduction contributes to moderation in salary increases and thereby improves competitiveness for industries not shielded from foreign competition. The second effect, however, operates only as long as taxes are in the process of being reduced (i.e. during the disarmament process). The tax reduction, however, gives a permanent improvement in competitiveness;

Table 4.18 The Tax Scenario 1992-2030 (Deviations from the Baseline, %)

Variable	1992	1995	2000	2010	2020	2030
Military consumption	-11.3	-45.7	-89.1	-100.0	-100.0	-100.0
Civilian Public consumption	0	0	0	0	0	0
Private consumption	-0.2	0.2	3.0	2.3	1.8	-0.2
Gross investment	-0.3	-0.8	3.0	1.5	0.9	-1.1
Exports	0.0	-0.1	0.0	0.5	1.1	1.8
Imports	-0.5	-1.5	-1.0	-2.6	-2.8	-3.9
GDP	-0.3	-0.9	-0.3	-0.2	-0.1	-0.5
Current account (in % of GDP)	0.2	0.7	0.7	2.0	3.5	6.6
Fiscal surplus* (in % of GDP)	-0.1	-0.3	0.5	1.5	3.4	7.2
Consumer prices	0.0	-0.5	-1.5	-2.5	-3.2	-4.4
Wage rate**	-0.3	-1.6	-3.8	-5.7	-7.0	-9.6
Employment	-0.3	-1.4	-1.6	-1.6	-1.6	-1.8
Unemployment rate	0.2	0.9	1.1	1.1	1.0	0.9

* A positive Fiscal surplus means an increased surplus or a lower deficit relative to the baseline.
** Excluding defense.
Source: Our own calculations using MODAG, September/October, 1992

in the longer run this increases exports and reduces import shares, thus contributing to higher output and employment.

In the short term both GDP and value added for the private sector decline, because households do not increase their demand enough to compensate for the loss of demand from the public sector. After ten years, the effect on GDP is positive, however, and in the long run total GDP is about the same as in the baseline scenario. Thus, the effect on output in the private sector is positive in the long run.

Lower tax rates means that a given level of real wages can be reached with a lower increase in nominal wages. Because of this and because unemployment increases, wages and salaries grow less than in the baseline scenario. Comparing the growth of wages and salaries with the *Disarmament* scenario we find lower wages and salaries in the short to medium run and higher ones in the long run, even if unemployment remains lower. This is because annual tax reductions have a direct negative effect on the growth of wages and salaries. When the disarmament process is complete, no further tax reductions are awarded relative to the baseline scenario (or other scenarios). The increase in private consumption and in investments has contributed to increased production and lower unemployment in comparison with the disarmament scenario. The pressure on the labor market then gives increased growth in wages and salaries and therefore lower growth in employment. In the long term, the level of unemployment will converge towards the unemployment in the *Disarmament* scenario, and the growth of wages and salaries to a level higher than in the *Disarmament* scenario.

The positive effect on demand from the private sector eventually outweighs the negative effects of the reduction of military demand. Industry production grows because of lower salary growth and improved competitiveness during the disarmament process. The general increase in production also gives higher investment. This effect is smaller, however, than the increase in housing investment. Production in the construction industry increases more slowly in the long run under this scenario, but because of the increased housing investment the negative effects are less than in the *Disarmament* scenario. Relative to the *Disarmament* scenario it is primarily the service sectors which experience increased production. This is a direct effect of increased private consumption. Employment is also directed towards these sectors.

The lower growth in wages and salaries (lower than in the disarmament scenario) leads in turn to increased exports. Increased private consumption yields higher imports, however, so that the balance of trade and the balance of payments deteriorate relative to the *Disarmament* scenario, but not relative to the baseline scenario.

The initial effect on the current account is close to zero. Subsequently it improves because of the lower level of economic activity and imports. After some years, mainland economic activity increases relative to the baseline scenario, and the income of the public sector and the fiscal surplus increase. Thus, even if the initial or first round tax reductions are equal to the cut in military spending, the fiscal surplus is higher. The negative employment and output could therefore have been counteracted by a more expansionary fiscal policy than assumed in this scenario – either through further tax reductions or through increased public expenditure.

4.9.5 Comparing the Scenarios

To get an overall picture of the scenarios let us compare results for some key economic indicators in graph form: Figure 4.3 shows the development of GDP over the entire simulation period for the three scenarios, measured as deviations from the baseline. We note a clear tendency towards convergence, although less so for the pure disarmament scenario. The *Health* scenario is consistently above the baseline, while the *Tax* scenario is almost consistently below. A separate figure for GDP generated in the private sector on the Norwegian mainland (i.e. excluding oil and gas) – not reproduced here – shows the opposite development for these two scenarios: *Tax* above and *Health* below the baseline. But this is swamped in Figure 4.3 by GDP generated in the public sector.

Figure 4.3 Gross Domestic Product 1992-2030 (Deviation from the Baseline Scenario, %)

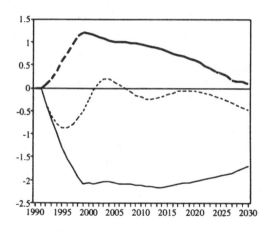

_____ Disarmament scenario   _ _ _ _ Tax scenario   ▬▬▬▬ Health scenario

Source: Our own calculations on MODAG, cf. Hove (1993), p. 15.

Figure 4.4 shows the level of unemployment during the same period. Here, the trend towards convergence is even more pronounced. The *Health* scenario is consistently ahead of the baseline scenario in reducing unemployment, while the other two scenarios lag behind. The decline of unemployment in the baseline is about as high as the maximum difference between the two extreme scenarios (*Health* and *Disarmament*), i.e. about 3%. By 2030 the *Health* and baseline scenarios are down to about 2% unemployment, while the two other scenarios are still above 3%. This may be interpreted as a long-term political advantage of *Health*. But the model itself contains an assumption that the long-run or equilibrium level of unemployment is about 2.5-3%, so we cannot put much emphasis on minor differences around this level.

Figure 4.4 Unemployment 1992-2030 (%)

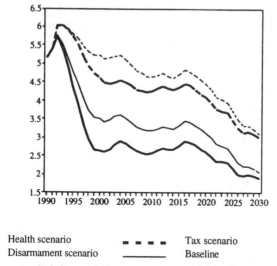

Health scenario   Tax scenario
Disarmament scenario   Baseline

Source: Our own calculations on MODAG, cf. Hove (1993), p. 15.

Figures for other indicators (not reproduced here) show a much lower degree of convergence. When it come to exports, for instance, the *Disarmament* and *Tax* scenarios deviate increasingly upwards, while the *Health* scenario deviates consistently downwards. For consumer prices and real wages before tax, the trends are the exact opposite: up in *Health*, down in *Disarmament* and *Tax*. Private consumption shows a more mixed pattern – with *Health* consistently and increasingly higher than the baseline, *Disarmament* below, and *Tax* first above, then converging. For gross investment, *Disarmament* is consistently (but not increasingly) below, *Tax* first above, then in the long term below, and *Health* first above, then converging. For imports, *Tax* and *Disarmament* go off in a negative direction, while *Health* converges.

Although the unemployment rates do not differ much between the three scenarios by 2030, employment levels do. Lower unemployment in *Health* from the start and higher real wages increase labor supply in that scenario. Thus, while employment has increased in *Health* it is nearly 4% lower in *Disarmament*. The GDP effects are more equal in the three scenarios, mainly because *Tax* and *Disarmament* allocate more labor to private industry, where productivity is higher than in public health services. Unemployment levels tend to converge between the scenarios as a consequence of how the model is specified, but employment levels will not converge if labor supply differs between the scenarios. Depending on the level and sectoral allocation of labor, there may also be output differences between the scenarios.

One additional difference between *Tax* and *Health* should be noted. While both the current account and the fiscal surplus change very little in the *Health* scenario compared to the baseline, there is an increasing surplus in the *Tax* scenario. Thus, it would be possible to expand the public sector or reduce taxes further. This would bring the results of *Tax* more in the line with *Health*.

4.9.6 Short-Term and Long-Term Effects

We concluded in Section 4.5 that the short-term national effects of even an extremely rapid and drastic form of disarmament could be overcome, given the right set of countermeasures. Indeed, as we saw in Section 4.6, even with the restraint of having to give a substantial proportion to development assistance – not in itself a good national countermeasure – other domestic countermeasures can put employment and GDP growth back at the same level.

Our analysis of the long-term effects confirms that national adjustment problems can easily be overcome with a suitable set of countermeasures. By putting the peace dividend into local government health expenditure, we can immediately obtain positive net results in terms of GDP as well as employment. Giving priority to tax reduction yields higher growth in the private sector, excluding oil and gas, but the long-term development of GDP is about the same as in the baseline scenario. In *Health*, unemployment is clearly reduced relative to the baseline, while *Tax* represents a minor improvement on pure disarmament without countermeasures as far as unemployment is concerned. Towards the end of the simulation period unemployment levels in the *Health* scenario and the baseline converge, but this is mainly because the unemployment in all the scenarios approaches 2.5-3%

We are now in a position to say something about *the size* of the potential peace dividend. The reduction of unemployment during the 20 middle years of the simulation period is quite substantial, generally between 0.5 and 1 percentage points. 0.5 corresponds, by the year 2005, to 12,000 people moved from the ranks of the unemployed – and any Norwegian government would be pleased to achieve such a result.

If we use consumption (private and public civilian) as a measure of wealth, we see that the peace dividend will make Norwegians slightly more affluent, but not dramatically so. Table 4.19 compares the immediate and extended effects of conversion with countermeasures. The increased wealth is marginal – whether compared to the absolute level of wealth before conversion, or compared to the 28% real growth in GDP per capita anticipated in the baseline scenario.

But increased consumption is not the entire peace dividend. Increased spending for health programs will presumably lead to improved public health and thus to a higher level of welfare. The institutions of the welfare state are under strong pressure to economize. The peace dividend might arrive just in the nick of time to help preserve important elements of the welfare state, such as (almost) free education and medical care. Investment in the infrastructure of health and caring institutions (hospitals, old-age homes, etc.) increased so rapidly in the 1960s and 1970s that society has been unable to utilize these institutions to their full capacity. Thus, by giving priority to operating costs over investment, more welfare can be gained per additional unit of expenditure.

It is very difficult, however, to translate increased health spending into precise estimates of improved health or higher welfare. It would be simplistic to equate the welfare increase with the proportional increase in spending. The health system itself is so advanced in many ways that improvements in many of the traditional indicators of health do not necessarily imply higher welfare. For instance, increased health expenditure may produce further increases in life expectancy. But

Table 4.19 Private and Public Civilian Consumption per Capita, 1992 and 2010, Complete Disarmament with Health Scenario (1992 NOK '000 Except Where Noted)

	1992 Immediate effect	2010 Extended effect	Increase
Baseline scenario	115.2	147.2	28%
Disarmament with countermeasures (*Health* scenario)	115.7	156.9	36%
Increased wealth	0.4%	6.6%	

The 1992 results corresponds to the results reported in Table 4.7: immediate complete disarmament and transfer of all the funds to increased local government health expenditure. The 2010 results correspond to Table 4.17: gradual disarmament until total disarmament is reached in 2010, and transfer of all resources to local government health expenditure.

what if this increased life expectancy serves primarily to increase the proportion of old people suffering from serious infirmities like Alzheimer's disease? Is overall welfare increased, or is it conceivable that it may be reduced? And what if further reductions in infant mortality increase the proportion of severely handicapped children, who grow up to be severely handicapped adults? These questions lead us directly into the central issue of priorities in the modern welfare state; obviously, it would be beyond the bounds of this book to pursue them further here. We merely wish to point out that how a financial peace dividend can be translated into a welfare peace dividend is neither obvious nor simple.

For conversion studies - indeed, for any analysis of the economic consequences of policy choices - it is vital to be able to go beyond the effect on GDP. But for the time being, with regard to health or other aspects of individual welfare, this is as far as we can come. In the next section we turn to one aspect of welfare where we may say a little more: the effects on the environment.

4.10 Environmental Consequences

4.10.1 Military Activity and the Environment

There is a large and rapidly growing literature on the environment in relation to war and peace (Gleditsch, 1992b). Indeed, 'the environment has now become firmly established as an item on the agenda of peace research' (Brock, 1991, p. 407). Much of this literature deals with definitional linkages, such as the attempt to establish the concept of 'environmental security' (e.g. Westing, 1989). Others are concerned with the role of environmental factors in causing conflict or even triggering war (Homer-Dixon, 1991). A third set of issues relates to the environmental consequences of war – both actual effects such as defoliation in Vietnam and oilwell fires in Kuwait or hypothetical ones, as in scenarios for major war in Europe (Westing, 1990). And finally, there is the question of the peacetime environmental effects of the military establishment. This area is of direct interest to studies of conversion.

In peacetime, the military establishment has two main environmental effects. One is that money spent on defense might instead have been used on the environment (Brundtland et al., 1987, Chapter 11). To date, public expenditure on the environment has been relatively limited in most countries; hence a transfer of resources from the military establishment could mean a major increase in environmental expenditures. For instance, in the Norwegian Fiscal Budget for 1992, total expenditure of the Ministry of the Environment is only about 13% of the budget of the Ministry of Defense. Theoretically, then, if all these resources could be transferred, the environment budget could be increased ninefold. Deger & Sen (1992, Chapter 9, Table 10, p. 184) estimate that 'pollution control expenditure' varies between 0.9 and 1.5% of GDP for six leading OECD countries, while military expenditure varies between 1.0 and 6.6 % for the same countries. Presumably, Deger & Sen's high figures for pollution control must include private spending; even so, these countries – with the exception of Japan – spend between 1.5 and 4 times more on the military than on pollution control. The room for expansion is considerable. On the other hand, precisely because environmental spending is still a relatively small budget item in most countries, a major expansion could be effected by a contraction of almost any major ministry, by lowering the growth rates of the competing ministries, or by expanding taxation slightly. For instance, the total spending of the Ministry of the Environment makes up only about 23% of the subsidies for Norwegian agriculture, 6% of the budgeted expenditure for the Ministry of Petroleum and Energy or 2.6 % of the expenses budgeted for Norway's Comprehensive Pensions Scheme. If total public expenditure (excluding public pensions) were expanded to accommodate a doubling of environmental expenditure, it would have increased by only 0.9%. In practice, it is extremely difficult to say whether military expenditure competes with environmental expenditure more or less than with any public project. The same problem occurs as in studies of the priorities of military and social welfare spending: it may be possible to show empirically a negative relationship between them in the past, but that provides little guarantee that the money will be transferred in that particular direction after disarmament.

Apart from such budgetary priorities, the military establishment may have a stronger negative impact on the environment if it tends to consume particular resources which are especially useful for the environment. It is adequately documented that the military establishment consumes great quantities of scarce resources such as land, minerals, and qualified labor (Lumsden, 1981). However, the more relevant question in conversion terms is whether the military establishment systematically consumes scarce resources in excess of its share of the national product (6%) or of central government expenditure (20%). For instance, some estimates claim that military R&D claims as much as 20-25% of all R&D expenditure (Norman, 1981, p. 72; Deger & Sen, 1992, p. 169). If this figure is correct, it is evident that the military establishment consumes more of that particular resource than its share of the national product. If, however, the relevant comparison is with the military share of central government expenditure, then there is no difference to speak of. On the whole it seems relatively unlikely that military R&D consumes so much of overall R&D that the intellectual resources should not be available for important civilian purposes like environmental protection and improvement – assuming that funding is made available for these purposes. And that takes us back to the general issue of competition for budgetary priorities.

The second main peacetime impact of the military establishment on the environment relates to the ways in which the military uses land, water, and air. Military exercises in peacetime can have destructive effects on the environment, as can the production and storage of toxic weapons. For instance, Altes (1992, p. 65) argues that 'even in peacetime, armed forces all over the world are among the greatest polluters'. A more cautious judgement is exercised by Belousov et al. (1992, pp. 81f.) who indicate that while there 'is no doubt that military activity ... has a harmful effect on the environment' it is not so obvious that disarmament will affect the environment very much, since 'military activity accounts for a limited share of the total volume of components polluting the biosphere'. The environmental effect of disarmament may even be harmful, since no one knows for certain that the former military resources, once they enter the civilian part of the national economy, will be used in environmentally sound ways. So far, these authors state, we only have qualitative estimates of the environmental effects of conversion. In an extensive quantitative study of 21 Latin American countries, Looney (1992, p. 214) found that military expenditure contributes independently to environmental damage, even when one controls for per capita income and the share of industry output in GDP. However, dividing the countries up into three groups according the degree of seriousness of their environmental problems, Looney finds that for the countries with the most serious environmental problems, only per capita income is significant in accounting for differences in environmental effects.

4.10.2 Military Contributions to Pollution

Westing (1988, p. 262) concludes that the military sector in peacetime contributes to environmental disruption in a way which is 'roughly proportional to the size of the sector'. If this is correct, the environmental effect of disarmament should be nil, assuming that the civilian part of the economy expands proportionally. This depends, of course, on the nature of the countermeasures. Some tentative quantitative estimates are available in the Norwegian Defense Ministry Environment Plan (Ministry of Defense, 1990, 1992). This plan contains calculations indicating that military resource use is sometimes above, sometimes below the military share of the overall economy, as measured by the share of the national product. More precisely, the defense establishment in 1989 – according to the national accounts – consumed 3.3% of the national product, while it consumed 0.8% of all diesel fuel, 0.2 % of all petrol, 3.2% of all heating oil and 12.7% of all jet fuel. The total military emissions of CO_2 equivalents amounted to about 1.3% of the total Norwegian emissions – well below the military share of the national product. (This calculation ignores the relatively more frequent idling of engines in the military establishment, which produces higher emissions of CO, CO_2, and soot, but a more refined calculation would probably not produce very different results.) Thus, if a relative reduction in military activity occurs in Norway – as seems likely in the next few years – and the resources are transferred proportionally to all current private and public activities, it would seem that an important component of environmental pollution will *increase* and the environmental dividend will be negative! However, we cannot attach too much importance to such crude estimates; in the next section we report some model-based estimates. Of course, if conversion can be geared to environmentally benign activities, there will be room for an 'environmental dividend'. The Norwegian military establishment has proclaimed environmental consciousness as an important target; clearly, in a process of detente and disarmament, environmental standards must also be applied to the resource allocation of the peace dividend.

4.10.3 Disarmament and Greenhouse Gases

Economists are frequently criticized for limiting their investigations to a very narrow field of human accomplishment, such as economic growth, to the exclusion of other important goals (Daly & Cobb, 1989). Be that as it may, macroeconomic models can be adapted to include environmental variables such as energy consumption, emission of air pollutants, etc. Environmental effects are calculated from the results of the economic model with no feedback to the economic process (Alfsen, 1991, p. 4). The MSG and MODAG models have already been used extensively for the analysis of air pollution problems. Today, the paucity of reliable environmental data is probably as much of a problem as the models.

This section presents some model-based estimates of the environmental consequences of our three scenarios, calculated on a separate sub-model using results from our MODAG runs. We are unable to say anything about possible feedback from the environmental effects to the economy. The model consists simply of a set of linear relations between variables that are endogenous in MODAG, such as the use of fuels for transport and heating and emission of gases related to the burning of fuels. Similarly, the use of certain chemicals for industrial purposes is related to material inputs in each industry in the model. Thus the detailed input-output structure of MODAG, along with a fairly disaggregated industry modeling, enables us to make reasonable linkages between variables of the model and variables related to emission of greenhouse gases as well as other pollutants.

The effects of the three scenarios on some pollutants are shown in Table 4.20. In order to discuss the main results we may imagine that the pollutants depend on two main variables: level of GDP and composition of industry. The higher the level of GDP for a given industry composition, the more pollution there will be. A change in the composition of industries towards manufacturing will have the same effect, largely because Norwegian manufacturing consists of a relatively high proportion of energy-intensive sectors producing raw materials mainly for exports.

We may conclude that generally all scenarios show lower emission of greenhouse gases than the baseline scenario. In some cases there are some small increases in emissions but mainly for pollutants that are not considered to be a major problem (SO_2, CO, and Lead[22]). The emission of CO_2 is reduced in all scenarios. Thus, there are environmental dividends in addition to the peace dividend. From an environmental perspective the *Tax* and *Health* scenarios are slightly less favorable than *Disarmament* without any countermeasures. The main

Table 4.20 Effect of Conversion on the Emissions to Air of Greenhouse Gases and Other Pollutants (Differences from Baseline in %)

	Disarmament		Health		Tax	
	2010	2030	2010	2030	2010	2030
CO	-1.1	-0.3	0.1	-0.7	0.7	0.5
CO_2	-1.8	-1.9	-1.1	-1.7	-0.7	-1.2
NO_x	-2.8	-3.4	-1.8	-2.6	-1.6	-2.5
N_2O	-0.6	-0.9	-0.1	0.0	-0.2	-0.6
SO_2	-0.5	1.0	-1.3	-2.8	0.7	1.8
Lead	-1.0	-0.6	0.8	0.9	1.4	0.1
Soot	-1.6	-1.9	-1.0	-1.3	-0.9	-1.4
VOC	-0.9	-1.4	-0.1	-0.0	-0.1	-0.9

CO = Carbon monoxide, CO_2 = Carbon dioxide, NO_x = Nitrogen oxides (NO and NO_2), N_2O = Nitrous oxide, SO_2 = Sulfur dioxide, VOC = Volatile organic compounds.

reason for this is that *Tax* and *Health* result in somewhat higher GDP levels than *Disarmament*.

The *Health* scenario generally does better in terms of environmental effects than the *Tax* scenario, even though GDP is higher in *Health*. The reason for this result is the composition effect referred to earlier. While the higher wages in *Health* lead to loss of competitiveness and less output (and thereby use of energy) in most manufacturing sectors, the opposite is true for *Tax*. This fact is also reflected in the figures for exports in Tables 4.17 and 4.18 above. The reason why there is more emission of Lead and VOC in *Health* compared to *Tax* is mainly the higher level of private consumption in *Health*, which leads to the more extensive use of cars. As noted earlier, there is some scope for additional government spending in the *Tax* scenario, as public finances show a higher surplus than in *Health*. If this surplus were used, the GDP effect would make *Health* look comparatively more favorable in environmental terms than it does in Table 4.20.

4.10.4 An Environmental Dividend?

Of course, the *process* of conversion itself may also have some environmental costs. Disarmament treaties presuppose that weapons are *destroyed*; but if this is done carelessly, the destruction itself may cause more pollution in the short run than if the weapons had remained. The most difficult cases are weapons of mass destruction, like nuclear and chemical weapons. Too dangerous simply to leave alone, they also contain substances so lethal that they cannot merely be left to the elements after dismantling. If one assumes that a technical solution can be found, this is a question of a one-time expense for cleaning up after the arms race. In the long run, this short-term 'peace penalty' will be outweighed by the peace dividend.

When the industrialized world starts disarming, it is of course possible that environmentally harmful byproducts of the arms race will be dumped onto the Third World. French nuclear testing in the Pacific is an old example of international military pollution. Charlin & Varas (1992) have shown that the Third World already serves as a dumping-ground for dangerous waste from the North. It will no doubt be a tempting prospect to include toxic military waste in shipments to the Third World, but so far there has been little systematic research on this issue. Another tempting possibility is to dump military waste in no man's land, as the Soviet Union did when it buried old nuclear ship reactors in the Barents Sea.

Nevertheless, the main problem still concerns the environmentally unsound use of the peace dividend. It is not hard to write pessimistic scenarios, of course. If military activities are curtailed and highly polluting private consumption is increased correspondingly, consumption of fossil fuel products is very likely to increase. However, our own calculations present a somewhat more optimistic picture than those of the Ministry of Defense. In fact, the countermeasures which we had selected for economic reasons also seem to yield an environmental dividend. We are not aware of similar calculations from other countries. Many countries have the same capability as Norway for building environmental standards into national planning models, and no doubt the Norwegian models will also be improved. This should facilitate more precise calculations of the environmental effects of conversion and improve international comparability.

Notes

1. This alternative was suggested to us by the Norwegian member of the Thorsson committee, Sten Lundbo.

2. The McCloy-Zorin declaration is reprinted in United Nations (1965), pp. 87f. A good critical review of such proposals is found in Myrdal (1976), particularly Section 3.4 'Propaganda Game with General Disarmament Plans'.

3. Conversion of the nuclear weapons complex is discussed by Bischak (1988) and of chemical weapons by Lock (1992) and Evstafiev & Gregoriev (1992).

4. Calculated from data given in Table 1.3, p. 14 of the *SIPRI Yearbook*, 1989.

5. Cf. the Report from the Defense Commission, *NOU*, 1992:12, p. 27.

6. We return in greater detail to the question of public opinion in Chapter 7.

7. *NOU*, 1978: 9. The dissenting views are found on pp. 253-298. Cf. also Kielland (1971, 1979). Galtung & Hansen (1981), and a committee report from the Liberal Party, Venstre (1980). Galtung has also published extensively on the question of non-violent defense (Galtung, 1976) and on non-offensive defense (Galtung, 1984), but with scarcely any specific reference to the Norwegian military establishment.

8. Cf., for instance, Adams & Korb (1991) and Bischak (1991), particularly his own contribution (Ch. 5).

9. The minority view was presented by Arent Henriksen from the Socialist Left Party, cf. *NOU*, 1978:9, pp. 278.

10. Cf. Bowitz & Cappelen (1990), discussed below in Section 4.8.2. For a review of the Commission's extensive local conversion studies, see Chapter 6.

11. For comparisons between the Nordic countries, see Gleditsch et al. (1992). Annual figures for all countries are reported in the *SIPRI Yearbook*.

12. Cf. *Langtidsprogrammet 1994-1997* [Long-Term Program 1994-97], *St.meld.* no. 4 (1992-93), particularly Appendices I and II.

13. For an overview of literature about disarmament and development see Wängborg (1979abc).

14. For further details about Norwegian ODA, see Bjerkholt et al. (1980), Chapter 3 and Ministry of Foreign Affairs (1992ab). More detailed information is available in the annual reports of NORAD

(the Norwegian Agency for International Development) and in the annual budgets of the Ministry for Foreign Affairs and Ministry for Development Cooperation (for several years a separate ministry).

15. The basis for this estimate, considerably lower than that published in the *Fiscal Accounts*, is explained in Bjerkholt et al. (1980), p. 54.

16. For details, see Bjerkholt et al. (1980), pp. 70ff.

17. The simplifications and method of calculation follow closely those used by Cappelen (1978), except that we have assumed that import shares will grow by 2% per year and real wages at the same rate as labor productivity.

18. *Langtidsprogrammet 1982-85* [Norwegian Long-Term Program 1982-85], *St.meld.* no. 79 (1980-81). Appendix II in this report presents three scenarios for the period 1979-2000, all calculated using MSG-4. We used the 'medium' alternative.

19. MSG adjusts private consumption to maintain full employment. A reasonable interpretation is that this is achieved through tax reduction, but the level of direct taxation is not specified in the model.

20. Details are given in Cappelen et al. (1992), Table 4.1, p. 70.

21. Cf. Cappelen et al. (1984b) and references therein.

22. The SO_2 problem in Norway is mainly imported from Europe through acid rain and domestic emissions are very small. Lead emissions have already been substantially reduced in Norway as an increasing number of cars have converted to lead-free gas. The baseline scenario assumes that this trend continues.

5

Global Conversion

5.1 The International Context

Conversion is an issue that is international in scope. It is very unlikely to come about except as the result of a change in international relations. The end of the East-West conflict signals the most promising starting-point for large-scale international conversion since the end of World War II. Furthermore, conversion is international because militarization of the economy has consequences beyond national boundaries. Military production involves imports of components and raw materials. It also generates pressure for exports, as the released production capacity is unlikely to have a domestic market. Moreover, hundreds of thousands of troops, mainly from the USA, are currently stationed abroad – with economic consequences for the sender as well as the host country, and dislocations when forces are withdrawn.

The magnitude of the problem may be illustrated by some data from a critique of the US defense budget after the Cold War. As late as October 1992, the USA alone had nearly 300,000 troops stationed in foreign countries, in addition to close to 50,000 personnel afloat in foreign areas (CDI, 1993, p. 7). Indeed, the Center for Defense Information claims that only 2.5% of the US defense budget is spent in the defense of the Continental United States, in addition to 14% on nuclear forces, while the rest is being spent abroad (1993, p. 6). How much of the money spent on foreign military missions is forward defense of the home country, and how much involves 'defense of foreign countries', is a difficult definitional issue – to the extent that the strategic doctrine allows the two to be separated at all. But there can be no question that, for today's remaining global superpower, the military establishment is an important international economic actor.

For countries at the 'receiving end' of the relationship, too, the economic implications of defense cooperation can be quite significant. At the end of the Cold War there were 250,000 US military personnel in West Germany. The gross economic impact of this force was somewhere between 0.5% and 1% of GDP, at a time when West German domestic military spending made up about 3%.[1] In Iceland, which has no domestic military forces at all, the economic value of the US bases as of 1986 was calculated to be about 1.4% of GDP (Duke, 1990, p. 113), as much as the domestic military spending of most European neutrals at the time. As we have shown in Chapter 3, Norway had a very 'open economy' in the early 1950s as far as the defense sector was concerned, mainly due to the US military assistance program, but the economic importance of outside assistance soon declined. It increased again in the 1980s but never to the point where it would matter very much in terms of national conversion.

Various international economic models have been used to study the international economic ramifications of armaments. In this chapter we will briefly review some such models (Section 5.2). Then we discuss some probable consequences for the global economy of major arms cuts (Section 5.3). Finally, we take a look at some consequences for Norway (Section 5.4).

5.2 International Models

Various models have been developed for the analysis of international economic interrelations. Most of these describe the world system in broad economic terms, including national accounting concepts such as GDP; but demographic variables, energy, natural sources, environmental variables, and even political processes may also be included. Relationships may be specified at the national, regional, or global level. Such models differ widely with regard to coverage, degree of detail, time horizon, methodological approach, and empirical foundation. Naturally, there are also considerable differences in the quality of the models, although the criteria for a quality comparison may not be obvious.

For our purposes, the basic requirement is that main economic relationships should be modeled in a realistic way, including a specification of the military sector. The model should include as large a part of the world economy as possible, preferably specified by country. Furthermore the model should be well corroborated and reliable.

From a methodological point of view we may distinguish between computable general equilibrium models (CGE), input-output models (IO), and econometric models. There is something to be said for each of these three. CGE models depict equilibrium situations and tend to downplay the adjustment process of moving from one equilibrium to another. For comparing situations with different levels of global armaments this approach might be found attractive. IO models emphasize the flows of goods and services among industries, and between regions and countries. With strong emphasis on the feasibility or alternative uses of resources, this should be the preferred approach. And thirdly, econometric models emphasize the actual functioning of the economic system under consideration; they might be the preferred choice if the emphasis is on tracking, year by year, the macroeconomic effects of a step-by-step disarmament process. Fortunately, these approaches are not mutually exclusive: Both CGE and econometric models will often include an input-output representation at some level of specification, and IO models may include elements typically found in the other two approaches. Of the Norwegian models used in Chapter 4, MODIS is a typical input-output model; its successor MODAG includes various econometric elements, while retaining an input-output core (far more aggregated than in MODIS). The MSG model, on the other hand, is a CGE model – in fact one of the first to be constructed. But MSG also has an input-output core, the same as that in MODAG.

Among the many available global models, two seem particularly well suited to our purposes and three somewhat less so. First, a brief description of the latter three: The *FUGI* model (Future of Global Interdependence) has been an ongoing project at Soka University in Japan from around 1973. More than 150 countries are now represented by separate sub-models. The project, sponsored by the Japanese government through the Ministry of International Trade and Industry (MITI) and the Economic Planning Agency (EPA), has been used for analyzing conversion as well as environmental issues (Onishi, 1990, 1991). Secondly, the OECD has a model called *Interlink* with a module for each OECD country but with an emphasis on the larger OECD countries (Richardson, 1988). There is little disaggregation of the private business sector in Interlink, and public expenditures are also highly aggregated. Consequently, the model is not suitable for an analysis of disarmament without some modifications to the structure. Thirdly, the *GLOBUS* model, developed at the Wissenschaftzentrum in Berlin, is the best known example of a model which goes beyond economics in its inclusion of political processes both internationally and in government decision-making (Bremer, 1987). The model was sponsored by the West German Ministry of Research and Technology and the West Berlin Senate. The GLOBUS project ended officially in 1988, but the model continues to be used and developed by its various contributors. It has been applied to disarmament, the New International Economic Order, transformation processes in Eastern Europe (Eberwein, 1992) and other current policy issues.

Now to the two models that seem more appropriate to our purposes: *LINK* and the *World Model. Project LINK* is in fact a global model system rather than a model. The project was started in 1968, initiated by the Committee of Economic Stability and Growth of the US Social Science Research Council (Hickman & Ruffing, 1991). Lawrence Klein of the University of Pennsylvania has been a key figure in this project since its inception; he is also largely responsible for the US model included in the model system. From the beginning, the large industrial countries were included in the model system; today there are nearly 80 models included. Most of these are 'domestic' models run by institutions in the respective countries. Some have been constructed at the LINK center, especially models for developing countries. Some of the participating models cover a whole region, such as 'Africa Least Developed Countries'. The individual countries are tied together by means of a trade matrix. Market growth and import prices are endogenous in the system. Interest and currency rates are modeled only to a limited extent, however.

The most characteristic feature of the LINK project is that the individual models belong to institutions in the participating countries. In Norway this is Statistics Norway, in the UK the London Business School, in France the Institut National de la Statistique et des Études Économiques, in the Netherlands the Central Planning Bureau, in China the State Information Centre, etc. The implications of this are both positive and negative. The models are more closely tied to national expertise, but on the other hand they differ in specifications, in levels of aggregation, etc. – in short, they are less standardized and it may be technically more difficult to implement a given set of measures in all countries. There is probably no modeling system which covers the world outside the OECD area as well as the LINK system does. This model is now run by the United Nations Department of Economic and Social Development.

There is a high level of activity in the LINK project and a great deal of development work is going on, especially around international trade services and currency rates. There is also a development project which aims at disaggregating world trade in commodities, but here further work is required on the national models. In principle it should be possible to use LINK via international electronic networks, at least after an initial period of familiarization with the system in New York or Philadelphia. For the future, the LINK network would seem to be a most promising development as a flexible tool for relatively quick and updated analyses of changes in international economic relations, such as disarmament. We have not, however, been in a position to use LINK in this study.

Development of *The World Model* started in 1973 under the direction of Wassily Leontief, then at Harvard University. The project later moved to Brandeis University and then to New York University, where it is currently under the direction of Faye Duchin. The United Nations has sponsored the World Model for several studies of global problems (Leontief et al., 1977; Leontief & Duchin, 1983b; Duchin et al., 1992).

The World Model divides the world into 15 regions,[2] each represented by means of an input-output model. These regional models are tied together through international trade and financial transactions. The input-output models for each region give a fairly detailed description of production, consumption, energy use, pollution, demography, and the flows of goods and services. The model system has been used for a wide variety of purposes since 1977 – especially in the areas of technological change, use of natural resources, pollution, sustainable development, and disarmament. The World Model is unique in its high level of detail with respect to economic structure. It can also draw on a very large database. On the other hand, the model is incomplete in important respects with regard to the functioning of the world economy, so some caution should be exercised in interpreting the results.

The following section presents computations made on the World Model in 1982. It would have been preferable to make new computations, but this has not been possible for financial and practical reasons. However, we hope that the relatively general results that we report are not too much affected by the fact that a decade has elapsed since these calculations were made. We carried out computations for Norway at the same time, so the international results are compared with calculations for the Norwegian economy.

In our 1982 study we asked two separate but related questions: *What would be the global effect of disarmament measures* such as those we have studied at the national level? This is discussed in Section 5.3. In the final section we discuss the second question: *What effects would international disarmament have on the Norwegian economy?*

5.3 Can Disarmament Buy Development?

The question of the global consequences of disarmament has been addressed in various UN reports and in a number of theoretical, political, and speculative writings. However, there are few empirical and model-based studies. Among those based on the World Model are Leontief (1978, 1980), Leontief & Duchin (1983ab), Duchin (1983), and Duchin et al. (1992).

A World Model computation describes a possible path that could be followed by the world economy over, say, a 30-year period. As in our national computations, a *baseline scenario* is compared with scenarios which encompass alternative policy choices. Leontief & Duchin (1983b) looked at three arms control scenarios, labeled DIS1, DIS2, and DIS3. In all of these, government military purchases were reduced, compared to the baseline scenario's values. For each region except North America and the Soviet Union, the proportion of GDP allocated to military purchases was assumed to fall to 75% and 60% of the baseline scenario value by 1990 and 2000 respectively. For North America and the Soviet Union, the importance of maintaining military parity between the two superpowers dictated a slightly different treatment: the future military purchases of the two superpowers were assumed to be the same in all three scenarios and in sum equal to two-thirds of the military purchases in the baseline scenario. These arms control scenarios did not actually involve any disarmament relative to current military spending. In fact, military spending was assumed to be about 40% higher in 2000 than in 1980, while superpower arms spending rose by 35%. However, arms spending was assumed to decrease relative to the baseline scenario.

In DIS1, reductions in military spending were not accompanied by any other changes in exogenous assumptions, while in DIS2 additional economic aid was provided from a number of donor regions. The additional aid was set in 1990 to 15% of the savings in military expenditure (i.e. the difference between the baseline values and the values in the arms control scenario) and 25% in 2000. The third scenario, DIS3, differed from DIS2 only in assuming considerably lower imports of military goods for most regions. This assumption has very minor effects compared with DIS2, but leads to somewhat higher production and consumption levels in the poorer developing countries, due to the reduced burden of imports of military goods.

The donor regions consisted of the eight richest regions, including all the developed regions (except South Africa and Medium Income Western Europe) as well as the Middle East and African Oil Producers and Centrally Planned Asia. The recipients included the four poorest regions in the model; they shared the additional aid between them in fixed proportions.

The baseline scenario forecast a dismal future for the poorest regions in terms of per capita consumption (in Africa, as well as Resource Poor Latin American countries). Per capita GDP and per capita consumption were lower in 2000 than in 1970 for two of the regions and only marginally higher for the others. China started out at a similarly low level, but the baseline scenario predicted more than a 100% increase in per capita consumption over the 30-year period to 2000. In retrospect, these assumptions do not seem too wide off the mark.

Disarmament (DIS1) resulted in an increase in all aspects of economic activity, including increased per capita consumption in all regions, generally around 3-5% relative to the baseline figures by the year 2000. Under scenario DIS2, even though the degree of disarmament was modest, substantial additional development aid was generated, compared to the levels in the baseline scenario. The aid was transferred to the poorest regions as a credit to their balance of payments, enabling them to increase their imports. Per capita consumption increased spectacularly in the low-income regions, without any significant loss of consumption in the high-income regions. The gap between rich and poor was not much reduced, however. If measured as the *difference*, the gap was generally higher in DIS1 and DIS2 than in the baseline scenario. However, when measured as a *ratio*, the gap was reduced in DIS2.

In our own study using the World Model (Cappelen et al., 1982) we employed somewhat more radical scenarios:

DIS Military expenditure reduced across the board to 85% of the 1980 level in 1990 and 70% in 2000

CON-LO Military expenditure reduced across the board as in the DIS scenario; the difference between current level and 1980 arms spending transferred 100% to developing regions

CON-HI Military expenditure reduced across the board to 70% of the 1980 level in 1990 and 40% in 2000; the reduction transferred 100% to developing regions

In the detailed specifications of the scenarios we have largely followed Leontief & Duchin (1983b). Our scenarios differ from theirs mainly in the degree of disarmament. We relate the reductions in military spending in 1990 and 2000 to actual levels in 1980, while Leontief & Duchin in their scenarios defined reductions in military spending as divergences from the hypothesized baseline scenario. While we define the levels of military spending and the additional development aid in our scenarios without reference to the baseline scenario, we rely on the baseline scenario of Leontief & Duchin for all other assumptions in our projections for 1990 and 2000. The baseline scenarios are used as the reference in evaluating the results.

Military spending is reduced proportionately for all countries, and in the same proportion for all kinds of military spending. (Thus, we did not adopt the special parity assumption used by Leontief & Duchin for the two superpowers.) The financial resources released are transferred to the developing regions from the donor regions in the form of increased financial transfers. Three regions (less affluent countries in Southern Europe, Resource Rich Latin American countries, and South Africa) were neither donors nor recipients. The distribution of aid on recipients was Arid Africa (15%), Low Income Asia (45%), Resource Poor Latin America (10%), and Tropical Africa (30%), following the assumptions made by Leontief & Duchin.

One of the assumptions made in 'closing' the World Model, i.e. to determine the overall constraints required to solve the model, was that employment in developed countries is equal to the estimated labor force. When changes were introduced in the model's exogenous variables (e.g. reduced military spending), it was implicitly assumed that the economy would adjust by absorbing the released labor power through growth in consumption. This constraint mirrored the one that was made in the MSG model (cf. Section 4.7.3 above), and seemed reasonable against the background of the low unemployment levels in developed countries in the 1960s and the early 1970s. In view of the higher unemployment in all major Western countries it now seems more dubious, however. In any case, this means that we are unable to report any results for employment. Tables 5.1 and 5.2 report our main results for GDP and Private consumption. (Similar computations for imports and exports may be found in Tables 4.4 and 4.5 in Cappelen et al., 1982.)

Table 5.1 GDP 1980-2000 (at Constant 1970 Prices): Baseline Results (in USD '000 Mill.), Disarmament and Conversion Results (in Percentage Deviations from the Leontief-Duchin Baseline Scenarios)

	1980	Projection to 1990				Projection to 2000			
	Leontief-Duchin	Leontief-Duchin	Our scenarios %			Leontief-Duchin	Our scenarios %		
	Base	Base	DIS	CON-LO	CON-HI	Base	DIS	CON-LO	CON-HI
Developed countries, of which:	4,044	6,006	1.3	1.4	4.7	7,856	3.3	3.4	4.3
High Income Western Europe	980	1,526	0.8	0.8	0.9	1,893	1.8	1.8	2.3
Receiving regions, of which:	328	404	14.1	51.9	101.6	574	5.5	62.9	136.1
Arid Africa	24	29	12.6	178.8	349.5	41	25.1	172.2	526.6
Low Income Asia	162	203	24.6	44.4	87.2	279	5.5	62.9	122.1
Resource Poor Latin America	105	109	0.9	22.3	43.9	173	1.9	25.3	49.3
Tropical Africa	37	62	3.9	68.7	134.3	81	4.9	87.9	171.8

For specification of the three scenarios, see p. 113 above.
Source: Leontief & Duchin (1983b) and our own calculations, cf. Cappelen et al. (1982), p. 20

Table 5.2 Private Consumption 1980-2000 (at Constant 1970 Prices): Baseline Results (in USD '000 Mill.), Disarmament and Conversion Results (in Percentage Deviations from the Leontief-Duchin Baseline Scenarios)

	1980	Projection to 1990				Projection to 2000			
	Leontief-Duchin	Leontief-Duchin	Our scenarios %			Leontief-Duchin	Our scenarios %		
	Base	Base	DIS	CON-LO	CON-HI	Base	DIS	CON-LO	CON-HI
Developed countries, of which:	2,641	3,798	3.5	2.9	3.1	4,997	7.3	6.6	7.4
High Income Western Europe	683	1001	1.9	0.7	0	1,251	3.8	2.1	1.3
Receiving regions, of which	264	297	4.2	59.4	89.6	393	8.2	117.2	179.2
Arid Africa	19	21	17.8	204.7	398.6	29	37.5	342.3	658.7
Low Income Asia	132	155	3.5	48.7	95.1	199	7.4	128	153.7
Resource Poor Latin America	84	76	0.8	22.1	43.8	100	2	34.4	67.2
Tropical Africa	28	44	6.2	91.3	177.5	64	7.3	109.8	213.9

For specification of the three scenarios, see p. 113 above.
Source: Leontief & Duchin (1983b) and our own calculations, cf. Cappelen et al. (1982), p. 20

The overall impression is that the economic effects of disarmament for the developed regions are positive, but small. GDP and Private consumption increase between 1.3% and 7.4%, depending on the scale of conversion and the time-span. For the four receiving regions the changes are generally much larger, with percentage increases for all regions together between 5.5% and 136.1% for GDP and 4.3-179.2% for Private consumption. The increases vary dramatically among the recipient regions, from 0.9% to 526.6% for GDP and 0.8% to 658.7% for Private consumption. The smallest changes occur for Resource Poor Latin America and the highest for Arid Africa (which includes both Egypt and Israel). These results cast some doubt on the wisdom of using fixed proportions for distributing additional development aid.

It is notable that all percentage changes for GDP and Private consumption are positive for donors and recipients alike. For GDP the increase over the baseline is higher than in CON-LO compared to DIS and even higher in CON-HI. Thus, additional aid financed from the resources released by disarmament does increase the level of production in the developed regions as well. This is because much of the additional aid will be channeled back to the developing countries to pay for imported goods. The additional aid stimulates overall productivity in the developed regions through the effect on the industrial distribution of labor.

In terms of Private consumption, the developed regions are better off with disarmament without any additional aid. The loss in Private consumption from DIS to CON-LO is hardly significant compared with the gains for the recipient regions. More radical conversion recovers some of the loss for developed regions, and by the year 2000 Private consumption is actually higher in the developed regions in CON-HI than in DIS.

Data on imports and exports, not reproduced here, corroborate this picture. In all scenarios, both forms of trade increase over the baseline, for donor as well as recipient regions. The changes from baseline to DIS are not very extensive; they are also quite balanced in overall economic activity brought forth by the reduction in military expenditures. The poor developing countries, which in the model are constrained mainly by their balance of payments, are free to use the reduction in imports of military goods for more beneficial ends. Imports of these regions increase little compared with gains made in GDP and Private consumption.

In CON-LO and CON-HI, aid means trade. The poor regions are allowed a relaxation of their balance of payments constraint equal to the reduction of military expenditures of the donor countries. Imports of these regions increase considerably: by 2000 the imports of Arid Africa are almost four times as high in CON-HI as in the baseline. Exports also increase, but not as much.

In the developed regions, exports increase twice as much as imports. Countries in the poor regions buy development-promoting goods from the developed countries. The increased development transfers are then returned to the developed countries as payments for exports. Thus, transfers may promote development in poor countries and continued growth in rich countries.

The overall impression from these results – that all regions gain not only from disarmament, but also from the redistribution of resources released by disarmament – may be somewhat superficial. The regions of the model are large entities.

Although there is an element of homogeneity imbedded in the model's definitions of regions, there is no particular reason to assume that the effects will be distributed completely evenly among all the countries in a region – this applies to developed as well as developing countries. Results are also contingent upon the realism and reasonability in the assumptions of the baseline scenario itself. Furthermore, there is the underlying assumption that the recipient countries will be able to exploit the benefits of additional aid to promote expansion and growth of their economies – rather than, for instance, building white elephants or filling up accounts in Swiss banks. The model probably exaggerates how significant the balance-of-payments constraint is to development relative to other constraints.

Table 5.3 presents some results for the distribution of the global product between donors, aid recipients, and other regions in the year 2000. The table indicates a slight improvement of the relative position of the receiving countries as a whole. Compared to the distribution of the world's population, the fairly radical efforts at disarmament and conversion assumed in CON-HI go only a very limited part of the way toward closing the gap between the rich and the poor.

Table 5.3 Relative Distribution of the World GDP in 2000 between Donors and Recipients (%)

	Baseline	DIS	CON-LO	CON-HI	Population
Donating regions	90	90	86	83	44
Receiving regions	6	6	9	12	49
Other regions	5	5	5	5	7
World total	101%	101%	100%	100%	100%
in USD '000 Million	10,389	10,625	11,038	11,510	6,248

Source: Leontief & Duchin (1983b) and our own calculations, cf. Cappelen et al. (1982), p. 23

An even more pessimistic picture is presented in Table 5.4, where countries are divided into developed and developing, with the developing countries further subdivided into resource-rich and resource-poor. A slight improvement is found for the resource-poor developing countries, but none at all for the resource-rich. A more optimistic conclusion from these calculations is that whatever modest redistribution is achieved occurs without any *absolute* reductions for donor regions or developed countries. This should make the redistributive aspects of the conversion package easier to digest in developed countries.

Table 5.4 Relative Distribution of the World GDP in 2000 between Developed and Developing Countries (%)

	Baseline	DIS	CON-LO	CON-HI	Population
Developed countries	76	76	74	71	23
Developing – Class I	15	15	15	15	13
Developing – Class II	9	9	12	14	64
World total	100%	100%	101%	100%	100%
(in USD '000 Million)	10,389	10,625	11,038	11,510	6,248

Developing Countries Class I are resource-rich developing countries; class II the resource-poor countries.
Source: Leontief & Duchin (1983b) and our own calculations, cf. Cappelen et al. (1982), p. 23

5.4 Effects for Norway

The Norwegian economy is a small and open one. In 1982 total exports amounted to 45% of GDP and imports 40%. (Ten years later, the figures are a little smaller, but not much.) Thus, any major change in the world economy, including global conversion, must be expected to affect the Norwegian economy. Changes in the demand for Norwegian goods and services on the world market cause cyclical variations as well as influencing growth in the Norwegian economy.

According to our calculations on the World Model, global conversion will not lead to increased problems of supply shortages due to resource limitations. Changes in prices due to conversion seem to be of minor importance. The World Model has considerable limitations, however, in forecasting the price effects of shifts in demand. In our calculations for Norway we have therefore taken Norwegian imports of goods and services as being determined by domestic factors alone.

The indirect effects of global conversion on the Norwegian economy are assumed to appear exclusively through changes in the demand for Norwegian exports. Norway's major trading partners are countries in the same region, High Income Western Europe (WEH). No less than 84% of Norway's exports went to this region in 1980, followed by North America (3.4%); no other region exceeded 2%.[3] The WEH region absorbs most of Norway's considerable exports of crude oil and natural gas, in addition to its more traditional exports. As an approximation we have assumed that all Norway's exports have the same sectoral distribution as its exports to WEH.

The macroeconomic consequences of conversion for the WEH region presented in the previous section include higher growth in GDP and exports. In scenario CON-LO, imports of manufactured goods to WEH were approximately 4% larger in 1990 than in the baseline scenario, while imports of services (including transport) increased by 2%. There was also an increase in imports of natural resources. We have translated the results for imports to WEH by commodity into corresponding assumptions of Norwegian exports.[4]

In Chapter 4 we analyzed extensively the effects of national conversion on employment and other economic indicators. In Table 5.5 we compare the short-term effects of immediate and complete disarmament in 1980 with the effects derived from a structural shift in the world economy due to global conversion. The final column of the table shows the net short-term effects. Given the assumptions of the World Model, the global results cannot be considered as being of a 'short-term' nature. Hence, this is a somewhat hypothetical exercise. It does, however, bring out the degree to which international conversion may replace the national compensatory measures ordinarily needed to combat undesired economic consequences of disarmament. The export effects are calculated by means of impact tables obtained from MODIS IV, the national budget model which served as the main analytical tool in the 1980 study.

In order to apply the impact tables to the present problem we have aggregated the commodities to six commodity groups (cf. Cappelen et al., 1980). It is evident that any national economic problem caused by unilateral conversion becomes sharply reduced when conversion is seen in a global context. The remaining minor loss of employment can also be overcome by early retirement schemes for military personnel, or by other specifically chosen countermeasures. Interestingly, GDP increases slightly even if employment decreases. This is due to a reallocation from the labor-intensive military sector to the more capital-intensive export sector. We should also point out that this result is based on the transfer policy which is least labor-intensive for Norway (purely financial transfers), since this same form of transfer was assumed in the World Model scenarios.

Table 5.5 Short-Term Effects on the Norwegian Economy of Unilateral Conversion Compared to the Export Effects of Global Conversion (%)

	National conversion	Export effect from global conversion	Net Effect
Employment	-0.84	0.61	-0.23
GDP	-0.56	0.63	0.07
Imports	-0.47	1.20	0.73
Balance of payments	-0.29	0.41	0.12

The national conversion results correspond to those in Tables 4.2-4.4 above, but with a more modest degree of disarmament. The increase in exports is calculated by using the increases in exports given in Appendix 2 of Cappelen et al. (1982), on the basis of the 1978 value of the exports. Balance of payments is calculated in % of GDP; a negative sign means an increased deficit or a reduced surplus.
Source: Cappelen et al. (1982), Table 5.2, p. 27. The corresponding absolute figures can be found in op.cit., Appendix 3, p. 40

The effects in Table 5.5 are based on the *moderate* disarmament scenario (15% reduction), while we have generally reported the most drastic disarmament scenario (complete disarmament) in Chapter 4. The Norwegian results can easily be multiplied up to the required degree of disarmament, but this is not necessarily true for the World Model results. The point here is that global disarmament would have favorable effects for Norway and that short-term negative effects of unilateral disarmament would be counteracted by global conversion, regardless of the scale of disarmament.

Norway is only one of 17 countries in the WEH region. We assume that the results for the entire region hold for each country – of course, a simplification. Nevertheless, the region is homogeneous enough to make this assumption not entirely unrealistic.

How much would global conversion matter to the Norwegian economy? In Table 4.11 we compared GDP and other economic indicators in 1990 and 2000 under the baseline scenario and the Disarmament scenario, using the general equilibrium model MSG. In Table 5.6 we make a similar comparison between the Disarmament scenario (DIS) and the CON-LO scenario, which involves feedback to the Norwegian economy from the increased transfers to development assistance. Where there are any changes at all, they tend to be in a favorable direction – exports increase, the balance of trade improves, while GDP remains the same, and there is only a slight decrease in Private consumption. But the changes are very small compared to the changes assumed by the LTP scenario for the Norwegian economy. Indeed, they are so small that they would hardly be noticeable to the population at large.

Table 5.6 Long-Term Macroeconomic Effects in Norway of Disarmament and Global Conversion, 1980-2000

Effect on	Baseline 1980 (NOK '000 mill., 1980 Prices)	Deviations from Baseline 1980 (%)				Relative change (%) DIS to CON	
		1990		2000		1990	2000
		DIS	CON	DIS	CON		
Military consumption	7	-15	-15	-30	-30	0	0
GDP	241	29	29	60	60	0.0	0.0
Imports	103	39	40	80	80	0.7	0.0
Exports	108	24	27	47	50	2.2	1.9
Private consumption	118	32	31	80	77	-0.6	-1.4
Investment*	70	39	40	69	168	-1.0	0.0
Employment	1 691	4	4	4	4	0	0

* Excluding additions to stocks.

DIS = Disarmament scenario as defined in the first row; CON = Conversion scenario CON-LO as defined on p. 116.

Source: Recalculated from the MSG calculations in Cappelen et al. (1982), Table 5.3, p. 31. Cf. also Table 4.11 above

Table 5.7 gives a basis for evaluating global conversion as a countermeasure, by comparing its effects with those of the other compensatory measures discussed in Chapter 4. We may eliminate the negative effects of disarmament entirely by devoting about three-quarters of the released resources to a domestic countermeasure that holds high employment potential; but the negative effects could also be reduced by extending conversion, by choosing a transfer model which has more favorable domestic effects, or by exploiting the effects of global conversion. In addition to the effects on our four economic indicators, Table 5.7 also gives a 'conversion index' (measuring what fraction of military expenditure is converted to development aid in one year) as well as the type of transfer assumed in each case. An overall comparison comes out quite favorably for the global conversion vs. the unilateral conversion alternatives.

Table 5.7 Effects of Unilateral Conversion, and Four Alternatives Designed to Decrease Negative Effects (%)

Alternatives	Effects in 1978 on					
	Employment	GDP	Imports	Balance of payments	Conversion index	Type of transfer
0 Moderate unilateral conversion	-0.84	-0.56	-0.47	-0.29	15	Financial
1 Extended conversion First year effect	-0.06	-0.04	-0.04	-0.02	1.2	Financial
2 'Best' transfer model	-0.27	-0.12	0.17	-0.06	15	Commodity
3 With domestic countermeasures	0	-0.02	-0.06	-0.02	3	Financial
4 Global conversion	-0.23	0.07	0.73	0.12	15	Financial

Conversion index in this Table means the fraction of military expenditure converted to development aid in one year. *Balance of payments* is calculated in % of GDP. A negative figure means an increased deficit or a reduced surplus.

Source: Cappelen et al. (1982), Table 6.1, p. 34

This is one result which we cannot generalize to other countries. The outcome of global disarmament is particularly favorable for Norway. While this need not be a zero-sum game – the shift in spending worldwide could lead to growth from which most countries could benefit – countries with heavy arms exports would probably lose more in the short run than would Norway. However, even for these countries the effects of national disarmament are likely to overshadow the effects of disarmament in other countries.

Notes

1. Cf. Bebermeyer & Thimann (1990), pp. 113f. Duke (1989), p. 387;

2. The regional classification scheme is found in Leontief & Duchin (1983b). It is also reproduced in Appendix 1 of Cappelen et al. (1982).

3. Detailed data for 1974, 1977, and 1980 are found in Cappelen et al. (1982), Table 5.1, p. 25, based on *NOS* 'Utenrikshandel' (External Trade), an annual publication from Statistics Norway.

4. A detailed presentation of the conversion-induced increase in exports by commodity is given in Cappelen et al. (1982), Appendix 2.

6

Local Conversion

6.1 Three Levels of Conversion

The economic effects of conversion may be analyzed at three levels: *global*, *national*, and *local*. The national and global levels, discussed in the previous two chapters, are both important because they correspond to actual decision-making. The national level of decision-making remains the most important when it comes to decisions about the future size and shape of national military forces. On the other hand, the international level should not be ignored altogether, since UN resolutions and NATO decisions, formal disarmament agreements as well as informal action-reaction processes contribute significantly to shaping national decisions about arms procurement.

With subnational geographical units, we are no longer at a level where independent decisions about the military establishment are made. Yet the economic prospects of such units may also have a bearing on national decisions. Local communities and particular industries may act as pressure-groups in order to secure funding for a new (or continued activity in an old) part of the military establishment. Firms, of course, may make important decisions of considerable relevance to arms production, arms exports, and military resource use. Many studies of conversion have focused on the individual firm. Here, however, we are mainly concerned with *public* decision-making and will largely ignore the private decision-making of firms and individual citizens.

The local level is particularly important to studies of conversion because it is here that the social effects of disarmament may be observed most clearly. If an arms factory goes out of business or a base is closed down, the effects at the national level may be negligible, but at the local level this may spell havoc for individuals and local communities. Norway is no exception – indeed, Northern Norway is particularly strongly affected by the end of the Cold War.

6.2 Local Attitudes

Local attitudes to the military establishment are of two radically different kinds. On the one hand, there will frequently be resistance to the establishment of a military facility in a local community. Military establishments often require large areas and tend to displace traditional activities, particularly other area-intensive activities in the primary sector. They represent a clear danger in wartime, as potential objects of military action ranging from missile or air attack to invasion. The establishment of military installations, shooting ranges, mountain-top communications towers, etc. has frequently met with local or environmental protests.[1] In the 1980s dozens of municipalities, including some with important military harbors, declared themselves to be 'nuclear-free'. Formal decisions about arms control and disarmament are, of course, not made at this level. But when municipal councils pass such resolutions they should probably be interpreted not only as a part of a political campaign to have all of Norway (or Scandinavia) declared a nuclear weapon-free zone, but also as an indication of a very real fear that any connection with nuclear weapons – whether in the form of transit of nuclear weapons in harbors or airfields or the deployment of nuclear-related weapons systems – means an additional danger in wartime for that particular community.

Yet, once a military establishment is in place, a diametrically opposed attitude usually takes precedence. The arms factory or the military base now becomes a benefactor of local industry, a source of employment, and a source of revenue for the municipality. Since war is dangerous in any case and since wartime hazards are more remote than everyday benefits like employment and public expenditure, it is understandable that the bird in the hand prevails over the two in the bush.

We are not aware of systematic local attitude surveys on such issues, but one illustration may be provided by the local campaign in Aukra (in the northwestern part of Southern Norway) in the early 1980s. Very strong local opposition developed to the establishment of a relay station for the NATO communications system Cross Fox, designed to provide communication to NATO's Strike Fleet Atlantic (Johansen, 1984). In April 1981 58% of the registered voters in the municipality signed a petition, after the military had distributed written information to all households. The municipal council unanimously voted to ask the military authorities to move the station to an uninhabited area. The station's functions had a fairly tenuous connection to nuclear war preparations, but the danger of nuclear war played a considerable role in the campaign. On the other hand, when *Folkereisning mot krig* (the Norwegian section of the War Resisters' International) and its journal *Ikkevold* tried in 1983 to mobilize local public opinion against military airfields, antisubmarine warfare installations, and intelligence installations, the campaign encountered a mixture of local hostility and apathy. This was so despite the fact that the campaign followed hard on the heels of four years of a major national campaign against NATO's decision to deploy new intermediate-range missiles in Europe and for a Nordic nuclear weapon-free zone, and that the installations selected had fairly well-documented links to nuclear war preparations (Johansen et al., 1986).

The Norwegian military is now well established in a number of communities, and in most places has been a stable source of local employment and revenue for several decades. We assume, therefore, that any negative attitudes grounded in the fear of becoming a target in wartime and resentment against the displacement of traditional activities, have given way to an appreciation of the positive peacetime economic benefits of the military presence. Of course, just as the end of the Cold War gives many of these local military installations lower priority in the 1990s, these military and political changes drastically reduce the physical danger associated with the presence of a military base – for anyone who has not already succeeded in suppressing any thought of the local consequences of a war. Thus, since the probability of war is lower, the net positive effect of military spending becomes higher, and local resistance to disarmament may increase.

6.3 Studies of Local Effects

There is an enormous literature on local effects of conversion, but most of it is oriented toward the individual firm or military base. Generally, this literature is not very helpful from our perspective. It is virtually impossible for a national government to plan conversion in such a way that no single firm is adversely affected. The probable consequence of such a requirement would be a complete freeze on any change in the location of military industries and facilities. Taken to its extreme, an ambitious policy of conversion might require that no individual would be adversely affected by conversion. This scarcely seems realistic. Our aim must be to survey the main effects of conversion at the industry and local level, with a view to mapping the nature and extent of the adjustment problem and suggesting possible *general* countermeasures at the subnational level.

Conversion studies are frequently undertaken for a community or firm which is in a symbiotic relationship with the military, but where a radical union or outside critics of the military for ethical reasons want to lessen or eliminate the dependency on military demand. Britain's Lucas Aerospace is the classic case. After a period of declining military employment, a joint shop stewards committee took a lead from Tony Benn, then Minister of Industry in the Labour government. The shop stewards solicited suggestions for conversion from a number of research institutes and worked out a detailed conversion plan which they made public in January 1976. A number of detailed suggestions were made for how the company could adapt to changing circumstances using the engineering and technical skills of the existing staff. The Lucas workers got considerable international publicity for their ideas, but little response from the management. Despite extensive public discussion, little ever came of the conversion proposals.[2]

Other firms have had to face the problem of conversion when military demand is sharply reduced or eliminated. A firm which has a diversified line of production may be able to build up its civilian production at the same time as its military production is built down. However, if a firm is totally dependent on military production it will be in a weak position when it comes to seeking alternative customers. Its most obvious strategy will be to require the government to maintain a demand, for whatever product it can offer. The Russian military-industrial complex after the end of the Cold War offers an illustration of this problem. Many firms were totally dependent on military production. Some firms in the military sector also produced consumer goods – for instance the defense industry is claimed to have a 'near-monopoly' on such household goods as sewing machines and washing machines (Cooper, 1991, p. 323) – but these products are made because firms are ordered to, not because of any organic relationship with the market. These civilian products are not competitive by international standards and can survive in the Russian market only if shielded from foreign competition. Clearly, the production capacity left vacant by the reduction in military demand can be compensated in the short term only by preserving the command economy in the civilian sector. When conversion coincides with attempts to introduce a market economy, the military factories do not stand much chance in the competition.

In China conversion from military to civilian production has taken place since the late 1970s on a grander scale than in any other country. The conversion has been part and parcel of the economic reforms initiated by Deng Xiaoping and has been accompanied by modernization of the arms industry and a more commercial arms export orientation. The conversion policy was made possible by the detente with the Soviet Union and the more amiable relations developed towards the USA, Japan, Taiwan and others. There has of course also been pressure from within for utilizing the valuable resources tied up in the immense military production capacity for civilian purposes. Folta (1992) provides an overview of the overall reforms of the defense industry. The conversion has not implied a massive transfer of production capacity from the military to civilian domain; the civilian goods are produced within military run facilities.[3] The conversion process has, however, involved a massive transfer of technology from the military to the civilian sector and taken away the almost complete separation between defense and civilian industry. Even within the defense sector there were separate vertical structures and a policy of self-sufficiency which discouraged lateral ties between industrial ministries and caused huge inefficiencies of lack of specialization. The conversion process has been one of the major factors behind the success of the economic reforms in China, and has benefited the military sector as well as the Chinese consumers.

The conversion, modernization, and restructuring of the Chinese military-industrial complex have reduced the financial burden. In 1977 the official defense budget's share of total state expenditure was 18%; it decreased to 8% in 1986-89, and subsequently rose again to about 10% (Folta, 1992, p. 20). In 1985 China announced that the military forces would be reduced by one million men – one-quarter of the total military manpower.[4]

The USA offers a number of relevant studies of local conversion. Its economy is particularly interesting from the viewpoint of conversion, because of the high level of military spending in the post-World War II period, but also because of the considerable variations in spending occasioned by the Korean and Vietnam wars. The USA has experienced not just one but three postwar mobilizations in the past 50 years – in addition to the present demobilization after the end of the Cold War.

Benoit (1962) reports some data on military employment by state in 1960. Several states exceeded the national average by a factor of four. For employment in major defense industries in percent of total manufacturing employment, Kansas headed the list with 30.2%, while the national average was 7.3%. For the Department of Defense payroll in percent of all personal income, Alaska was the extreme case with 26.5%; the figure for the USA as a whole was 2.9%.[5] A study from the early 1990s indicated that defense employment is now more evenly spread over the states, although a few states exceeded the national average in defense dependency by a factor of between 2 and 3 (Adams, 1992, p. 25).

The 'base closure' problem is a well-known headache in US politics (Leitenberg, 1978). A publication from the US Congress (1973) examined a large number of base closures in the 1960s and early 1970s. A peak was reached in 1965, with 149 separate 'actions' (consolidation, reduction, realignment, or closure), eliminating a total of 53,010 jobs. Over the period 1961-73 a total of 1371 'actions' eliminated

317,693 jobs (US Congress, 1973, p. 14).[6] Many of these actions are described as 'horizontal', affecting military establishments across the country. Towards the end of the period more actions were classified as 'vertical' – affecting fewer communities, but hitting each of them more severely. Two extreme cases were Brunswick, GA and Mineral Wells, TX, which each lost one third of all jobs in the community as a result of base closures (1973, p. 16).

A later Congressional report on economic adjustment (US Congress, 1979, p. 297) noted that over the period 1961-77 economic assistance was provided to over 200 communities. A summary of 75 completed cases of community adjustment reported that 78,765 civilian jobs were now located in the former defense facilities to replace the loss of 68,000 previous Defense Department civilian or contractor jobs. Another 10,540 new jobs off-base were directly attributable to the economic adjustment efforts. In 72 out of the 75 cases the former defense facilities had been converted to new commercial or educational uses (1979, p. 298). The report notes that beyond the first few years, it is difficult to measure the exact effects of federal countermeasures. But on the whole, these experiences would seem to yield relatively favorable results. A particularly attractive factor in conversion of defense facilities is that it makes available large land areas which invite major new industrial or commercial construction. An even later report states that for the period 1961-81 about 90,000 defense jobs were replaced by 120,000 new jobs in 94 localities (US Congress, 1985, p. 7).

The US debate about base closures always contains a strong political element. Although members of the Congress may favor public savings and base closures generally, they prefer that the savings are made elsewhere. Members of Congress, particularly those with high seniority in the right committees, are often able to attract new bases and prevent the closure of old ones. This attitude found a telling illustration in a statement by a Representative from the congressional district which had Grumman as a large local contractor. He commented on the future of the A-6 naval fighter-bomber:

> I'm the congressman from that district and I'm on the Armed Services Committee. It's my job, whether I think the A-6 is good or not, to support it.[7]

As noted by a senior official in the Department of Defense in 1985:

> It is no secret that some major installations were not closed in the seventies because of political concerns and these problems are still with us today.[8]

This testimony indicated that about 100 of the 900 major bases in the USA were candidates for closure, and that the savings in annual operating costs would be about USD 500 million for every 20 bases shut down. However, in 1977 the Congress acquired great influence on the base closure process and it became harder for the Department of Defense to shut down a base if a Member of Congress opposed it strongly enough (US Congress, 1985, p. 11). Between 1978 and 1988 no US bases were closed down at all, but the process reopened at the end of the 1980s (Adams, 1992, p. 27).

With the end of the Cold War the USA faced a fourth round of conversion since World War II. This time, substantial cuts are being made in overseas bases, particularly in Western Europe, as well as in the Continental United States. A study made by the Congressional Budget Office (1992) found that the limited cuts in military spending in 1991 would have unequal impact in the states, but that no state would suffer a decline in output greater than 3%; the national average being 0.6%. Larger cuts would also have greater regional impact but the cuts would be felt mostly in coastal states, whereas the last major recession in 1981-82 affected mainly the heartland.

6.4 Effects by Industry

In all countries with an extensive military establishment, the severity of the conversion problem varies strongly from one industry to another. For example, for the USA Benoit reported that in 1958 about 95% of the employment in the aircraft and missiles industry was directly or indirectly dependent on military demand, while the figure for the entire private sector was only 5.6%.[9]

An noted in Chapter 3, Norway has developed an extensive and diversified military industry in the postwar period. Among the 64 members of the Norwegian Defense Industry Group (NFL), several are industrial conglomerates, and a report from a subcommittee of the Defense Commission (Thulin et al., 1990, p. 6) estimates that these 64 include 250-300 separate firms, accounting for 85-90% of domestic military supplies. The firms range from civilian products (food, clothing, furniture) to specifically military products. Although military forces are heavily overrepresented in Northern Norway, military industry is concentrated in Southern Norway, with at least half the number of employees of NFL membership in the Oslo area (op.cit., p. 8).

The total number of employees in NFL member-firms is 46,845, or roughly comparable to the total number in the armed forces. However, since many of these firms are only partially dependent on military deliveries, these figures tell us relatively little about the military dependency of manufacturing industry as a whole. The Thulin Committee Report estimates that the three 'civilian' product groups mentioned in the previous paragraph account for about 1450 person-years of employment. The final report of the Defense Commission itself claims that 12,000-14,000 jobs in Norwegian industry are supported by military demand (*NOU*, 1992:12, p. 139). But no estimate is provided of how many of these would disappear if the military establishment were abolished. Since – after disarmament – former military personnel would still to some extent be eating products from the Norwegian food industry and even (although to a lesser degree) be clothed in products from the Norwegian textile industry, the jobs lost would clearly be fewer than 12,000-14,000. For 1970 and 1980 we estimated the number of strictly military jobs in Norway's two major arms factories at Kongsberg and Raufoss (Table 6.1) – and obtained a much lower number.

The government's industry-promoting strategy has not been altogether successful. In particular, the compensation agreements have been criticized for making the military products more expensive, without yielding corresponding benefits. This subject is, of course, highly politicized. One of the few impartial studies was carried out in 1991 by a private consulting firm, on contract to the Thulin Committee. This study (ECON, 1991) listed a number of advantages of such

Table 6.1 Military Employment in Norway's Two Major Arms Factories, 1970 and 1980

	1970		1980	
	Number of jobs	% of employment in municipality	Number of jobs	% of employment in municipality
Kongsberg Våpenfabrikk	1,525	19	2,106	21
Raufoss Ammunisjonsfabrikker	885	17	1,044	17

Sources: Employment in military production: Our own estimates on the basis of the annual reports from the companies. Total employment in the municipalities of Kongsberg (in the district of *Buskerud)* and Vestre Toten, (in *Oppland)*, home of Raufoss. Census reports for 1970 and 1980 (*NOS* various issues). Cf. Gleditsch et al. (1987), pp. 46-47. KV has later been dismantled, with military production continuing in the successor Norsk Forsvarsteknologi.

compensation agreements (technology transfer, transfer of quality control procedures, improved market access, the buildup of long-term cooperative relationships between industry in Norway and abroad, increased activity levels in certain firms) but also several disadvantages (higher purchasing costs, ineffective use of resources in the case of parallel production, interrupted collaboration, and a freezing of the Norwegian industrial structure). On the whole, ECON concluded, such agreements gave insufficient macroeconomic gains, and results had not corresponded to the promise. Since the information about alternative courses of action is so sparse – in particular it is not known what prices would have been if the compensation strategy had been abandoned – ECON was unable to reach any firm conclusion. However, it did recommend that the military establishment should seek to obtain a double bid, one with compensation and one without, in order to reduce uncertainty about the price paid for the compensation.[10] The Thulin Committee concluded that no definite conclusions could be drawn about the compensation agreements but felt that the proposed double-bid system would be impractical. The Committee recommended that compensation agreements should be concluded only where there were real transfers of technology, competence, or market access or where long-term cooperative relationships could be established, but not in order to gain short-term advantages with respect to the balance of payments or national or regional employment (Thulin et al., 1991, pp. 45-47). The committee also concluded that continued liberalization of the arms industry would be to Norway's advantage, but that the current high degree of protectionism in the industry makes it necessary for Norway to use national protection measures like the compensation agreements.

In our 1992 study using MODAG we calculated some effects by industry. Table 6.2 shows the effects of disarmament on value added by Norwegian industry, given for the *Disarmament, Health,* and *Tax* scenarios, as defined in section 4.9 above. Results are reported for one year only, 2010 – the year when the disarmament is assumed to be complete. The differences between the baseline and the three disarmament scenarios are rather small.

Subdivisions are also given for different kinds of manufacturing: Production of nondurable consumer goods – including foods and textiles – is affected negatively by the general decline in consumer goods due to the reduction in military demand. This reduction is compensated for in *Health* and even more so in *Tax.* Firms producing mainly raw materials – included in the categories Paper and pulp, Industrial chemicals, and metals – do not produce much for the military sector and benefit from the increased competitiveness in the disarmament scenario; they benefit even more in *Tax*. In *Health*, cost competitiveness is reduced compared to the baseline scenario, and the output in these sectors is reduced. For Machinery we find the same differences between the scenarios. In Norway, this sector is less intimately connected to the military sector than in many other industrialized countries, since Norway has no domestic production of military vehicles or aircraft. Thus, disarmament enhances output in this sector rather than decreasing it, except in *Health* where the output is negatively influenced by the lower cost competitiveness. The products of Miscellaneous manufacturing are mostly inputs to Construction, hence the results for these two are closely related. In addition, this sector includes the production of ammunition, which is used by the military establishment, as well as by the construction industry. Apart from the 4% decline in the Machinery sector in *Health*, none of the manufacturing sectors changes by more than 2.6% in either direction in any scenario. By and large even un-compensated disarmament has very marginal impact on any part of industry except perhaps construction.

As is apparent from Table 6.2, the choice of countermeasures influences the impact on the manufacturing sector. Disarmament without countermeasures implies lower consumption and higher exports, and favors the most export-oriented manufacturing sectors, i.e. those which produce raw materials as well as machinery. If the countermeasures promote employment in the public sector (as in *Health*) the manufacturing sector as a whole – except that part which produces consumer goods – will suffer in the long run. If taxes are reduced there is a general improvement in cost competitiveness favoring manufacturing in general, above all in the export-oriented sector. Thus, drastic compensatory measures, especially designed for the manufacturing sector, would hardly seem necessary.

Table 6.2 Effects by Industry for Three Scenarios

Value added in	Deviations in 2010 from Baseline scenario (in %)		
	Disarmament scenario	Health scenario	Tax scenario
Manufacturing	-0.3	-1.9	1.5
of which			
Non-durable consumer goods	-0.1	0.3	1.0
Paper and pulp	1.0	-1.6	2.3
Industrial chemicals	0.9	-1.2	2.2
Metals	0.6	-1.2	1.5
Machinery	0.9	-4.0	2.6
Shipyards	-0.2	0.0	-0.2
Miscellaneous	-1.8	-2.5	1.2
Construction	-5.5	-2.3	-1.8
Services, private	-1.8	0.3	1.6

Source: Hove (1993), Tables 2-5

This confirms a similar analysis conducted in 1980, using the MODIS model (Bjerkholt et al., 1980, section 4.4.1). Whether under the condition of pure disarmament plus increased transfers to developing countries or under the condition of disarmament with domestic countermeasures, the changes for the individual industries were generally very small. The main factor which affected particular industries was the choice of commodity transfer policy. Since the commodity transfer policies which we have called 'egoistical' and 'altruistic' both involved a strong component of fishing vessels, there is a considerable positive effect on the manufacturing category 'Ships, boats, and other transport', whereas under the 'benevolent' exports the manufacturing category 'Machinery, etc.' is the main beneficiary. For the transfer policy which involved expanding current aid without changing its composition, none of the industry categories changed by more than 3%.

As mentioned, Norway is a net weapons importer and has not really succeeded as an arms producer or exporter, despite trying hard. Hence, it is scarcely unexpected that disarmament has little impact on any broad category of manufacturing. If we keep subdividing industries we will of course come up with sectors which may suffer more from disarmament, like weapons and ammunition, but these are generally limited to a few firms. Disarmament primarily affects public administration; and since it is in public administration that we have concentrated our countermeasures (at least in the *Health* scenario) it is not surprising that the net effect should be very limited. We therefore turn to a different disaggregation, the geographical, where the conversion problems are greater.

6.5 Local Effects in Norway

The two main administrative sub-units in Norway are the *fylke*, which we refer to as *district,* and the *kommune,* or *municipality.*[11] Both are political units with their own elections (held simultaneously every four years, mid-way between national elections), their own civil service, their own taxation, and their own budgets. Public identification may well be stronger with a local community that is smaller (or larger) than the municipality and even with traditional areas between the municipality and the districts. Nevertheless, Norway's approximately 440 municipalities (the exact number has varied) and 19 districts are convenient sub-units for analyzing conversion at the local level, mainly because most public and private statistics are collected with reference to those sub-units. Traditionally, until private cars became widely available in the 1970s, a municipality might be said to represent the maximum extent of daily commuting to work, while the district might represent weekly commuting. Thus, these two subdivisions represented (again we must emphasis *very roughly*) important limits to labor mobility. Today, however, commuting distances are greater than before, and daily commuting across municipal boundaries is very common. In the smaller districts of Eastern and Southern Norway, daily commuting may occur across an entire district and even between districts.

In addition to these two administrative subdivisions, we shall use a third division, frequently found in discussion of military matters; one that divides

Norway into five geographical *regions* (These regions have no administrative competence). Figure 6.1 gives the administrative division of Norway into regions and districts as of 1993. The number of municipalities for each of the 19 districts is also shown.

Figure 6.1 Administrative Division of Norway, 1993

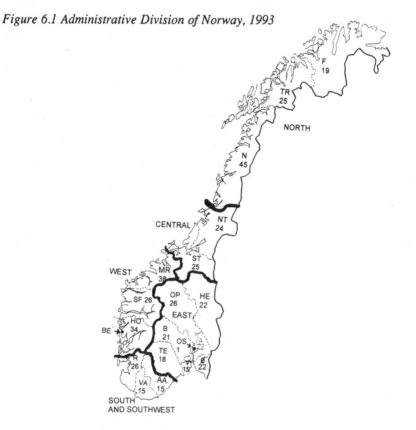

Heavy lines indicate the boundaries between the five *regions*. Broken lines separate the 19 *districts*. The capital of Oslo is a separate district, while the second largest city, Bergen, was a separate district until 1972. The figures indicate the number of municipalities in each district in 1993. Letter codes for districts are as follows:

Ø =	Østfold	Te =	Telemark	MR =	Møre og Romsdal
Os =	Oslo	AA =	Aust-Agder	ST =	Sør-Trøndelag
Ak =	Akershus	VA =	Vest-Agder	NT =	Nord-Trøndelag
He =	Hedmark	R =	Rogaland	N =	Nordland
Op =	Oppland	[Be =	Bergen]	Tr =	Troms
Bu =	Buskerud	Ho =	Hordaland	F =	Finnmark
Ve =	Vestfold	SF =	Sogn og Fjordane		

Source: This map is based on the one found in the 1970 Census (*NOS* A-679, p. 21), updated with the present number of municipalities from the 1993 edition of *Statistical Yearbook* (also in the *NOS* series).

Using census data involves several problems. One is that definitions vary somewhat from census to census. In 1950, military employment was specified by district. The figures included persons with military employment as the main source of income. This excluded conscripts altogether. At the municipal level, military employment was lumped with public administration generally. In 1960 all data on military employment, at any level, were included in the larger category of 'public administration and defense'. Data on *military work* were, however, provided under occupational groups, at the national and district level; however this excluded civilians employed by the military establishment. At the municipal level, employees with military work were grouped with people with unspecified work. In the 1970 census the data were more complete. At the district level we find not only total military employment, but also specifications for officers, civilians, and conscripts. At the municipal level, data on military work are available, but no data on total defense sector employment. In the 1980 census data on conscripts are available at the municipal level, but classified according to their permanent residence rather than their place of employment. Military work is lumped with `unspecified' and in the data by sector the military are grouped with public administration and services. The 1990 census was carried out by means of publicly available registers supplemented by a 10% sample survey; occupation was not among the variables collected for the entire population. Whatever might be said for this system, it was not designed to aid research on military employment or the study of conversion!

The changing classification of conscripts mirrors a real argument as to where they should be counted in conversion studies. Clearly, if conscription is reduced (in coverage or duration) conscripts are more likely to spend the freed time in their municipality of residence. If they become unemployed, they do so at home rather than where they have been serving their time as conscripts. If they find new jobs, these jobs are as likely to be at home (or in an entirely new location) as in the place of temporary residence. On the other hand, it is not completely realistic to count conscripts only at their permanent residence, since they do generate a certain amount of economic activity in their temporary municipality.

The confusion over the statistics of military employment is not accidental. When, in the early 1980s, we applied for permission to compute (from available census data) tables on military employment by district, the application was rejected by the Defense Ministry on security grounds. The argument was that the enemy might deduce the size of military installations on the basis of military employment figures by district. Since there is no district in Norway with less than several dozen military installations, large and small, this argument errs on the side of caution. At the municipal level such an argument makes more sense – assuming of course that the size of a particular military installation is important to the enemy and, if important, cannot be ascertained in other ways. In any case, this rejection put an effective end to any realistic study of conversion at the local level in the early 1980s. At the time, Norwegian authorities were concerned with conversion at the national and international level as a topic for discussion in the United Nations, but there was little urgency about engaging in conversion planning for Norway itself – a planning which would necessarily have to be based on data about the local problems that might be generated.

By the time the most recent Defense Commission was appointed in 1990, the situation had changed. Disarmament now seemed a more realistic possibility and the overly cautious security practices of the Norwegian military establishment had been challenged in several ways (Gleditsch & Wolland, 1991). The Defense Commission subcontracted a number of studies of the local effects of conversion. Its main subcommittee for the study of local effects noted that its work required 'a great deal of innovation on the data side' (Aamo et al., 1990, p. 7).

What *economic indicators* should be used at the local level? At the national level we have relied mainly on employment and GDP. At the local level we shall look mainly at *employment*, in addition to *tax income* for the municipality. In an early study of local effects of military activity in Northern Norway, Andreassen (1972) also used military purchases of goods and services and revenue in retail trade. But these must be assumed to serve mainly as proxies for the more interesting and relevant variables of employment and tax income.

In view of the inconsistencies in the data collection and secrecy constraints, it is difficult to produce a consistent time series, but Table 6.3 gives a fair impression of the great shift to the North in Norwegian defense policy. What political and military developments lie behind these figures?

In 1946 the first Norwegian postwar Defense Commission was appointed by the Cabinet to outline the future direction of Norwegian defense policies. Its final report (Ministry of Defense, 1949) was issued in October, half a year after Norway had joined NATO. In the analysis of threats and challenges, numerous references were made to the experience of World War II, where Norway had been occupied from its southern approaches. The report argued that Norway might be drawn into war because of its geographical position. Norway would be important for the great powers as a base area for aircraft, and for naval forces. Also noted was the importance of Norway for the control of exits from the Baltic and from the Murmansk area.

In the first postwar years, most of Norway was seen as strategically important. The early emphasis on the defense of Southern Norway may, however, be explained with reference to three factors. First, the overwhelming concentration of population in the South (78% in 1950, even if we assign the Central region to Northern Norway). Second, the large Soviet fleet in the Baltic. Third, the fact that Germany was still an occupied country and a burden on the Western military effort, rather than a contribution to it.

West German integration into the Western political and military system started in the early 1950s. What had been a burden soon turned into a military asset for Western Europe in general and for Norway and Denmark in particular. The outbreak of war in Korea in 1950 and the subsequent establishment of a peacetime integrated command structure further stimulated West German rearmament. The Norwegian government now argued that the 'defense of Northern Norway should be given special consideration' (*St.prp.* no. 122, 1950, p. 5). The decisive movement of defense efforts towards Northern Norway came after the NATO Defense Ministers' Meeting in December 1954. After that meeting NATO also decided to base the common defense on nuclear weapons. Accompanying this change was the introduction of a 'forward defense strategy', made possible by the combination of nuclear weapons and West German rearmament. The combination of these changes led to the following assessment for Norway:

This implies that the threat of invasion of Southern Norway is reduced considerably. In Southern Norway we can count on having some time available for mobilization and other preparations. The commission therefore suggests a gradual shift in our continental preparedness, with the main emphasis placed on Northern Norway. (Ministry of Defense, 1955)

This suggestion became official policy and was visibly reflected in defense planning throughout the 1950s and 1960s.

The rationale guiding Norwegian military defense planning during most of the period 1950-80 was therefore that the limited national resources could be used most effectively in Northern Norway. Threats from the south and southeast would be met primarily by West Germany and Denmark, and these two countries were therefore seen as crucial for the security of Norway as such.

The second Defense Commission was set up in 1974, and delivered its report in 1978. This report confirmed what has already been said about Northern Norway, but also recommended strengthening the defense of the rest of the country, in particular that of Central Norway (*NOU,* 1978:9, p. 97). Subsequently, public concern was expressed about the new threats to Southern Norway posed by the expansion of the Soviet Navy, Soviet long-range aircraft, special forces, etc. However, these concerns have only to a limited degree been translated into policies which could effect the regional distribution of labor in the military sector.

The report of the third Defense Commission was written as the Cold War was coming to an end. By late 1990, warning time for a major attack on the NATO area was expected to be weeks rather than days, and an isolated attack on Northern Norway was judged improbable. The buildup in Northern Norway continued nevertheless. Of the NOK 3,600 million budgeted for military construction in 1990, 56% was to be spent in Northern Norway. This was hardly a reflection of the prevailing threat perception in 1990, but must rather be interpreted as a delayed result of the renewed Cold War in the 1980s.

The results of this historical process can be seen in Table 6.3. Counting conscripts at place of employment, the share of military employment in Northern Norway is about 9% – or three times the national average. The process of shifting a large part of the military establishment to the North was by and large completed by 1970, with no clear upward or downward trend since then. The absolute size of the peacetime military establishment has always been larger in the Eastern region than in Northern Norway (with 40% and 33% of the national total respectively). But the 'sharp end' of the military is overrepresented in the North, where the main buildup would occur in the event of a mobilization.

Although Finnmark is closer to the Russian border, Troms has a much heavier military concentration. Finnmark is relatively flat and in greater danger of being overrun in a surprise attack, while Troms has a topography better suited to defense; also, forces stationed there will have extended warning time. Thus, the bulk of the standing army in Northern Norway is found in Troms rather than Finnmark, with a heavier concentration of radar, intelligence, and early warning sites in Finnmark. The military headquarters for Northern Norway, as well as some major naval bases, are found even further south, in Nordland.

Table 6.3 Military Share of Employment, by Region (% of Total Employment)

Region	Permanent military employment (Officers and Civilians)				Total military employment by permanent residence	Total military employment by place of employment			
	1950	1960	1970	1990	1970	1975	1980	1984	1990
East	1.0	1.6	1.6	1.3	2.7	2.3	2.4	2.4	2.3
South/ Southwest	1.0	1.6	1.3	1.0	2.6	2.5	2.4	2.4	2.5
West	0.5	0.5	1.1	1.2	2.5	1.4	1.5	1.5	1.8
Central	1.1	1.7	1.8	1.7	3.3	2.7	2.7	2.7	3.5
North	0.9	2.6	4.1	4.0	6.0	8.6	9.0	8.8	8.8
Total	0.9	1.5	1.8	1.5					
Total, including conscripts					3.1	2.9	3.0	3.0	3.0

Sources: 1950: Folketellingen 1. desember 1950, tredje hefte [Census, 1 December 1950, vol. 3], *NOS* XI 221, pp. 100-101, 218-219; *1960:* Data from the Census Tract Data Bank (Alvheim, 1981), aggregated to the regional level; *1970: Folke- og boligtelling 1970, hefte 2* [Census 1970, vol. 2], *NOS* A-693, pp. 148-149, 220-221. *1975, 1980, 1984:* Regional distribution of budgeted military work by region, adjusted by later figures for the national total of military work actually performed, both from the annual defense budget. Data on total work performed from annual national account publications, with the regional distribution from *Folke- og boligtelling 1980* [Census 1980], *NOS* various issues. *1990:* Aamo et al. (1990), pp. 16, 18

Disaggregating further to the district level, we find that all the three districts (*fylker*) in Northern Norway are above the national average in military employment (Table 6.4).

Table 6.4 Military Employment, the Oslo Area and Northern Norway

District	1970 No. of employed by permanent residence		1989 Permanent jobs by place of employment		1990 Total military employment	
	absolute figures	%	absolute figures	%	absolute figures	%
Oslo Area						
Oslo	4,834	2.3	3,736	1.9	5,145	3.7
Akershus	5,507	4.3	2,981	1.5	5,311	2.8
Northern Norway						
Nordland	4,390	5.3	2,798	3.3	4,518	5.3
Troms	3,585	7.4	3,134	5.7	8,144	14.7
Finnmark	1,487	5.5	787	2.9	2,147	7.8
Total	44,533	3.1	25,895	1.5	50,126	3.0

Sources: 1970: Census Tract Data Bank and Census 1970, cf. Gleditsch et al. (1987), p. 20. *1989:* Recalculated from Årethun (1990), p. 18. In the 1970 figures conscripts are counted in their place of residence, whereas in the 1989 figures they are counted in the district where they serve. *1990:* Aamo et al. (1990), p. 16

More detailed data in an earlier report (Gleditsch et al., 1987) indicate that between 1950 and 1970 all districts but three (Telemark, Sogn og Fjordane, and

Møre og Romsdal) increased their military dependency in terms of employment, and those three were insignificant in military terms to begin with. But by far the greatest changes took place in the three Northern districts.

At the municipal level, we would expect to find even higher levels of military dependency. At this local level, a single large military base can make up a sizeable proportion of the employment. Table 6.5. lists all the municipalities with military dependency (excluding conscripts) exceeding 15% in Spring 1990. The table also provides some data on the proportion of taxes deriving from military personnel.

Table 6.5 shows that a small number of municipalities have extremely high military employment. Further, the military dependence of these municipalities has grown over the past 30 years, with one exception in Northern Norway (Sørreisa, where military dependence has remained about the same after 1970) and one in Southern Norway (Ullensaker, near Oslo, where military employment has grown in absolute terms, but decreased in relative terms). The municipalities' dependence on the tax income from military personnel parallels the proportion of regularly employed military and civilian personnel in the armed forces. An additional source of income for the municipalities is municipal fees of various kinds (e.g. property taxes). Andøy is an extreme case, with municipal fees from the military establishment representing nearly half the total tax revenue.

Table 6.5 Military Dependency by Municipality, 1960, 1970, and 1990 (%)

Municipality	Permanent military employment only (officers and civilians)			All military jobs (including conscripts)	Taxes from military personnel
	1960	1970	1990	1990	1989
Tjeldsund (N)	16.4	38.2	53.1	65.4	33.8
Målselv (Tr)	17.3	34.1	43.1	66.4	38.4
Bardu (Tr)	28.5	37.4	36.7	65.4	36.9
Ørland (NT)	22.4	24.7	31.6	40.0	25.9
Andøy (N)	*	20.2	23.4	29.6	23.7
Evje og Hornnes (AA)	13.7	20.8	22.8	50.5	14.8
Porsanger (F)	*	11.9	20.2	45.0	22.3
Ullensaker (Ak)	23.0	19.5	16.5	25.3	2
Sørreisa (Tr)	*	15.8	15.7	-	2

N, Tr etc. refer to names of districts, cf. Figure 6.1.

* not computed (less than 10%).

** not given in source.

Vadsø (F) had 10.6% military employment in 1970. It is probably for security reasons that this municipality has been left out of the list in Aamo et al. (1990), which claims to include all municipalities with military dependence exceeding 5%. The most likely explanation for the omission is that the only military facility of any size in Vadsø is a signals intelligence site (Wilkes & Gleditsch, 1979, 1981). *Sources: Employment 1960, 1970:* The Census Tract Data Bank. *1990:* Aamo et al. (1990), pp. 17, 19. *Taxes, 1989:* Aanesen (1990), cited from Aamo et al. (1990), p. 26

If we compare the military dependence of the municipalities with heavy dependence on military facilities with the military dependence of the two munici-palities which host the two major Norwegian arms factories (Table 6.1 above), we note a much heavier dependence in the case of the former. Moreover, the two arms factories are both located in the Eastern region, where population is much denser, communication facilities are superior, and overall chances of alternative employment much better. In addition, these two arms producers are both diversified companies, with some possibilities for alternative employment within the company itself. There are major uncertainties here, but what can be stated is that *the military establishment itself plays a much greater economic role in Norway than does military industry. Thus, to the extent that there is a Norwegian conversion problem, it is one of compensating for the loss of military bases rather than for reduced activity in military industry.*

6.6 Indirect Local Effects

In the four national studies from 1964 to 1992 summarized in Table 4.2, we found a multiplier for employment between 1.3 and 1.6. Thus, the direct employment effect of immediate complete disarmament in 1992 was 2.7%, and the indirect effect 0.9%. We cannot assume that the same multiplier will apply in all geographical sub-units, however. First, because Southern Norway has a more diversified industrial structure, we might expect a greater proportion of the purchases made by the military establishment and its employees to benefit local business, whereas in Northern Norway more of the indirect effects would 'leak' to other regions. In fact, a study carried out for the Defense Commission in 1990 showed that the operating costs, excluding salaries, of the military establishment closely mirrored the distribution of employment. On the other hand, a very substantial proportion (45%) of purchases of equipment goes abroad, and the Oslo area claims a lion's share relative to Northern Norway. Where Northern Norway really does well is in construction: fully 55% of all military construction activity is carried out by firms located in Northern Norway, well above the region's share of military employment (28%). The reason for this is simply that a relatively large share of military construction takes place in Northern Norway. However, military construction varies considerably from one year to the next and 55% may not be fully representative. For the total purchases of goods, the three districts in Northern Norway come out with about the same share as in military employment.

For areas with high military dependency, two qualitatively different (and opposite) processes complicate the picture. With high military dependency there is little room for other employment and the indirect effects cannot be as large as at the national level. (To take an extreme example: if local military employment dependency is 100%, the indirect employment effects by definition must be zero.) On the other hand, when military dependency is extremely high, disarmament may threaten the very foundation of the community: after disarmament there may not be enough customers for a local store, not enough pupils for the local school, not enough business for the local branch of a bank or the post office. It becomes virtually impossible to sell a house, because the property market collapses. And when the very infrastructure of the community is threatened, this endangers the whole community.

In a study for the Defense Commission, Johansen (1990; cf. Aamo et al., 1990, p. 23) estimated the local employment multipliers to be in the range of 1.3-1.6. Interestingly, this is exactly the range we have found for the national employment multiplier over nearly 30 years of studies. Extrapolating from Johansen's calculations of the effects of a 10% cut in military activity, Table 6.6 gives the loss of employment in the three districts in Northern Norway for disarmament with no countermeasures. These calculations take no account of any 'threshold effects', but simply assume that all the indirect effects are linear. In addition, these results should be interpreted as short-run effects of disarmament where tax rates and other government expenditures are unchanged and government financial savings are increased. As shown in Chapter 4, this scenario will result in changes in relative prices and competitiveness that in the long run will produce quite different multipliers.

Table 6.6 Loss of Employment, Immediate Disarmament without Countermeasures, 1990 (%)

Nordland	8
Troms	18
Finnmark	9
All of Norway	4

Source: Recalculated from Johansen (1990), cf. Aamo et al. (1990), p. 24

Data for the indirect employment effects at the municipal level are not available, but Aanesen (1990) provides some data for the tax income of the most defense-dependent municipalities.

6.7 Local Countermeasures

The various countermeasures which we discussed at the national level hold differing degrees of promise at the local level. *Development assistance* might be a favorable local countermeasure if given as commodity transfers, with a concentration on fisheries. Because of the rather unstable resource situation for the fisheries, the most prudent policy might be to give away fish products in resource-rich periods and excess fishing-vessels in resource-poor periods. This would hardly make for a very consistent aid policy in the long run, however. *Global disarmament* is far too unpredictable – there have been no calculations on the regional effects of the (in any case rather uncertain) national gains in terms of increased exports. *Tax reductions* might work well in many local communities, but the relatively one-sided and traditional nature of economic activity in Northern Norway makes it more likely that the main benefits would come in the South.

This leaves the various countermeasures involving an expansion of other public consumption, either by general transfers to the municipalities or by the expansion of specific programs in health or social services. The advantage of such countermeasures is that they can relatively easily be provided in a regionally skewed form, to compensate for particular problems in the North or other regions. In theory they could also be linked directly to reductions in military activity, but this would probably have to be done at the district rather than at the municipal level, as the level of municipal services in neighboring municipalities might otherwise become strikingly different. This would not be without precedent. Some Norwegian municipalities receive considerable leasing income from their rights to national hydropower. Recently, as conservationist and environmental interests have worked for postponing or conserving indefinitely undeveloped hydro resources, some municipalities have demanded economic compensation for *not* having their hydroelectric power potential exploited – so far with little success.

We tested the effects of regionally biased countermeasures using the REGION model – a multi-regional input-output model at the level of the district (fylke). This analysis was based on national disarmament scenarios which in turn used the MSG growth model (cf. section 4.7.3 above). The MSG model assumes that wage-rates adjust so that there is always full employment. In the short and medium term this assumption is obviously at variance with reality. However, in the long run – 20 years in our case – it is not unreasonable to assume that prices and wages can be flexible enough to secure full employment, or something close to it. The following scenarios were developed:

DIS   50% reduction of military expenditure in the period 1984-93 and complete disarmament by 2003. Government expenditures for civilian purposes unchanged and tax reductions equal to lower military expenditures.

CON   Disarmament as in DIS. Half the budget savings transferred to public health programs in accordance with the regional distribution in the baseline scenario, the other half given as tax reductions.

NOR   Disarmament as in DIS and total transfers to public health programs as in CON, but with the regional distribution skewed so that the three districts of Northern Norway get twice as much (in relative terms) of the additional health programs as other districts.

Basic results for the three scenarios are given in Table 6.7. The effect of disarmament is very moderate in most regions. A negative effect of uncompensated disarmament is most clearly felt in Northern Norway. The conversion scenario is relatively similar to the disarmament scenario as far as effects in Northern Norway are concerned. By contrast, the NOR scenario yields a net positive effect in Northern Norway. In a sense, the regional bias of the countermeasure is slightly stronger than what would have been needed in order to compensate for the greater military employment in Northern Norway.

The two main economic mechanisms behind the results in Table 6.7 are the following: First, there are macroeconomic and national differences between the scenarios. DIS has lower public expenditures and higher private expenditures compared to the other two scenarios. Thus private consumption as well as investment are higher in DIS. Total GDP is also higher in this scenario. These differences imply differences in the sectoral allocation of labor and capital, with relatively more employment in industries producing consumer goods and invest-ment goods. One consequence is to modify the 'de-industrialization' feature of the baseline scenario. Secondly, the various sectors in the economy are not evenly distributed geographically. Changes in the allocation of total output between sectors therefore affect the regional pattern of employment. The South/Southwest and Central regions benefit more from disarmament mainly because these regions have the highest employment, in relative terms, in manufacturing. Their relative shares of military employment are close to the average of 2.8% in 2003.

The regional effects on employment from the various scenarios do not take into account that bottlenecks may appear due to the regional reallocation of labor. Employment figures in Table 6.7 are in a sense determined solely from the 'demand side', except for the national aggregate which is solely determined from the 'supply side'. In order to analyze the possible inconsistency between aggregate or national supply and regional demand, Skomsvold et al. (1987) relied on a regional demographic model that projects regional labor supply based on demographic forecasts combined with assumptions regarding labor participation rates by age, sex, and region. This regional model is calibrated so that total labor supply is the same as in the national model. One can then study the labor market balance by region according to two models. The gaps between regional labor demand and supply that appear have to be filled by inter-regional migration since there is no gap at the national level. The absolute regional excess demand (the absolute difference between labor demand and supply by region) is calculated to 7.1% of the labor supply in 2003 in the baseline scenario. In all the three other scenarios in Table 6.7 this figure is lower, implying that disarmament to some extent is likely to modify regional imbalances in the labor market. Differences between the three scenarios are small, with the lowest in DIS (5.9%), while NOR has 6.2%. The latter figure could be reduced if we 'fine-tuned' the regional bias in health expenditures a bit more. Thus we conclude that, if there is a regional imbalance in the labor market in the baseline scenario, it is at least not increased by disarmament even if no particular measures are taken to increase employment in the North.

In studies performed for the Defense Commission in 1990, the Norwegian Institute for Urban and Regional Research (NIBR) used an updated version of the REGION model, developed by Statistics Norway, to calculate the effects of a similar package of disarmament with countermeasures. Unlike the case when we attempted to use the model in our previous analysis (Skomsvold et al., 1987), REGION now provides a reasonably accurate specification of the military sector. As in our 1987 study, REGION is used as a 'top-down' model where scenarios at the national level largely determine the regional effects. The NIBR study is based on MODAG simulations at the national level. Moreover, like the MODAG model, it does not take for granted the full use of labor resources. Under the current conditions of high unemployment it will therefore produce more realistic estimates of the probable changes in employment likely to result from disarmament and countermeasures. NIBR looked at a more modest disarmament scenario (10% reduction of military spending) in an uncompensated version as well as a version with full conversion to local government spending. NIBR found that the employment multipliers varied little from district to district, and concluded that disarmament with countermeasures could be carried out with very minor adverse effects in all districts, with the possible exception of Troms.

Two weaknesses of these studies are that they do not take account of (a) possible threshold effects or (b) the effect of reduced exercises involving allied reinforcement troops. In 1990 such exercises involved an income for the municipalities in 'inner Troms' (mainly Bardu and Målselv) of NOK 12 million, plus an estimated private consumption by the soldiers involved of another NOK 6 million. A third factor of uncertainty is that many transfers from the central government to local

Table 6.7 Employment in the Baseline, DIS, CON, and NOR Scenarios, 2003

	Employment in Baseline			Relative change in scenario		
	(in '000 Person-Years)		Military	(in % of employment in Baseline)		
Region	Total	Military	in % of total	DIS	CON	NOR
East	1,012	14	1.4	-0.6	-0.2	-0.7
Oslo/Akershus	557	11	2.0	-1.1	-1.4	-2.0
South/Southwest	255	6	2.7	5.1	0	-0
West	341	8	2.3	-1.2	1.2	0.9
Central	163	5	3.1	1.8	1.8	1.2
North	201	11	5.5	-3.0	-2.5	1.0
Nordland	101	4	4.0	-3.0	-3.0	1.0
Troms	68	5	7.4	-3.0	-3.0	1.5
Finnmark	32	2	6.3	-3.0	-0.0	0.0
Total	1,972	55	2.8	0	0	0

The net employment effect of 0 in all scenarios is an assumption in the model, cf. Section 4.7.3 above.
Conscripts are counted at their permanent residence.
Source: Our own calculations using MSG. For additional detail, see Skomsvold et al. (1987), Table 4

government are based on the population in the municipality. The Aamo Committee Report therefore concludes that its estimates of the probable losses of employment and tax income for the most defense-dependent municipalities 'may be severely underestimated' (Aamo et al., 1990, p. 29).

In a subsequent study, Dedekam (1992) found that the employment multipliers for the seven most defense-dependent municipalities varied from 1.52 to 1.80. He looked at two alternative scenarios. A 'normal scenario' was based on interview data in the municipalities (for Evje in Southern Norway, for instance, it showed that two-thirds of civilians in the military establishment would like to stay if they lost their jobs in the armed forces, whereas 92% of the military would move). A crisis scenario assumed that everyone who lost his or her job in the military establishment would move. In addition there would be a 'soldier effect', based on data on the consumption patterns of conscripts. Within the framework of the 'normal scenario' Dedekam found that a 10% reduction in military activity in six municipalities (neighboring Bardu and Målselv were merged for the purpose of this analysis) would result in a reduction of employment from 3.4% to 7.4%, and a reduction in municipal income of between 2.9% and 7.2%. In the crisis alternative the maximum losses were 8.2% loss of employment (Tjeldsund) and 7.5% of municipal tax income (Bardu-Målselv). Dedekam concluded that 'it is probably correct to say that the effect was far less than many had expected' (1992, p. 179). If we accept the linear assumption, the maximal losses in the case of complete disarmament are 82% loss of employment and 75% loss of municipal tax income; it is questionable whether many could have expected more drastic results than this.

Finally, in the second committee report on regional effects on disarmament (Aune et al., 1991) the seven vulnerable municipalities were analyzed in somewhat greater detail, with some comments on individual industries that might be endangered. This committee again assumed that 'threshold values' existed below which military activity could not be reduced without danger of collapse for the local community, but was unable to determine how to establish such threshold values. As an internal countermeasure within the military, the committee suggested that activity in the military establishment might be rearranged so that institutions and activities currently located in Southern Norway would be moved to Northern Norway to compensate for reductions there. This strategy would transfer the burden of a regional policy on to the military establishment. In a situation of increasing resource constraints, the military are likely to be extremely reluctant to take on this task. Regional policy may be an important political goal, but it is hardly part of national security, as traditionally conceived. The committee also recommended to government to resolve such questions *before* making decisions affecting the defense-dependent municipalities. At the time of writing (late 1993) it would seem that this call was issued too late to have much effect.

Despite all the disasters which may befall the defense-dependent municipalities (and particularly certain local communities within them) these changes may well be overshadowed by four other processes of change which will affect Norway generally and Northern Norway in particular.

The first is increasing unemployment. As we have pointed out, the end of the Cold War coincided with the highest registered unemployment in the post-World War II period. Traditionally, unemployment has been higher in Northern Norway: in 1986, for instance, it was 4.1%, as against a national average of 2.2%. Thus, any unemployment resulting from uncompensated disarmament would hit most severely the region where the problems were already greater. However, in 1992 there were only minor regional differences in unemployment, now close to 6% on average.

Secondly, oil and gas exploration is about to reach Northern Norway. The introduction of an oil economy has had profound effects on Southern Norway, positive as well as negative. If substantial finds of oil and gas are made offshore of Northern Norway, they will probably have much greater impact on employment and municipal income in the region as a whole than reductions in military activity. But such benefits will obviously not reach all muncipalities in Northern Norway.

A third factor is the changing resource situation in fisheries. As late as the turn of the decade, Norwegian fisheries were in a sad state of affairs, hit by resource depletion, overinvestment, and market failure. On all these three counts, the situation now seems to be changing. In particular, strict regulations on cod fishing during the 1980s have produced cohorts which can be harvested in much larger numbers than just a few years ago. In addition, the fish processing industry in Finnmark, which has suffered from over-capacity, now has Russian trawlers delivering their catches to Norway.

Finally, what does the end of the Cold War imply for a region that has been a remote appendix to a country with virtually all its cooperation directed towards the West and the South, and with cooperation to the East blocked by an Iron Curtain considerably tighter than that in Central Europe? There is a centuries-old tradition of trade in the Northern Cap (or Barents Sea region). If Russia succeeds in establishing a stable political system and a viable market economy, Northern Norway could benefit considerably from regional cooperation. This is already happening to some extent in the fisheries, in addition to increased tourism. The future economic consequences are hard to predict, but here is potentially the most important regional peace dividend.

This chapter ends with a series of question marks, and so it must. The question of local effects of conversion was ignored, even suppressed, by the Norwegian authorities until the Cold War had already ended. By then military and political priorities had been changing before researchers or committees could complete the studies that were meant to lay the basis for informed decisions. In such a situation it is easy to err on the side of caution. Traditionally, local reactions to base closures have been hostile. In one controversial case, the suggested closure of the NATO communications system Ace High generated strong resistance from defense communications personnel. In a dramatic action, the employees' trade union at one of the stations in a remote location in Northern Norway, with no more than a dozen members, lobbied in the Storting and charged that closing down the system would represent a threat to national security. The Ministry of Defense responded by having the union's letter classified on the basis that it contained security information. Nevertheless, the Ace High system survived for several years but was eventually closed down. The perceptual problem here is that defense employees can easily point to the jobs that are in danger of being lost. Jobs that may be created on the basis of potential savings are much more ephemeral. Present employment is a tangible entity, while future employment is a statistical category, not inhibited by people of flesh and blood. Like unborn children, traffic fatalities, or the victims of future wars, those who would benefit from conversion cannot organize to fight for their interests. There is always a risk, then, that a local conversion debate may focus on the past, rather than on future prospects. In extreme cases it might even develop into a Cold War nostalgia. But to date the post-Cold War changes seem to have been accepted as more or less inevitable.

Notes

1. Military shooting-ranges have, for instance, led to the displacement of hikers' cabins and have come into conflict with the traditional Sami activity of reindeer-herding, adding an ethnic dimension to the environmental protest. Several such cases have ended in court, where the military establishment has generally prevailed, but has had to pay major compensatory damages to the industry.

2. For a brief review with several references, see Smith (1993) and Lindroos (1981). Lindroos also reviews other attempts at company-based conversion.

3. The share of civilian goods in the production of the four major defense industries - nuclear, astronautics, aeronautics and ordnance increased from 10% in 1978 to 80% in 1990 (Folta, 1992, p. 1).

4. Case stories of conversion in China are given in Folta (1992), Chapter 6 and in a number of papers in Chai & Zhang (1992).

5. Cf. Benoit (1966[1962]), p. 649.

6. These figures are *net* losses - the difference between jobs lost and jobs gained through the 'actions'.

7. Quoted from Adams (1992), p. 24.

8. Lawrence J. Korb, Assistant Secretary of Defense for Manpower, Installations, and Logistics in US Congress (1985), p. 2.

9. Cf. Benoit (1966[1962]), p. 646.

10. Our summary of the ECON report is based on Thulin et al. (1991).

11. We deliberately avoid the official translation 'county', which means a small unit (like *kommune*) in the USA and a large unit (like *fylke*) in the UK.

7

Defense Without Threat?

7.1 Norwegian Military Spending

Norway, like most small industrialized market economies in Western Europe, has a military sector of modest size. Throughout the Cold War, however, military spending was substantially higher than in earlier peacetime periods. The postwar level of military spending has hovered around 3% of the national product in real terms, while throughout the previous 50 years it had usually stayed around half that level. With the exception of a short period after the end of the Korean War, military spending continued to grow until recently. In this book we have sought to document that economic adjustment to disarmament in Norway will not be difficult. Indeed, if the end of the Cold War raises the prospects of a major reduction in military spending and a return to the traditional low peacetime level, Norway should be able to reap a peace dividend.

The bulk of the evidence, for Norway as for other industrialized countries, is that the national economic effects of disarmament will be beneficial, albeit small. Economic growth is likely to increase somewhat, as lower defense spending will create more room for investment. The foremost effect of military spending will be the loss of employment in the military establishment. This can be offset, for example, by expanding other public programs such as health care or by stimulating private demand through reduced taxation.

Total employment in the Norwegian military establishment today is slightly above 3% of the labor force. Including indirect effects, the proportion of the population dependent on the military sector may run as high as 5% – close to the current level of unemployment in the country. It would obviously be politically unacceptable to add to the ranks of the unemployed all those employed by the armed forces, or even a substantial number of them. However, if military spending could be redirected to other labor-intensive forms of public spending, such as social welfare and health, more jobs could be supported at the same level of public spending. If there were a wish to earmark a major share of the released resources for increased development assistance – an idea strongly promoted in the United Nations in the early 1980s – this would be possible without major negative effects if at the same time the remainder were spent in a way which boosted employment in Norway. Alternatively, reductions in personal taxation would expand private demand and increase employment. A third option would be to use the peace dividend to improve the balance of the central government budget. In the USA, where the rearmament of the 1980s was financed largely by budget deficits and public borrowing, reducing the deficit is an important political issue. In Norway, large oil revenues accruing to the government have prevented the government debt trap that many OECD countries have fallen into, but at the time of completing this book (late 1993) the government deficit in Norway is higher than ever.

'Pure disarmament' for Norway, i.e. disarmament with no countermeasures, may be interpreted as deficit reduction. We have found that over a period of 10-15 years, this alternative yields somewhat higher unemployment and lower economic growth. Hence, disarmament without explicit countermeasures is unlikely to have favorable effects on the economy. On the other hand, policies with appropriate countermeasures can yield much more beneficial results.

Although complete disarmament is hardly a realistic possibility in the near term, it is useful for conversion studies to look at such drastic disarmament scenarios as a 'worst case' in terms of economic dislocation. The national effects of the worst-case scenario appear to be manageable – even favorable, if appropriate countermeasures are chosen.

Local adjustment effects can be more serious, as we have shown in Chapter 6. Because of the prevailing threat scenario in the Cold War, most of Norway's standing forces have been located in Northern Norway, which is very sparsely populated. Altogether, the armed forces represent almost 9% of employment in Northern Norway, and up to 50% in selected municipalities. Counting indirect effects, such municipalities stand to lose up to two-thirds of their employment, or three-quarters of their tax revenue. Such communities would come close to financial ruin in the event of rapid disarmament, so special countermeasures would have to be devised for them. One unorthodox possibility could be to offer early retirement with full pension rights, tied to continued residence in the community. Alternative forms of public spending could also be given a regional twist. For instance, many health and social services are joint state/municipal programs. If a higher proportion were refunded from the state to municipalities in Northern Norway (or specifically to municipalities with major reductions in defense employment) this could facilitate alternative employment.

A worst-case scenario in terms of economic adjustment for one community may at the same time promise a peace dividend for another community or, indeed, for the country as a whole. Our most recent work using the MODAG model (reported in Section 4.9 above) shows that the combination of disarmament and lowered personal taxes yields a minor increase in GDP per capita – indicating that there is a potential peace dividend if a decision is made to collect it. Of course, whatever particular purpose is targeted as the main recipient of the resources transferred from the military will see the peace dividend as a major windfall. Norwegian development aid could be doubled, or environmental expenditure quadrupled, or a major effort made in funding better old-age care – just to take three examples from the current debate about public spending.

7.2 Prospects for a Peace Dividend

What are the political prospects for disarmament and for reaping the peace dividend? Three factors likely to influence the outcome will be discussed here: changes in threat scenarios, international comparisons, and the pressure of domestic priorities.

7.2.1 Threat Scenarios

If earlier events had not settled the issue, the statement made by Russia's President in January 1992 – that the USA is no longer an enemy but rather an ally – ended the Cold War and also the traditional Norwegian threat scenario involving attack from the East – whether in isolation or as a part of a general East-West conflagration. The Polar Strategy – attack by one superpower on the other through the Arctic – remains only as the very last and highly unlikely resort for deterrence purposes. The likelihood of 'horizontal escalation' – one superpower attacking the other in the North in response to a defeat in Central Europe or in the Middle East -seems equally remote. Thus, Norway's much-touted 'strategic location' (Gleditsch, 1985) is no longer an apt description: strategic peripherality would be a more appropriate term.

Various possible new threat scenarios have been suggested. In Southern Europe and in parts of the former Soviet Union, the removal of the East-West 'overlay' (Buzan et al., 1990) has re-opened old ethnic conflicts. The danger of escalation into a major European conflagration seems very low; moreover, Norway is not located close to any of these conflicts. For a while in 1990-91 it looked as if the Baltic republics' struggle for independence might lead to a major armed conflict near the Nordic countries. However, with the dissolution of the Soviet Union, the Baltic countries were quickly recognized, and now seem to be firmly established as independent states. War between Russia and Ukraine or other former Soviet republics – a low-probability event, but not one that can be completely dismissed would be unlikely to spread to the West. Experience from the recent conflict in Yugoslavia points clearly in this direction. The war is a tragic event for all the nationalities and ethnic groups in the divided country, and particularly for the Muslims in Bosnia. But the danger of escalation to any part of Europe north or west of this territory is almost nil, in spite of – or perhaps because of – the strong awareness of the fact that a violent episode in that very area sparked off World War I. The war in the former Yugoslavia has led to the deaths of ceasefire observers and disaster aid personnel; if a major peacekeeping, not to mention *peacemaking,* operation is launched, such casualties will become much greater. All the same, this is very different from the diffusion of an armed conflict into the territory of neighboring states. Ukraine and Russia are of course much larger. Any military conflict between them would have major political repercussions and might be very costly. But there is no clearly visible mechanism for the diffusion of such a conflict to the West. Any direct military impact on Western Europe seems unlikely, although the political effects might be considerable.

Other threat scenarios relate to the Middle East and in particular to the rise of Islamic fundamentalism or expansionist secular regimes. Such conflicts are even further removed from the Nordic region, but have a higher escalation potential. Several Nordic countries participated (in a non-combatant role) in the Gulf War in 1991, and considerable public concern was expressed that the war might spread to Scandinavia in the form of terrorist attacks. These fears proved unwarranted, but the possibility of contagion even to Northern Europe cannot be ruled out entirely in the future; it may also be used to justify increased security precautions such as telephone tapping, building security, and border controls. It is very unlikely, however, that such 'derived conflict' would involve regular armed forces in a way warranting continued high defense spending.

Yet another threat scenario relates to social unrest in Russia and the other former Soviet republics. The spectre has been raised of millions of refugees fleeing to the West to escape hunger, social chaos, and possibly a military coup d'etat. The realism of this scenario may be questioned; but even if it is accepted, most of the traditional armory of the military establishment seems rather unsuited for the task of stemming a tide of hungry refugees.

There remains what we might call an 'uncertainty scenario'. The political future of Russia is highly uncertain. Certain political extremists in Russia advocate reclaiming all former Czarist territory, including Finland and Poland. Were they to gain power and ally themselves with the remnants of the armed forces, Russia might once again undertake a major re-armament effort, and another arms race with the West could ensue. Even less extreme rulers might decide that Russian national pride has taken enough of a beating and try to restore great-power status by military means. What this scenario holds out, essentially, is a continuation of cold war, probably under a black or brown rather than a red political leadership. Even under such a scenario, however, any substantial re-arming with modern weaponry could hardly start until several years from now. Meanwhile, the Russian military establishment will scarcely be able to maintain its great stocks of weaponry. In particular, it seems very unlikely that it will be able to pay the salaries of its very large standing forces. Extensive demobilization seems on the cards, and with it will go most of the remaining conventional threat to Europe. The countries of Central Europe will no longer be allies of Russia, but neutral or even hostile in a war, and Belarus and the Ukraine will be buffers between Russia and Western Europe. Norway is now the only NATO country bordering directly on Russia (Turkey bordered on the Soviet Union, but not on Russia), but war between Russia and Norway is hardly imaginable except in the context of a general war in Europe.

Little can be said with any certainty about Russia's future military spending, except that it is likely to decrease drastically. Political statements by Russian political leaders have indicated a reduction of the army to roughly one-third of its present level and reduction of military spending by as much as a factor of eight, from about one-quarter of the national product to a 'normal' European level of about 3%. Whether, and how soon, this will come to pass is of course uncertain. However, such reductions will not lead to any local, bilateral balance of power (Russia's forces adjacent to Norway will still be much larger than Norway's); in economic terms it is less likely that the military share of GDP in Russia will fall below the current Norwegian level of about 3%. Therefore, it will probably still be argued in Norway that Russia has decreased its forces to a 'reasonable' level – while Norway has been at that level all along – and therefore no change needs to be made in Norway.

Barring a turn to extremism and re-armament in Russia, then, the Nordic countries seem likely to remain on the European periphery as far as armed conflicts are concerned. However, the uncertainty scenario is one that cannot be disproved in the short run – indeed, it is hardly falsifiable. Moreover, throughout the Cold War the 'Eastern threat' scenario remained tightly coupled with the apparent failure of low military spending in the 1930s and neutralism in the face of the growing threat from Nazi Germany. The German invasion of Norway in April 1940 remains a trauma in Norwegian security policy. Not unexpectedly, the prospect of lower defense spending in the face of a vanishing threat has led military officers and others to draw explicit parallels to the situation in the 1930s.[1] This line of thought has a number of weaknesses, however. One of them is that much of the struggle about defense expenditure in the 1930s, particularly in the first half of the decade, had strong domestic overtones in Norway. The labor movement, rising to political hegemony in 1935, feared that the military would be used to preserve the old order. Conversely, one reason why the Establishment was interested in strengthening the military was precisely its role as a guarantee against a seizure of power from the Left. Eventually, such mutual domestic suspicions were laid aside in the face of rising fascism and increased international tension, and a consensus emerged that some increase in defense spending was warranted. But on the whole, the Norwegian defense debate in the 1930s took place in a very different domestic climate.[2]

If threat perceptions in Norway change more slowly than in the USA, there may even be some short-term pressure for *increased* military spending in Norway. Decreased US commitment to the defense of Western Europe may become an argument for greater European self-reliance. For a long time the USA has been putting pressure on Western Europe to shoulder a higher share of the defense burden, for instance by sharing the expenditure for pre-positioning stocks for US reinforcements to Europe in wartime. More generally, the US has argued that Western Europe is a free rider on the overall security provided by US armed forces. An academic version of this argument is provided by applying the theory of collective goods to security in a military alliance: If the largest party to an alliance provides military security for all the members (e.g. through nuclear deterrence) then it is unnecessary for the smaller countries to contribute as much. If they are free to act on their own, they will therefore take a 'free ride' on the security provided by the alliance leader.[3] However, this argument disregards the possibility that a leading member of an alliance may be promoting (and funding) its own unilateral aims which are *not* part of the common security. Thus, pre-positioning for US forces in Norway may be a way of tying the US military establishment to the defense of Norway – but it is also a way of tying Norway to the US military establishment, whose goal is not exclusively to provide for the security of its European allies. Perceptions here are strongly colored by political views. Our conjecture is that once the threat from the East is gone, the willingness of Norway and other European allies to bail out the US Treasury for pre-positioning and other joint projects will cool markedly. But similarly, the Pentagon will be far less willing to spend its more limited funds on early warning of and preparedness for extremely remote contingencies in quiet corners of the world.

In conclusion, the disappearance of the dominant threat is unlikely to lead to any rapid major change in defense spending, but it will probably erode support for continued high military spending, and this will lead to reductions in the long run.

7.2.2 International Comparisons

With regard to military spending as a proportion of GDP, Norway slightly exceeds the *median* of the approximately 150 or so countries for which data are available. Because of the high relative spending of the major military powers, Norway's spending is lower than the *average* for the same countries. However, global figures are hardly a relevant comparison for policy purposes. For Norway, the two relevant reference groups are (1) Russia and other former opponents and (2) the allies and other West European countries.

As noted, Russia's military spending is declining; the same applies to its former allies in Eastern Europe. With the threat from the East reduced or even eliminated, reductions in the military spending of Norway's allies and neutral neighbors will probably have a more direct impact on Norwegian policy. Among the 15 NATO countries with a domestic military establishment (all except Iceland), 10 were listed in the *SIPRI Yearbook* with lower military spending in real terms in 1992 than in 1991. Seen over a period of several years, only Norway, Luxembourg, and Turkey had increasing expenditures.[4] Among the neutral countries the trend is also towards lower military spending, with Finland as the clearest deviant. The power of these examples will be strong. Since virtually all other NATO members and neutrals are closer to sources of current conflict than Norway, and several have great-power ambitions outside the area defined by the North Atlantic Treaty, they are inherently less likely than Norway to be immediately affected by the demise of the East-West conflict. If they nevertheless persist in cutting military spending, it will be more difficult to argue for continued high levels in Norway, despite Norway's common border with Russia.

7.2.3 Competing Priorities

The welfare state which emerged in Norway and other countries after 1945 presupposed an expanding public budget made possible by income and retail taxation in an expanding economy. Then in the early 1970s, the postwar boom in Western industrialized countries petered out, to be followed by more turbulent years with high unemployment. The policy focus shifted from demand management to supply-side factors. The bulging public sector came under attack as a source of deadweight loss through its tax financing, and privatization was called for as a better way in societies with high private incomes. This development came somewhat later to Norway, as North Sea oil revenues smoothed the path and reduced the need for contractive measures through the 1970s and most of the 1980s. In Norway, general government expenditure, including transfers, amounted to fully 60% of GDP in 1991. In the first half of the 1970s, high taxation levels had already encouraged a right-wing populism in protest against state 'confiscation'. The right-wing wave of the early 1980s also led the more centrist political parties to reconsider the dependence of the welfare state on an expanding public sector, with privatization, deregulation, and reduction in some public services as the inevitable result. Eventually, many of these changes came to be accepted by a Labor government faced with fiscal constraints.

Lower retirement ages, health benefits, and increased use of disability pensions will continue to lay claim to substantial public funds. The rising costs combine to increase the relative burden on those now in the labor force and will be exacerbated some decades ahead by demographic changes.

Attempted cutbacks in public budgets have, in turn, led to counter-reactions. In 1990 a strong protest by spokespersons for the retired gained such strength that an extra 'old age billion' (i.e. NOK 1,000 million) was added to the government budget. In retrospect, such extra grants may appear as political gimmicks and their long-term impact on the budget is unclear, but the political weight of the issue of old-age care remains. Considerable concern has also been expressed about the quality of Norwegian education in the face of shrinking budgets. The rapid rise of unemployment in the late 1980s (which even for a while brought Norway from close to the bottom level to an almost 'normal' European rate of unemployment) has occupied the center-stage in politics and has raised the question of priorities in public spending.

Thus, due to rising expectations and claims for public funding, a mature welfare state with little outright poverty is likely to experience greater, not less, competition for public funds. Contrary to the impression one may gain from looking at the rise in the absolute level of military spending, the military have fought a losing battle with civilian interest groups for much of the postwar period. As Figure 3.4 shows, the military share of GDP declined substantially from the peak in the early 1950s to the end of the 1970s. It rose slightly during the international rearmament in the 1980s, but has remained level since the end of the Cold War, and is now on a new downturn. The military share of total government consumption also declined substantially from the end of the Korean War until the end of detente in the 1970s, rose slightly in the 1980s and is now declining again. In this sense, the military are correct in their complaints that they have already been losers in the budget battle, although worse is probably to come.

The interaction of this continuing pressure on the budget with the disappearance of the traditional threat will probably pave the way for a gradual reduction in military spending. As the bitter experience in World War II recedes into the background, it will be less effective in blocking disarmament. Reduced military spending in Norway is less likely to come as a deliberate attempt to capture a peace dividend, with a plan for disarmament and a program for conversion of military facilities and industry.

7.3 New Roles for the Armed Forces?

If the old threat has gone and no credible major new threat is emerging on the horizon, what role – if any – remains for armed forces? The principle of national defense enjoys high standing in public opinion in Norway and is very unlikely to be discarded for a long time. However, the main task of the military will probably no longer be readiness for mass mobilization against a numerically superior enemy, nor to effect a holding action until allied help arrives. Rather, it seems likely that military power may have three tasks: (1) to maintain deterrence in the last resort (2) to serve as an instrument for maintaining Norwegian sovereignty, particularly over the large Norwegian economic zone (more than six times

Norwegian land territory) and (3) to participate in international peacekeeping operations. In addition, the military establishment may be given an increased role in disaster relief and environmental surveillance. However, these can only be supplementary tasks. If such functions dominate, the military establishment would become a civilian branch of government: it would be successfully 'converted'.

With the Norwegian military establishment for the first time in 45 years facing a long-term decline in military expenditures, it will also have to face the issue of how the armed forces may become more cost-effective. What parts of the military may be cut with the smallest loss in military effectiveness must be evaluated in relation to the main tasks. Three issues will be central to this debate: conscription, high-technology weaponry, and the future of Norwegian arms production.

7.3.1 The Future of Conscription

Norway's armed forces are limited in peacetime, but are based on very extensive mobilization in wartime. An expansion of the armed forces by a factor of eight, to some 320,000 (8% of the total population) would be the result of full mobilization. Since Norway in the past two centuries has not seen military action involving large land battles, it is difficult to know whether the high reliance on conscripts with basic training and refresher courses is a cost-effective defense strategy relative to a smaller, more professional, better-equipped force. That choice will not be made only on the basis of military effectiveness: an army based on conscription and large-scale popular participation is seen as a democratic guarantee for popular control of the armed forces. With the stabilization of Norwegian democracy, this principle may become less vital in the future. Fifty years ago the emerging labor movement and the military (and their political allies) viewed each other with strong mutual distrust, and the possibility of maintaining democratic procedures was called into question by both sides. Today, only very small fringe groups challenge the democratic consensus. Norway's military establishment may complain about political decisions, such as recent defense budgets, but conscription is hardly a major factor in their reluctance to use their power to challenge the democratic order.

In military terms, the main effect of conscription is to prepare for a very large army in case of full mobilization. The extreme among the Nordic countries, Finland, can mobilize 15% in wartime, with military spending at only half Norway's level: 1.5% of GDP. The historical reason for Finland's choice of priorities is probably its relative initial success in the Winter War against the Soviet Union in 1939-40, when the Finnish army was able to fend off much larger Soviet forces using superior tactics and intimate knowledge of the terrain. Such anti-invasion land defense is less relevant today. The three priority tasks probably require more specialized forces and better training. This may make conscription superfluous, at least in the form practised in Norway today.

Conscription may be modified. The intake of conscripts may be reduced by relaxing the medical criteria for exemption, making fully voluntary the choice between various forms of alternative service, having the conscripts serve for a shorter period, or drawing lots. Except for the lottery (in use in Norway up to 1910 and again between 1929 and 1936) all of these methods are now being used to some extent. Practice with regard to medical exemptions is liberal. Conscientious objection is higher than ever before, probably partly due to increasingly liberal legislation and court practice. The COs' own organizations have repeatedly expressed an interest in reforming the service to make it a meaningful part of an extended form of defense but little has been achieved in this direction so far. Together, medical exemptions and conscientious objection keep over a third of the conscripts outside the national defense. Since women serve in the armed forces purely on a voluntary basis, only about one-third of each cohort obtains relevant training. Recruitment to the Norwegian defense establishment is thus very far from 'universal'. Although individual freedom of choice may be seen as more democratic than a system of compulsory service, the traditional democratic basis of the service – equal burdens for all – is being eroded. A small fraction of the current cohort are being called up for the Home Guard for only six months' training – about half of the regular service. If the principle of general conscription becomes further eroded, for instance by introducing a lottery, it is questionable whether the institution can survive. Like taxation, conscription depends on a strong measure of legitimacy, and this can hardly be maintained if only a few are called on to contribute.

7.3.2 The Role of High-Tech Weapons

In 'the arms deal of the century' of the mid-1970s Norway replaced its aging fleet of fighter aircraft with a high-technology weapons system, the F-16. By the end of the 20th century (the end of this very decade!) the fleet of F-16s will be severely depleted, and the remaining planes will be 25 years old. New aircraft might cost NOK 100 million apiece, and the question has been raised whether it will still be possible for Norway to maintain a fleet of modern fighters. One option is to rely even more (perhaps exclusively) on allied reinforcements for air warfare. Another option would be to purchase much simpler fighters, suitable for close air support of land forces but not as fighter-bombers in an offensive role. Within the context of the likely future roles of the armed forces outlined above, it is questionable whether any large fleet of fighter aircraft is needed. Rather, main emphasis might be on surveillance aircraft for patrolling the Norwegian economic zone. In UN peacekeeping, it is unlikely that Norwegian combat aircraft would have any role to play.

Similar question-marks can be attached to other advanced and expensive major weapons systems, such as air-to-ship missiles, heavy tanks, and submarines, although the latter might play a role in enforcing Norwegian sovereignty under the surface of the sea. This does not necessarily mean, however, that the military establishment is certain to become a low-technology force. Various means of technical surveillance, radar, satellite imagery, night-vision equipment, etc. might be very important for the economic zone. Nevertheless, such technology would probably be a great deal cheaper than the latest major weapons systems.

The debate on these issues has just started. Spring 1992 saw the publication of the main report from the – largely civilian – Defense Commission (*NOU*, 1992:12) and a companion report from the Defense High Command (1992).

Characteristically, the military report describes a 'high' resource level scenario with 2.5% real growth over the rest of the century, in addition to a 'middle' scenario of zero growth and a 'low' scenario involving reduction to 80%, by the year 2000. That the high-growth scenario of the professional military corresponds to a growth rate which they in the past have criticized strongly for being too low, is indicative of a drastic change in perceptions with regard to what is politically feasible. By contrast, the majority of Defense Commission recommended zero growth. Specifically, the Commission proposed a growth in high-technology projects for the Air Force and Navy, and a sharp reduction in the activity of the Army. This re-orientation has led to some criticism that Norway's people-based territorial defense is being abandoned. On the other hand, proposals for new fighter aircraft and other expensive equipment face the same problem as building a new civilian airport in Oslo or other extremely expensive investment projects: decisions are so wide-ranging that they get deferred given any plausible excuse. Thus, barring any drastic change in Norway's immediate security environment, the recommendations of the Defense Commission are unlikely to maintain the resource base for the defense establishment in the long run.

A radical decision in favor of a clear disarmament scenario would have opened up the possibility of planning for the use of the peace dividend for civilian projects, at home in Norway or abroad. Such a decision would be controversial[5]. Currently it seems very unlikely. However, a less radical version of disarmament may very well come about by non-decision, indeed the figures for military consumption in 1993 may indicate that such a process has already started. In that case, the 'peace dividend' is likely to be consumed by whatever civilian projects happen to enjoy priority at the time, without any specific planning or debate.

Notes

1. One example is an article in *Aftenposten*, the major conservative daily, by H. F. Zeiner Gundersen, former Chief of the Norwegian Defense Staff and later Chairman of NATO's Military Committee, 10 February 1992.

2. Mutual fears between the labor movement and the military establishment are well documented in a number of works, most extensively in a forthcoming dissertation by Nils Ivar Agøy. For a preview, see Agøy (1992), which shows that there may even have been plans to use the military against a legally established Labor government - but this point is more controversial.

3. Cf. Olson & Zeckhauser (1966) Russett (1970).

4. The *SIPRI Yearbook* has not published complete military expenditure data for 1991 or 1992. The SIPRI figures for Norway deviate to some extent from our figures for military consumption from the national accounts.

5. While Norwegian public opinion remains strongly pro-defense and pro-NATO, it tends to favor the status quo rather than increasing military expenditure. There is also high support for such publicly-funded projects as old age care, education, and even development aid. Thus, if disarmament was seen as consistent with security, there would probably be wide public support for conversion. What appears to be the only study of Norwegian public opinion on conversion (Galtung, 1967) ranked social welfare and health, lower taxes, education, and technical assistance (in that order) as the most popular candidates for money released by disarmament - but the fieldwork was done 30 years ago. With information from the 1970s we concluded (in Bjerkholt et al., 1980, Section 4.5; on the basis of data from Ringdal, 1979) that public opinion in Norway was favorable to disarmament as well as to development aid, and that the two showed at least a moderately positive correlation.

Appendix A: Demographic, Economic, and Military Time Series for Norway

This Appendix provides data on Norwegian military consumption, military expenditures, the military use of manpower resources, as well as data on some other military, demographic, and economic variables. The collection has been extended back in time as far as reliable data are available, and forward as close as possible to the finalizing of the book manuscript.

Definitions

In this book we concentrate on measures of *military consumption*. Such figures are generally found in the Norwegian National Accounts *(Nasjonalregnskapet)*,[1] while figures for *military expenditures* are found in the Norwegian Fiscal Accounts *(Statsregnskapet)*, published annually in two *Reports to the Storting* (= Parliament). The first part of the accounts for each year is published in *Report to the Storting* no. 3 for the next session of the Storting. The second part is found in *Report to the Storting* no. 2 for the subsequent session. These figures differ somewhat from those published in various other surveys of Norwegian military expenditure, including the official Norwegian reply to the questionnaires of the UN Secretary-General.[2] To avoid confusion, we shall explain briefly the basis for the various figures.

Budgeted Military Expenditure is the figure for military expenditure found in each year's Annual Budget.

Military Expenditure is the total amount actually spent by the Ministry of Defense and its subsidiary agencies.

Military Consumption is a figure for the net real resources used for military purposes by state and local (municipal) authorities, according to definitions in the National Accounts.

Military Expenditure differs from *Budgeted Military Expenditure* in three ways:

1. It includes changes made during the budgetary process in the Storting
2. It includes supplementary appropriations made during the year
3. It excludes any funds made available in the Budget but not actually spent.

Military Consumption in turn differs from *Military Expenditure* in five ways:

1. It excludes (money) transfers to other organizations
2. It excludes gifts or sales of goods and services to other organizations
3. It excludes payments in advance or in arrears for goods to be consumed in other years
4. It includes expenditures for civilian preparedness activities, budgeted under the Ministry of Justice and other ministries
5. It includes military expenditure at the local (municipal) level.

Until 1961 military expenditures were calculated on the basis of a fiscal year running from 1 July to 30 June. All national accounts data have been recalculated on a calendar year basis.

Comparability Over Time

The transformation from current prices to constant 1970 prices has been done by comparing figures from various national accounts publications. Such a transformation - through several stages - inevitably implies some inaccuracy. In addition, a comparison on the basis of constant prices for a period of almost one century is somewhat fictitious, in the sense that the goods that could be purchased, for example, in 1970 are completely different from those available in 1910, due to general technological change. These columns may, however, serve as illustrations of *gradual* changes in military consumption.

Figures for military spending do not include the value of military assistance to Norway. For the first 25 years after World War II the value of such assistance was quite substantial. Nor does it include covert military funding hidden in other budgetary items, or the value of underpriced goods delivered to the military, such as conscript labor. These limitations are discussed in Chapter 3.

Table A.1 Basic Demographic, Military, and Economic Variables, 1887-1992 (in NOK Million, Except Where Otherwise Indicated)

| | | In current prices | | | | | | In constant 1970 prices | |
| | Mean population | Gross domestic product | | Military consumption | | Total government consumption | | Military consumption | |
Year	('000)	Old	New	Old	New	Old	New	Old	New
1887	1 969.8	659		9		34		101	
1888	1 976.6	710		9		34		99	
1889	1 984.3	770		10		36		106	
1890	1 996.9	780		10		36		105	
1891	2 012.5	802		10		37		102	
1892	2 026.0	799		10		41		104	
1893	2 037.8	809		11		43		117	
1894	2 056.7	816		11		44		119	
1895	2 083.1	832		14		48		153	
1896	2 111.7	875		20		55		216	
1897	2 141.7	919		20		58		216	
1898	2 173.8	998		20		60		202	
1899	2 204.1	1 065		24		69		232	
1900	2 230.5	1 115		22		71		206	
1901	2 254.9	1 101		21		73		201	
1902	2 275.5	1 088		19		73		184	
1903	2 287.8	1 081		17		71		167	
1904	2 297.5	1 081		15		69		147	
1905	2 308.6	1 105		16		70		155	
1906	2 319.2	1 187		16		71		150	
1907	2 329.0	1 265		16		74		144	

Table A.1 cont'd

		In current prices						In constant 1970 prices	
	Mean population	Gross domestic product		Military consumption		Total government consumption		Military consumption	
Year	('000)	Old	New	Old	New	Old	New	Old	New
1908	2 345.6	1 299		16		76		143	
1909	2 367.5	1 316		17		80		153	
1910	2 383.7	1 435		18		84		159	
1911	2 400.8	1 530		19		88		163	
1912	2 423.2	1 680		25		101		205	
1913	2 446.9	1 857		27		108		214	
1914	2 472.4	1 919		40		127		315	
1915	2 497.8	2 594		58		157		378	
1916	2 522.2	3 871		75		200		377	
1917	2 550.5	4 489		107		290		388	
1918	2 577.7	5 048		108		394		314	
1919	2 602.9	6 195		77		464		218	
1920	2 634.7	7 500		60		525		142	
1921	2 667.9	5 448		56		554		154	
1922	2 694.8	4 980		53		520		183	
1923	2 713.1	4 997		47		465		168	
1924	2 728.8	5 576		45		448		144	
1925	2 746.8	5 633		45		434		150	
1926	2 763.1	4 646		45		397		183	
1927	2 774.9	4 218		42		373		194	
1928	2 784.7	4 221		39		350		189	
1929	2 795.1	4 345		39		338		199	
1930	2 807.4	4 377		37		330		200	
1931	2 823.9	3 842		35		322		201	
1932	2 841.5	3 862		32		307		186	
1933	2 858.3	3 866		31		301		185	
1934	2 874.2	4 068		31		307		183	
1935	2 889.2	4 362		33		328		191	
1936	2 903.5	4 850		40		356		223	
1937	2 918.7	5 581		48		384		247	
1938	2 935.8	5 827		58		418		290	
1939	2 954.4	6 253		112		526		544	
1940	2 973.1								
1941	2 990.2								
1942	3 008.9								
1943	3 032.4								
1944	3 060.2								
1945	3 091.2								
1946	3 126.9	10 778		464		1 286		1 366	
1947	3 165.0	12 687		332		1 242		921	
1948	3 201.0	13 904		307		1 256		810	
1949	3 234.2	14 917	13 657	331	331	1 349	1 388	833	820
1950	3 265.1	16 425	15 073	353	353	1 467	1 511	837	822
1951	3 295.9	20 456	18 765	574	574	1 837	1 900	1 206	1 189

Table A.1 cont'd

		In current prices						In constant 1970 prices	
	Mean population	Gross domestic product		Military consumption		Total government consumption		Military consumption	
Year	('000)	Old	New	Old	New	Old	New	Old	New
1952	3 327.7	22 564	20 732	819	818	2 266	2 335	1 587	1 558
1953	3 360.9	22 884	21 013	996	994	2 577	2 664	1 906	1 875
1954	3 394.2	24 806	22 799	1 053	1 051	2 746	2 845	1 944	1 910
1955	3 427.4	26 376	24 278	891	888	2 711	2 820	1 612	1 577
1956	3 460.0	29 747	27 462	939	936	3 067	3 201	1 627	1 592
1957	3 491.1	31 775	29 248	1 009	1 007	3 350	3 538	1 672	1 637
1958	3 523.0	31 919	29 207	993	991	3 540	3 738	1 588	1 545
1959	3 552.9	33 946	30 958	1 063	1 061	3 862	4 090	1 663	1 638
1960	3 581.2	36 101	33 058	1 059	1 057	4 018	4 249	1 649	1 613
1961	3 609.8	39 245	36 062	1 141	1 138	4 370	4 633	1 734	1 694
1962	3 638.9	42 295	38 843	1 323	1 332	5 085	5 431	1 933	1 894
1963	3 666.5	45 661	41 682	1 414	1 425	5 592	5 977	2 014	1 951
1964	3 694.3	50 334	45 837	1 529	1 540	6 189	6 634	2 101	2 045
1965	3 723.2	55 828	50 563	1 862	1 874	7 111	7 608	2 441	2 386
1966	3 753.6	60 843	54 568	1 898	1 913	7 801	8 438	2 387	2 345
1967	3 786.0	66 902	59 700	2 078	2 149	8 881	9 615	2 524	2 579
1968	3 819.0	71 932	63 749	2 271	2 352	9 763	10 562	2 634	2 750
1969	3 851.0	77 930	69 418	2 522	2 549	10 831	11 674	2 795	2 825
1970	3 877.4		79 877		2 821		13 533		2 821
1971	3 903.0		89 107		3 035		15 978		2 849
1972	3 933.0		98 403		3 215		17 861		2 818
1973	3 960.0		111 854		3 505		20 390		2 845
1974	3 985.3		129 728		3 920		23 759		2 868
1975	4 007.3		148 701		4 750		28 701		3 095
1976	4 026.2		170 709		5 296		34 086		3 151
1977	4 043.2		191 534		5 741		38 625		3 116
1978	4 058.7		213 079		6 360		43 543		3 214
1979	4 072.5		238 668		6 789		46 585		3 292
1980	4 085.6		285 045		8 033		53 478		3 545
1981	4 099.7		327 674		10 243		62 616		4 043
1982	4 114.8		362 270		11 160		70 408		3 970
1983	4 128.4		402 197		12 569		78 214		4 172
1984	4 140.1		452 512		13 011		84 099		4 126
1985	4 152.5		500 200		14 441		92 653		4 294
1986	4 167.4		513 718		15 340		101 580		4 253
1987	4 186.9		561 480		17 763		116 045		4 510
1988	4 209.5		583 278		17 548		122 237		4 210
1989	4 226.9		621 383		20 458		130 998		4 686
1990	4 241.5		660 550		22 050		139 115		4 855
1991	4 261.7		686 686		22 218		147 478		4 782
1992	4 286.4		702 952		23 003		157 220		4 859
1993	4 312.0		733 580		21 650		161 619		4 455

Key: Old = Old definition in the national accounts, New = New definition.
Preliminary figures for 1993.

Sources:

Mean Population: 1887-1975: *Historisk statistikk 1978* [Historical Statistics 1978], *NOS* XII 291, pp. 46-47; 1976-93: *Statistisk årbok,* annual [Statistical Yearbook], *NOS* B 980, p. 38.

Gross Domestic Product, 1887-1960: Nasjonalregnskap 1865-1960 [National Accounts 1865-1960], NOS XII 163, pp. 340-343 (current prices). 1960-69, old definitions: Nasjonalregnskap 1953-69 [National Accounts 1953-69], NOS A 393, p. 14 (current prices). 1962-76, new definitions: Nasjonalregnskap 1949-62, revidert utgave [National Accounts 1949-62, revised edition], NOS B 239, pp. 22-23, Nasjonalregnskap 1962-78 [National Accounts 1962-78], NOS B 48, pp. 22-23, Nasjonalregnskap 1975-85 [National Accounts 1975-85], NOS B 629, pp. 22-23, Nasjonalregnskap 1989 [National Accounts 1989], NOS B 981, pp. 28-29. Statistisk årbok 1993 [Statistical Yearbook 1993], NOS B 980, p. 333. Økonomiske analyser no. 4, 1994.

Military Consumption, 1887-1974: As for Gross Domestic Product. 1975-1989: Nasjonalregnskap 1975-85 [National Accounts 1975-85], NOS B 629, pp. 50-51 table 7, Nasjonalregnskap 1991 [National Accounts 1991], NOS B 981, pp. 236-237 table 6.3. 1991: Statistisk ukehefte no. 19, 1991. Økonomiske analyser no. 3, 1993 and no. 4, 1994.

Table A.2 Relative Measures of Military Spending, 1887-1993 (%)

Year	Change in military consumption relative to previous year Old	New	Military consumption as a share of GDP Old	New	Military consumption as a share of total government consumption Old	New
1887			1.4		26.5	
1888	-1.9		1.3		26.5	
1889	7.1		1.3		27.8	
1890	-1.2		1.3		27.8	
1891	-3.2		1.2		27.0	
1892	2.4		1.3		24.4	
1893	12.0		1.4		25.6	
1894	2.3		1.3		25.0	
1895	28.0		1.7		29.2	
1896	41.5		2.3		36.4	
1897	0.3		2.2		34.5	
1898	6.4		2.0		33.3	
1899	15.1		2.3		34.8	
1900	-11.4		2.0		31.0	
1901	-2.4		1.9		28.8	
1902	-8.2		1.7		26.0	
1903	-9.5		1.6		23.9	
1904	-11.8		1.4		21.7	
1905	5.0		1.4		22.9	
1906	-3.2		1.3		22.5	
1907	-3.5		1.3		21.6	
1908	0.8		1.2		21.1	
1909	7.0		1.3		21.3	
1910	3.4		1.3		21.4	
1911	2.5		1.2		21.6	
1912	25.9		1.5		24.8	
1913	4.4		1.5		25.0	
1914	47.5		2.1		31.5	
1915	19.9		2.2		36.9	
1916	-0.2		1.9		37.5	
1917	2.8		2.4		36.9	

Table A.2 cont'd

Year	Change in military consumption relative to previous year		Military consumption as a share of GDP		Military consumption as a share of total government consumption	
	Old	New	Old	New	Old	New
1918	-19.0		2.1		27.4	
1919	-30.6		1.2		16.6	
1920	-34.9		0.8		11.4	
1921	8.8		1.0		10.1	
1922	18.9		1.1		10.2	
1923	-8.4		0.9		10.1	
1924	-14.4		0.8		10.0	
1925	4.3		0.8		10.4	
1926	22.0		1.0		11.3	
1927	6.1		1.0		11.3	
1928	-2.8		0.9		11.1	
1929	5.3		0.9		11.5	
1930	0.7		0.8		11.2	
1931	0.3		0.9		10.9	
1932	-7.2		0.8		10.4	
1933	-0.8		0.8		10.3	
1934	-1.2		0.8		10.1	
1935	4.4		0.8		10.1	
1936	16.8		0.8		11.2	
1937	11.1		0.9		12.5	
1938	17.3		1.0		13.9	
1939	87.6		1.8		21.3	
1940						
1941						
1942						
1943						
1944						
1945						
1946	4.3		36.1			
1947	-32.6		2.6		26.7	
1948	-12.0		2.2		24.4	
1949	2.8	2.2	2.4	24.5	23.8	
1950	0.3	0.3	2.1	2.3	24.1	23.4
1951	44.6	44.6	2.8	3.1	31.2	30.2
1952	31.2	31.1	3.6	3.9	36.1	35.0
1953	20.5	20.4	4.4	4.7	38.6	37.3
1954	1.8	1.8	4.2	4.6	38.3	36.9
1955	-17.3	-17.4	3.4	3.7	32.9	31.5
1956	0.9	0.9	3.2	3.4	30.6	29.2
1957	2.7	2.8	3.2	3.4	30.1	28.5
1958	-5.6	-5.6	3.1	3.4	28.1	26.5
1959	6.0	6.0	3.1	3.4	27.5	25.9
1960	-1.5	-1.5	2.9	3.2	26.4	24.9
1961	5.1	5.0	2.9	3.2	26.1	24.6
1962	10.8	11.8	3.1	3.4	26.0	24.5

Table A.2 cont'd

Year	Change in military consumption relative to previous year		Military consumption as a share of GDP		Military consumption as a share of total government consumption	
	Old	New	Old	New	Old	New
1963	2.9	3.0	3.1	3.4	25.3	23.8
1964	4.9	4.8	3.0	3.4	24.7	23.2
1965	16.7	16.7	3.3	3.7	26.2	24.6
1966	-1.9	-1.7	3.1	3.5	24.3	22.7
1967	7.2	10.0	3.1	3.6	23.4	22.4
1968	6.5	6.6	3.2	3.7	23.3	22.3
1969	5.3	2.7	3.2	3.7	23.3	21.8
1970		-0.1		3.5		20.8
1971		1.0		3.4		19.0
1972		-1.1		3.3		18.0
1973		1.0		3.1		17.2
1974		0.8		3.0		16.5
1975		7.9		3.2		16.5
1976		1.8		3.1		15.5
1977		-1.1		3.0		14.9
1978		3.1		3.0		14.6
1979		2.4		2.8		14.6
1980		7.7		2.8		15.0
1981		14.1		3.1		16.4
1982		-1.8		3.1		15.9
1983		5.1		3.1		16.1
1984		-1.1		2.9		15.5
1985		4.1		2.9		15.6
1986		-1.0		3.0		15.1
1987		6.1		3.2		15.3
1988		-6.7		3.0		14.4
1989		11.3		3.3		15.6
1990		3.6		3.3		15.9
1991		-1.5		3.2		15.1
1992		1.6		3.3		14.6
1993		-8.3		3.0		13.4

Key: Old = Old definition in the national accounts, New = New definition.

Table A.3 Military Employment, 1865-1993, Absolute and Relative Measures

Year	Military employment Person-years ('000) Old	New	MR	Person-hours (mill.)	No. of empl. ('000)	Total military salaries current prices (NOK mill) Old	New
1865	3					2	
1866	3					2	
1867	3					2	
1868	3					2	
1869	3					2	
1870	3					2	
1871	3					2	
1872	3					2	
1873	3					3	
1874	3					3	
1875	4					3	
1876	4					3	
1877	4					4	
1878	4					3	
1879	4					4	
1880	4					4	
1881	4					4	
1882	4					4	
1883	4					4	
1884	4					4	
1885	2					4	
1886	2					4	
1887	2					4	
1888	2					4	
1889	2					4	
1890	4					5	
1891	4					5	
1892	4					5	
1893	4					5	
1894	4					5	
1895	4					5	
1896	4					5	
1897	4					5	
1898	4					6	
1899	4					6	
1900	6					8	
1901	6					8	
1902	6					8	
1903	6					8	
1904	6					8	
1905	6					8	
1906	6					8	
1907	6					8	
1908	6					8	
1909	6					8	

... *Table A.3 Military Employment*

Total Employment					Military Employment as a Share of Total Employment (in %)					
Person-years ('000)			Person-hours	No. of empl. ('000)	Person-years			Person-	No. of	
Old	New	MR	(mill.)		Old	New	MR	hours	empl.	Year
654					0.5					1865
654					0.5					1866
654					0.5					1867
654					0.5					1868
654					0.5					1869
684					0.4					1870
684					0.4					1871
684					0.4					1872
684					0.4					1873
684					0.4					1874
731					0.5					1875
731					0.5					1876
731					0.5					1877
731					0.5					1878
731					0.5					1879
779					0.5					1880
779					0.5					1881
779					0.5					1882
779					0.5					1883
779					0.5					1884
775					0.3					1885
775					0.3					1886
775					0.3					1887
775					0.3					1888
775					0.3					1889
781					0.5					1890
781					0.5					1891
781					0.5					1892
781					0.5					1893
781					0.5					1894
818					0.5					1895
818					0.5					1896
818					0.5					1897
818					0.5					1898
818					0.5					1899
883					0.7					1900
883					0.7					1901
883					0.7					1902
883					0.7					1903
883					0.7					1904
897					0.7					1905
897					0.7					1906
897					0.7					1907
897					0.7					1908
897					0.7					1909

Table A.3 cont'd

	Military employment					Total military salaries	
	Person-years ('000)			Person-hours (mill.)	No. of empl. ('000)	current prices (NOK mill)	
Year	Old	New	MR			Old	New
1910	5					9	
1911	5					9	
1912	5					9	
1913	5					9	
1914	5					9	
1915	5					9	
1916	5					9	
1917	5					9	
1918	5					9	
1919	5					9	
1920	4					30	
1921	4					30	
1922	4					30	
1923	4					30	
1924	4					30	
1925	4					30	
1926	4					30	
1927	4					30	
1928	4					30	
1929	4					30	
1930	5					18	
1931	5					16	
1932	5					13	
1933	6					12	
1934	6					12	
1935	7					12	
1936	7					12	
1937	8					12	
1938	9					13	
1939	12					40	
1940							
1941							
1942							
1943							
1944							
1945							
1946	32					159	
1947	29					110	
1948	28					122	
1949	31	31				156	147
1950	32	32				139	130
1951	39	39				215	202
1952	46	46				284	267
1953	46	46				333	313
1954	50	50				379	357

... *Table A.3 cont'd*

Total Employment					Military Employment as a Share of Total Employment (in %)					
Person-years ('000)			Person-hours	No. of empl. ('000)	Person-years			Person-hours	No. of empl.	
Old	New	MR	(mill.)		Old	New	MR			Year
920					0.5					1910
920					0.5					1911
920					0.5					1912
920					0.5					1913
920					0.5					1914
984					0.5					1915
984					0.5					1916
984					0.5					1917
984					0.5					1918
984					0.5					1919
1 062					0.4					1920
1 062					0.4					1921
1 062					0.4					1922
1 062					0.4					1923
1 062					0.4					1924
1 111					0.4					1925
1 111					0.4					1926
1 111					0.4					1927
1 111					0.4					1928
1 111					0.4					1929
1 199					0.4					1930
1 167					0.4					1931
1 194					0.4					1932
1 206					0.5					1933
1 230					0.5					1934
1 253					0.6					1935
1 290					0.5					1936
1 322					0.6					1937
1 233					0.7					1938
1 370					0.9					1939
										1940
										1941
										1942
										1943
										1944
										1945
1 387					2.3					1946
1 413					2.1					1947
1 430					2.0					1948
1 454	1 373				2.1	2.3				1949
1 464	1 385				2.2	2.3				1950
1 460	1 383				2.7	2.8				1951
1 468	1 391				3.1	3.3				1952
1 461	1 387				3.1	3.3				1953
1 479	1 406				3.4	3.6				1954

Table A.3 cont'd

Year	Military employment					Total military salaries	
	Person-years ('000)			Person-hours (mill.)	No. of empl. ('000)	current prices (NOK mill)	
	Old	New	MR			Old	New
1955	44	44				434	408
1956	45	44				489	460
1957	45	44				526	494
1958	46	44				555	521
1959	45	43				583	550
1960	45	43				621	584
1961	44	43				656	618
1962	43	41	49.1	103.3	49.4	721	679
1963	44	42	50.4	105.5	50.7	795	749
1964	46	44	49.9	104.8	50.1	880	829
1965	45	43	51.4	106.3	51.6	954	899
1966	44	42	51.0	105.9	51.3	1 002	944
1967	46	44	51.7	106.8	52	1 133	1 101
1968	48	45.9	51.9	104.1	52.2	1 210	1 176
1969	49	46.6	53.2	103.2	53.5	1 359	1 300
1970		46.3	52.3	101.3	52.6		1 373
1971		45.3	51.4	99.3	51.6		1 479
1972		45.1	52.0	100.1	52.2		1 635
1973		46.3	51.2	98.7	51.5		1 802
1974		45.3	50.0	96.2	50.2		1 905
1975		45.3	51.2	98.8	51.5		2 260
1976		46.5	52.1	96.8	52.4		2 673
1977		46.5	51.1	93.2	51.4		2 885
1978		49.7	52.7	93.5	52.9		3 270
1979		48.3	53.0	93	53.2		3 374
1980		48.4	51.8	91.1	52.3		3 662
1981		48.7	52.1	92	52.6		4 100
1982		49.4	54.6	96.1	55.5		4 733
1983		49.4	54.6	96.8	55.6		5 139
1984		48.9	52.1	91.7	53.1		5 380
1985		48.9	51.5	90.6	52.5		5 751
1986		48.6	51.6	91.4	52.6		6 255
1987			52.6	93.5	53.5		6 923
1988			51.9	92.4	52.9		7 362
1989			53.2	93.6	54		7 760
1990			55.7	97.8	56.5		8 511
1991			54.7	95.7	55.4		8 643
1992			53.3	94.1	54.1		8 738
1993			53.4	94.5	54.2		8 854

Key: Old = Old definition in the national accounts, New = New definition, MR = Most recent definition.

... Table A.3 cont'd

Total Employment					Military Employment as a Share of Total Employment (in %)					
Person-years ('000)			Person-hours (mill.)	No. of empl. ('000)	Person-years			Person-hours	No. of empl.	Year
Old	New	MR			Old	New	MR			
1 478	1 410				3.0	3.1				1955
1 473	1 406				3.1	3.1				1956
1 475	1 409				3.1	3.1				1957
1 457	1 389				3.2	3.2				1958
1 463	1 394				3.1	3.1				1959
1 470	1 401				3.1	3.1				1960
1 483	1 423				3.0	3.0				1961
1 488	1 431	1 429	3 002.9	1 554.9	2.9	2.9	3.4	3.4	3.2	1962
1 503	1 451	1 436	3 003.0	1 561.8	2.9	2.9	3.5	3.5	3.2	1963
1 513	1 465	1 439	3 030.2	1 566.8	3.0	3.0	3.5	3.5	3.2	1964
1 525	1 479	1 455	2 984.7	1 579.7	3.0	2.9	3.5	3.6	3.3	1965
1 527	1 489	1 462	3 000.2	1 587.4	2.9	2.8	3.5	3.5	3.2	1966
1 539	1 509	1 472	2 995.2	1 597.6	3.0	2.9	3.5	3.6	3.3	1967
1 543	1 519	1 474	2 934.6	1 599.7	3.1	3.0	3.5	3.5	3.3	1968
1 554	1 528	1 484	2 882.4	1 613.5	3.2	3.0	3.6	3.6	3.3	1969
	1 547	1 504	2 896.2	1 640.4		3.0	3.5	3.5	3.2	1970
	1 558	1 512	2 881.2	1 655.2		2.9	3.4	3.4	3.1	1971
	1 565	1 523	2 856.1	1 673.1		2.9	3.4	3.5	3.1	1972
	1 571	1 528	2 853.3	1 684.4		2.9	3.4	3.5	3.1	1973
	1 593	1 541	2 853.4	1 706.3		2.8	3.2	3.4	2.9	1974
	1 596	1 554	2 874.4	1 738.6		2.8	3.3	3.4	3	1975
	1 624	1 597	2 872.4	1 796.7		2.9	3.3	3.4	2.9	1976
	1 657	1 633	2 881.7	1 842.9		2.8	3.1	3.2	2.8	1977
	1 675	1 644	2 862.3	1 876.4		3.0	3.2	3.3	2.8	1978
	1 686	1 661	2 858.4	1 904.8		2.9	3.2	3.3	2.8	1979
	1 714	1 692	2 920.6	1 948.0		2.8	3.1	3.1	2.7	1980
	1 722	1 701	2 929.2	1 967.1		2.8	3.1	3.1	2.7	1981
	1 718	1 700	2 909.7	1 969.6		2.9	3.2	3.3	2.8	1982
	1 709	1 689	2 888.8	1 963.2		2.9	3.2	3.4	2.8	1983
	1 725	1 708	2 892.8	1 975.3		2.8	3.1	3.2	2.7	1984
	1 772	1 757	2 957.4	2 028.4		2.8	2.9	3.1	2.6	1985
	1 832	1 805	3 036.9	2 089.8		2.7	2.9	3.0	2.5	1986
		1 848	3 137.0	2 133.2			2.8	3.0	2.5	1987
		1 839	3 024.6	2 117.1			2.8	3.1	2.5	1988
		1 789	2 940.5	2 067.3			3.0	3.2	2.6	1989
		1 778	2 899.0	2 050.5			3.1	3.4	2.8	1990
		1 755	2 861.9	2 033.9			3.1	3.3	2.7	1991
		1 745	2 868.5	2 028.3			3.1	3.3	2.7	1992
		1 744	2 869.5	2 027.8			3.1	3.3	2.7	1993

Key: Old = Old definition in the national accounts, New = New definition, MR = Most recent definition.

Sources:

Military Employment, Person-Years:
Old definitions: 1865-1920: Census taken for the various years. 1865: Departementet for det indre. C. No. 1, *Resultaterne av Folketællingen i Norge*, 1. Januar 1866 [Results of the Census 1 January 1866], p. 189; 1875: Det Statistiske Centralbureau, C. No. 1, *Resultaterne av Folketællingen i Norge* 1. Januar 1876 [Results of the Census 1 January 1876], pp. 142-143, 1885: *NOS Tredie Række*, No. 53, pp. 10-11; 1890: *Folketællingen i Kongeriket Norge 1. Januar 1891* [Census in the Kingdom of Norway 1 January 1891]. *NOS Tredie Række* No. 236, pp.186-187; 1900: *Folketællingen i Kongeriket Norge 3. December 1900* [Census in the Kingdom of Norway 3 December 1900], *NOS Fjerde Række* No. 111, pp. 118-119; 1910: *Folketællingen i Norge 1. December 1910* [Census in Norway 1 December 1910], *NOS* V, 211, p. 4; 1920: *Folketællingen i Norge 1. desember 1920* [Census in Norway 1 December 1920], *NOS* VII, 103, p. 72. 1930-60: *Nasjonalregnskap 1865-1960* [National Accounts 1865-1960] *NOS* XII 163, pp. 332-333. *Nasjonalregnskap 1953-69* [National Accounts 1953-69] *NOS* A 393, p. 48.

New definitions: *Nasjonalregnskap 1949-62, revidert utgave* [National Accounts 1949-62, revised edition], *NOS* B 239, pp. 122-123. *Nasjonalregnskap 1962-78* [National Accounts 1962-78] *NOS* B 48, pp. 204-205. *Nasjonalregnskap 1968-79* [National Accounts 1968-79] *NOS* B 141, pp. 198-199. *Nasjonalregnskap 1976-1986* [National Accounts 1976-1986], *NOS* B 715, pp. 202-203.

Most recent definition: Harildstad (1989), pp. 21-23. 1987-89: *Nasjonalregnskap 1989* [National Accounts 1989] *NOS* B 981, pp. 178-179 and later editions.

Military Employment, Person-Hours:
Harildstad (1989), pp. 15-17. *Nasjonalregnskapsstatistikk 1989* [National Account Stastistics 1969] *NOS* B981, pp. 168-169 and later editions.

Total Employment, Person-Years:
Old definitions: 1865-1929: *Langtidslinjer i norsk økonomi 1865-1960* [Trends in Norwegian Economy 1865-1960], *SØS* no. 16, p. 29. This source gives 'Labor force' and includes unemployed persons under their ordinary profession. 1930-60: *Nasjonalregnskap 1865-1960* [National Accounts 1865-1960] *NOS* XII 163, pp. 328-329. *Nasjonalregnskap 1953-69* [National Accounts 1953-69] *NOS* A 393, p 47.

New definition: 1960-1969: *Nasjonalregnskap 1949-62, revidert utgave* [National Accounts 1949-62, revised edition], *NOS* B 239, pp. 122-123, *Nasjonalregnskap 1962-1978* [National Accounts 1962-1978] *NOS* B 48, pp. 204-205. *Nasjonalregnskap 1976-1986* [National Accounts 1976-1986] *NOS* B 715, pp. 202-203.

Most recent definition: Harildstad (1989), pp. 12-13. 1987-89: *Nasjonalregnskapsstatistikk 1989* [National Accounts Statistics 1989] *NOS* B 981, pp. 176-177 and later editions.

Total Employment, Person-Hours:
Harildstad (1989), pp. 12-13. 1979-89: *Nasjonalregnskapsstatistikk 1989* [National Accounts Statistics 1989] *NOS* B 981, pp.164-167 and later editions. The figures include self-employed personnel.

Total Employment, Number of Employees:
Harildstad (1989), pp. 12-13. 1979-89: *Nasjonalregnskapsstatistikk 1989* [National Accounts Statistics 1989], *NOS* B 981, pp. 188-191 and later editions. The figures include self-employed personnel.

Military Salary Costs:
1865-1930: *Langtidslinjer i norsk økonomi 1865-1960* [Trends in Norwegian Economy 1865-1960], *SØS* no. 16, pp. 116-119. 1930-60: *Nasjonalregnskap 1865-1960* [National Accounts 1865-1960] *NOS* XII 163, pp. 162-163 or pp. 192-193. 1960-69: *Nasjonalregnskap 1953-1969* [National Accounts 1953-1969] *NOS* A 393, pp. 28-29.

New definitions: *Nasjonalregnskap 1949-62, revidert utgave* [National Accounts 1949-62, revised edition], *NOS* B 239, pp. 68-69. *Nasjonalregnskap 1962-1978* [National Accounts 1962-1978], *NOS* B 48, pp. 108-109. *Nasjonalregnskap 1976-1986* [National Accounts 1976-1986], *NOS* B 715, pp. 110-111. *Nasjonalregnskapsstatistikk 1989* [National Accounts Statistics 1989], *NOS* B 981, pp. 154-155 and later editions.

Preliminary figures for 1993.

Notes

1. Note that the definitions in the National Accounts have been changed. Calculations based on the new definitions have been made back to 1962 and based on old definitions up to 1969.

2. The first was dated 10 November 1977.

Appendix B: Models

In this Appendix we outline the main features of five models used in our studies of the national and international effects of military spending. Three of them (MODIS, MSG, MODAG) were developed in Statistics Norway primarily for use in government planning and policy-making. Two of the present authors (Bjerkholt, Cappelen) had major responsibilities in the development and use of these models for many years. The fourth model, REGION, was also developed in Statistics Norway for the study of regional economic development in Norway, while the fifth, the World Model, was developed by Wassily Leontief and associates for the study of international economic issues. Also presented here is the theoretical framework developed by Nicholas Kaldor, elaborated by John Cornwall, and used by us with some modifications for the study of the economic effects of defense spending in the OECD countries.

We employ the models basically to calculate the effects of demand shifts on Gross Domestic Product, Imports, and Employment. The primary impulse is a shift in military expenditure; this impulse may generate further demand through the mechanisms of the economy (indirect effects) or through policy actions (countermeasures). An important feature of the models used is the sectoral disaggregation, but we illustrate the simple logic of the calculation at the most aggregate level.

MODIS and MODAG

We first describe the two models used in our study of national effects of disarmament. MODIS and MODAG have a number of features in common. We deal with these first, and then discuss specific characteristics of each model. More detailed descriptions of these models are available elsewhere (MODIS in Bjerkholt & Longva, 1979; MODAG in Cappelen & Longva, 1987, and Cappelen, 1992).

The total supply and demand of goods and services in an economy can be expressed in the overall balance equation:

(1) $\quad E + B = C + G_c + G_m + I + A$

where

E = Gross Domestic Product (GDP)
B = Imports
C = Private Consumption
G_c = Government Purchases of Goods and Services (Civilian)
G_m = Government Purchases of Goods and Services (Military)
I = Gross Investments (including changes in inventories)
A = Exports

All variables are measured in constant prices; thus, changes can be interpreted as volume changes.

The starting-point in the calculation is a change, ΔG_m, in Government Purchases of Goods and Services (Military). The direct consequences of a reduction in military demand are reductions in domestic production and imports. As the overall balance equations must still hold, the reductions in GDP and imports must equal the reduction in demand:

(2) $\Delta E_1 + \Delta B_1 = \Delta G_m$

The reduction in military demand entails reduced incomes for military personnel and others directly employed in the military sector. Reduced military purchases will furthermore lead to reduced incomes from industrial activity. Through the consumption relations of the model, this loss of income and output will lead to reduced private consumption and investment; this, in turn, implies further reductions in GDP and imports:

(3) $\Delta E_2 + \Delta B_2 = \Delta C + \Delta I$

In MODIS the term DI was zero by assumption.

If the government puts into effect countermeasures of increased civilian government consumption, these can be expressed as

(4) $\Delta E_3 + \Delta B_3 = \Delta G_c$

Such countermeasures will also generate changes in income and private consumption as above. An alternative countermeasure may be to encourage increased private consumption directly, e.g. through tax reductions.

Finally, if the reduction of armaments in Norway is part of an international reduction, Norwegian exports in response to military demand in other countries may be affected. On the other hand, alternative public spending in other countries may affect Norwegian exports positively. Changes in exports presuppose corresponding changes in domestic production and imports:

(5) $\Delta E_4 + \Delta B_4 = \Delta A$

The total effects can be written in aggregate terms as

(6) $\Sigma E_i + \Sigma B_i = \Delta C + \Delta G_c + \Delta G_m + \Delta A$

Much of the concern over the effect of reductions of military expenditure relates to the sectoral pattern of released resources and whether it matches the counteracting demand.

Production capacity made available by reduced military expenditure may be wanted for high priority demands like domestic welfare spending, development aid, etc. But to the extent that the production capacities are tied to specialized military production, they may not be utilized for other purposes and will have to be left idle. Released capital equipment is usually tied for use in the industry in which it is invested. Similarly, released labor power may be convertible to a limited extent only, depending on its qualifications and its regional distribution. Thus, the total volume of released resources may not be easily aggregated to a simple figure.

MODIS was used by Statistics Norway and the Ministry of Finance from 1960 until 1990. In the early 1960s this model was a rare example of a computer-based model actually used for practical policy purposes on a current basis. Its successive generations were known as MODIS I to MODIS V. MODIS IV, which we used for the calculations in our 1980 study, contained several thousand variables and several hundred equations. It distinguished around 200 commodities, while domestic production was subdivided in about 150 industries. The demand for individual commodities was added up from a great many demand components, such as intermediate demand from the 150 industries, the demand for around 50 items of household consumption, investment demand for several types of capital, demand for government consumption by a large number of items, and export demand by commodity. The model took into consideration that different demand components had different import propensities.

All demand components – apart from intermediate demand and the demand for household consumption – were exogenous. For any given exogenous demand vector, the model worked out the consequences for the composition of supply between imports and domestic production and for the industrial distribution of domestic production. An increase in the demand for, say, paper products led to increased demand for pulp and forestry products and to increased demand for all inputs used in the production of paper, pulp, and forest industry, including additional demand for paper products.

The model also included relations for price determination and for income generation at the same level of detail. Exogenous demand generated income in the form of wages and profits in the domestic industries. Through relations of estimated consumption behavior this income in turn led to household consumption through a multiplier process. A contraction of exogenous demand led to further contractions of total demand unless the contraction was offset by compensatory measures. The representation of household demand in the model included a detailed representation of the direct and indirect tax structure.

The main strength of MODIS was its ability to assess the direct and indirect effects of exogenous changes in demand upon the industrial pattern of production and upon household consumption, through the multiplier processes briefly described above. The individual industries in the model used labor as a production factor in highly varying degrees of intensity. Through the model's detailed industrial representation it was thus possible to arrive at fairly reliable estimates of implications for labor demand of various exogenous changes.

Our more recent studies use MODAG, designed in 1983 to succeed MODIS. MODAG is much more aggregated than MODIS, with about 25 sectors and 40 commodities. Altogether it has about 1,750 endogenous variables, about 250 stochastic equations, and 1,500 nonstochastic equations and identities. The input-output structure is, apart from aggregation, the same in the two models. On the price side, the commodities in MODAG may in principle have three different prices, depending on origin and use: import price, export price, and domestic price (price of Norwegian goods delivered to the home market). Import prices are exogenous, as is the exchange rate. Most other prices are determined by unit costs by sector, as well as the competing import price and an index of capacity utilization. Unit wage costs depend on productivity, which again is given by factor demand equations where the number of hours by sector depends on relative factor prices, output, and capital stock. Capital stock is determined via investment equations where output is the most important factor, but where profitability is also included. Exports are determined mainly by demand equations relying on the Armington (1969) approach. However, exports of oil, gas, and net receipts from shipping services – one-third of Norwegian total export revenues in the early 1990s – are exogenous. Imports are determined by import shares, which depend on relative domestic/import prices. Import shares differ by commodity and domestic user. Consumer demand depends on household income disaggregated by socio-economic groups as well as financial variables. Labor supply is disaggregated by sex and age, and is fairly inelastic with regard to real wages adjusted for taxes. Wage growth by sector is determined by equations where unemployment enters in a nonlinear way. Additional explanatory variables are taxes, productivity, and prices.

MODAG, like MODIS, is mainly Keynesian in character in the short and medium term, although its multipliers are fairly small, due to the openness of the Norwegian economy and the high marginal tax rates for households. In the long run more neoclassical results emerge, mainly due to the assumptions about the labor market, which imply a movement towards a nonaccelerating inflationary rate of unemployment (NAIRU), as changes in demand lead to changes in wages and competitiveness which crowds in or out the tradable sectors of the small and open Norwegian economy.

In MODAG, government spending is disaggregated into four sectors: Military, Health and social services, Education, and Administration and miscellaneous. For the latter three sectors the model also distinguishes between central government and local government spending. The expenditure is subdivided into labor costs, equipment, and other material inputs. The three cost categories differ with regard to import content. Equipment such as major weapons systems is mostly imported; other material inputs have import shares around 0.4-0.5, while labor remuneration has no direct effect on imports. (Military wages and salaries do, of course, generate imports via changes in household income and consumer demand, but no more than other wages and salaries.) The importance of this breakdown is well illustrated by the relative decrease in the military labor costs of total military spending from 50% in 1965 to a third in the early 1990s. There have been changes over time in the relative composition of equipment and other material inputs as well. Civilian government expenditure has a much higher labor cost share, about two-thirds. Thus, a switch from military to civilian consumption has a pronounced direct impact on labor demand.

MSG

The MSG ('Multi-Sectoral Growth') model originates from a study by Leif Johansen (1960). We used the version MSG-4 in our 1982 study where we linked the World Model (described below) to conversion results for Norway. MSG-4 is a multi-sector neoclassical growth model which determines the prices and quantities of about 30 industries within an input-output framework so that demand equals supply in markets for commodities as well as production factors (Longva et al., 1985). The supply of labor is exogenous. The model calculates a long-term growth path of the economy. The production factors comprise labor, capital, energy, and other intermediate inputs. For given wage rates, rates of return on capital, and trends of technical change, the model determines the cost minimizing techniques in terms of input coefficients and the prices that cover total costs. Changes in the pattern of household consumption are calculated from total consumption and relative prices, using an expenditure system. The breakdown of government spending is roughly the same as in MODAG.

Imports are calculated from import shares differentiated by commodity and purchasing sector. Exports and government expenditures are exogenous, while private consumption and investment are endogenous. The given wage rate and the rate of return on capital, together with the industrial distribution of demand, determine the overall demand for capital. The level of household consumption is determined so as to ensure full capacity utilization. In this sense, private consumption is determined as a residual, given the productive capacity and other demand. If exogenous demand, e.g. exports, is increased, private consumption will be reduced.

The main advantage of large modeling systems like MODIS, MODAG, or MSG is that they represent structure (sectoral differences) as well as a broad set of economic relationships. These models are used extensively in the analysis of the Norwegian economy and in Norwegian policy studies. A disadvantage of large models is the lack of transparency and, hence, the difficulty for non-experts to discern the exact relationships. No model can answer all kinds of questions with regard to the economic consequences of conversion. It is important for the interpretation of results to know which effects are and which are not included. The models have been used by several government agencies for a long time; this provides some assurance that bugs have been eliminated and that reasonable results are produced.

The World Model

The World Model was originally developed under UN auspices to study the impact of prospective economic issues and policies in the Second United Nations Development Decade (Leontief, Carter & Petri, 1977). It has also been used extensively to study the effects of world-wide disarmament measures (Leontief, 1980; Leontief & Duchin, 1983ab). The following describes the model as of 1982 when we used it in our own work. For a more recent description, see Duchin et al. (1992).

The World Model is a multi-purpose model, undoubtedly one of the more successful attempts to extend the flexible and comprehensive input-output approach to the world economy. The 1982 version divided the world economy into 15 regions (eight developed regions, three developing with major mineral resource endowments, and four other developing). Each region was described in terms of about 45 sectors of economic activities, half of which were manufacturing industries. The model focused particularly on food production, scarce raw materials (including energy) and pollution. Four categories of agricultural products, six metals, and three primary energy goods were measured in physical units within the model, together with eight types of pollutants. The economy of each region was represented in the World Model by an input-output matrix which is a detailed and consistent description of the structure and the use of war materials, labor, capital, and intermediate and finished goods, including the emission and abatement of pollutants.

While each of the regions is treated separately in some respects, the model also brings them together through various linking mechanisms. These include exports and imports of around 40 goods and resources, capital flows, aid transfers, and foreign interest payments.

In the model all interregional trade goes through a world 'pool' of traded goods, without identifying the region of origin of any region's exports. Imports are specified as a given ratio of imports to domestic output. Thus, every region draws an amount from the world pool of specific products in accordance with its domestic consumption and its import coefficients. On the export side, each region is assigned a given share of the total export pool for each commodity. Changes in international trade are thus generated by changes in the need for imports and they, in turn, lead to corresponding changes in exports. Imports and exports are calculated as gross figures including intraregional trade, i.e. imports and exports among countries in the same region. This simplified treatment of international trade in the model leaves out many factors which are important in determining the amount and direction of trade.

We used the model to assess the implications of various model solutions for Norwegian exports. Norway is a small country within the larger regions in the model, High Income Western Europe (WEH). Norway has only 1.5% of the population of that region, which includes most countries in EFTA and the European Community. For a complete regional classification as of 1982, see Leontief & Duchin (1983b) or Cappelen et al. (1982), Appendix 1.

The World Model of 1982 had 1970 as the base year and was solved at ten-year intervals. The computed solutions describe possible paths that could be followed by the world economy from 1970 to 2000. (Some runs were extended to 2030.) The *baseline scenario* of the World Model projected current trends into the future. Other scenarios were created by changing the values of exogenous variables and sometimes the structural coefficients. Results were given as deviations from the baseline scenario.

There are also alternative ways of 'closing' the model, that is determining the overall constraints required to solve the model. These constraints correspond to the economic constraints under which the economies are assumed to operate. One such constraint imposed in our use of the model was that *employment in developed countries was equal to the estimated labor force*. This meant that when changes such as reduced military expenditure were introduced, it was implicitly assumed that the economy adjusted by absorbing the released labor power through growth of consumption in the respective regions. This constraint seemed reasonable enough on the basis of the high employment in the 1960s and the early 1970s, but appears more dubious in view of the developments in most Western countries since the end of the 1970s.

On the whole, the World Model is well suited to deal with a wide range of problems in international economic relations. One of its strong points is the built-in consistency provided by the input-output framework for each region and the balance equations for commodities and resources across regions. As already mentioned, however, the database is dated and sparse in relation to the superstructure erected on it. The results should therefore be interpreted with some caution.

The Kaldor/Cornwall Model

In our study of military spending and economic growth in the OECD countries (Cappelen, 1984ab; Chapter 2 in this book) we modified a model developed originally by Kaldor (1966) and further elaborated by Cornwall (1977).

Kaldor postulated a linear relationship between the growth rate of GDP and the growth rate of manufacturing output and estimated this relationship using data for the OECD countries for the period 1953-54 to 1963-64 (on the average). He found the direct effect of manufacturing growth on GDP growth to be 0.6. Cornwall obtained an almost identical result using a different sample period. Even if we do not attach too much significance to the exact magnitude of this parameter, its value is significantly greater (in statistical terms) than the share of manufacturing output in total GDP (approximately one-third in most OECD countries). How can we explain this disproportionate contribution of the manufacturing sector in accounting for the rate of growth of GDP?

If economic growth is a process of transformation and redistribution of resources – as distinguished from the notion of balanced growth with increasing amounts of factors of production – the importance of manufacturing may be explained partly by its high level of productivity. When surplus agricultural labor is employed in manufacturing, the overall productivity increases, and so do income, demand, and production. Furthermore, the manufacturing sector is often said to be characterized by increasing returns to scale (Verdoorn's law). Thus, manufacturing output grows more quickly, productivity increases faster as well, and this has positive effects on the growth rate of the whole economy.

A third factor emphasized by Cornwall is that the manufacturing sector promotes growth in non-manufacturing sectors as well. New technology is embodied in new capital goods produced by the manufacturing sectors, and their use increases other sectors' productivity as well as their productive capacities. Fertilizers and machinery increase productivity in agriculture. More machinery and other inputs from manufacturing result in increased production and reduced employment in agriculture.

Since the manufacturing sector is usually the most important producer of tradable goods, the growth in production of manufactured goods is important in financing the growth of imports (assuming unchanged terms of trade). Countries unable to finance their growing needs for imports when GDP grows may then have to pursue a more deflationary economic policy in order to slow down the rate of growth of imports and thus of GDP.

Our unified Kaldor/Cornwall model consists of three equations:

(1) GDP_g $=$ $a_0 + a_1\text{MANU}_g + a_2\text{MIL}\% + a_3\text{INV}\%$
(2) MANU_g $=$ $b_0 + b_1\text{WORLD}_g + b_2\text{MIL}\% + b_3\text{INV}\%$
(3) $\text{INV}\%$ $=$ $c_0 + c_1\text{GDP}_g + c_2\text{MIL}\% + c_3\text{NONMIL}\%$

GDP_g and MANU_g are growth rates of GDP and manufacturing output, respectively.

To the basic Kaldor/Cornwall equation (1) we have added two explanatory variables: Military Expenditure as a percentage of GDP (MIL%) and the Gross Investment Ratio (INV%). [1] The national accounts treat capital formation in the military sector as government final consumption, not as investments. Parts of this capital formation may, however, be of use to the civilian sector of the economy as well. The military expenditure share of GDP may have a direct effect on growth due to resource mobilization and modernization (spinoff effects), as suggested by Deger & Smith (1983). The Gross Investment Ratio is included in order to pick up effects of increased capital stock (capacity). A priori we expect both these variables to enter the growth equation with positive signs.

The second equation is the growth equation for output in manufacturing. As suggested by Cornwall, MANU_g is assumed to depend on INV%. (More precisely, Cornwall relates MANU_g to INV% in the manufacturing sector, not in the economy as a whole.) The manufacturing sector produces a substantial part of the capital goods in the economy, and this in turn increases capacity both in manufacturing and in the rest of the economy. INV% also picks up the effect on the growth potential of induced technological change which is related to the level of investment as new technology is embodied in new capital goods. We have also included the growth rate of the world market, defined as the growth of world exports of manufactured goods (WORLD_g), in order to pick up the effect of export-led growth. In addition, we are interested in testing for the effects of MIL% on MANU_g. MIL% may take account of possible spinoff effects on the development of new technology in manufacturing which may be embodied in new capital goods and increase MANU_g. The idea is that military spending consists partly of R&D expenditures which lead to the development of new better arms, and that by-products of these innovations may be used in civilian production as well.

Finally, in the third equation, INV% is related to GDP_g through various mechanisms. First of all, we may think of a simple acceleration model of investment where economic growth increases investment because of the demand for new production capacity. Secondly, a more rapid rate of growth in GDP may generate a distribution of income between wages and profits that increases capital accumulation. [2] Furthermore, INV% is related to the share of government final expenditures in GDP. The inclusion of MIL% and NONMIL% (the part of government final expenditures used for civilian purposes) is basically a way of modeling crowding-out effects. Government expenditures in general have to be financed either through taxes on private income, or borrowing which may increase interest rates; in both cases there may be adverse effects on investment. Government expenditures may crowd out private consumption rather than investment, if taxes are paid mainly by households rather than by firms. In some cases a high investment ratio may be financed by borrowing from abroad. Both these factors seem to explain why Norway has maintained a very high investment ratio even if NONMIL% has increased substantially over the past 20 years.

In the *structural form* of the model, as given above, MIL%, WORLDg, and NONMIL% are exogenous variables. The set of three equations can be solved to give GDP_g, $MANU_g$, and INV% as functions only of exogenous variables:

(4) $GDP_g = u_0 + u_1 MIL\% + u_2 WORLD_g + u_3 NONMIL\%$
(5) $MANU_g = v_0 + v_1 MIL\% + v_2 WORLD_g + v_3 NONMIL\%$
(6) $INV\% = w_0 + v_1 MIL\% + w_2 WORLD_g + w_3 NONMIL\%$

This is the *reduced form* of the model.

Too much significance should not, of course, be attached to this simple model. One purpose of our 1984 study was to test a model which was very different from the other models used in our other studies, in order to test the robustness of our previous results. But it tells us something about what variables to look for when we want to find out how fast GDP has to grow in order to maintain full capacity utilization (but not necessarily full employment). We do not deny that the change in military expenditure relative to GDP (i.e. $\Delta G_M/Y$) may be relevant in accounting for GDP growth, but we have tried to refute the idea that it would be '... a dimensionally incorrect procedure' to include the level of military expenditure relative to GDP in this equation, as Faini et al. (1980, p. 498) have claimed.

Notes

1. This is the formulation used by Smith & Smith (1980) and will also be further developed below.

2. On the other hand, with reference to the neoclassical life-cycle model of consumption, a high growth rate may increase the consumption ratio. Consumers may want to redistribute their expected discounted life income ('human wealth') if they believe that this rate of growth will persist.

References

[Titles of items published in languages other than English are generally given in English translation in square brackets.]

The German letters ä, ö, and ü appear in their usual position in the alphabet, as if they were written ae, oe, and ue. The Scandinavian letters æ (ä), ø (ö), and å appear at the end of the alphabet.

Authors who have published under slightly varying names – Ron Smith/R.P. Smith/Ronald P. Smith is a case in point – are generally cited under a single form of the name, to avoid confusion.

Abell, John D., 1990. 'Defence Spending and Unemployment Rates: An Empirical Analysis Disaggregated by Race', *Cambridge Journal of Economics*, vol. 14, no. 4, pp. 405-414.

Abell, John D., 1994. 'Military Spending and Income Inequality', *Journal of Peace Research*, vol. 31, no. 1, February, pp. 35-43.

Aben, Jacques & Ron P. Smith, 1987. 'Defence and Employment in the UK and France: A Comparative Study of the Existing Results', pp. 384-398 in Schmidt & Blackaby, 1987.

ACDA, see US ACDA

Adams, F. Gerard & Jere R. Behrman & Michael Boldin, 1992. 'Defense Expenditures and Economic Growth in the Less-Developed Countries: Reconciling Theory and Empirical Results', ch. 10, pp. 123-132 in Chatterji & Forcey, 1992.

Adams, Gordon, 1992. *The Role of Defense Budgets in Civil-Military Relations*. Washington, DC: Defense Budget Project.

Adams, Gordon & David Gold, 1987. *Defense Spending and the Economy: Does the Defense Dollar Make a Difference?* Washington, DC: Defense Budget Project.

Adams, Gordon & Lawrence J. Korb, co-chairs, 1991. *Responding to Changing Threats. A Report of the Defense Budget Project's Task Force on the FY 1992-FY 1997 Defense Plan*. Washington, DC: Defense Budget Project.

Agøy, Nils Ivar, 1992. 'Forsvarsminister Quisling og den indre militære sikkerheten' [Defense Minister Quisling and Internal Military Security], *Historisk Tidsskrift*, vol. 71, no. 2, pp. 123-169.

Ahlström, Christer; with Kjell-Åke Nordquist, 1991. *Casualties of Conflict. Report for the World Campaign for the Protection of Victims of War*. Uppsala: Department of Peace and Conflict Research, Uppsala University.

Alexander, J. Davidson, 1994. 'Military Conversion Policies in the USA: 1940s and 1990s', *Journal of Peace Research*, vol. 31, no. 1, February, pp. 19-33.

Alfsen, Knut H., 1991. 'Use of Macroeconomic Models in Analysis of Environmental Problems in Norway and Consequences for Environmental Statistics', *Discussion Paper*, no. 61. Oslo: Central Bureau of Statistics.

Altes, E. J. Korthals, 1992. 'The Arms Race, Development and the Environment in Peacetime', ch. 3, pp. 65-79 in Gleditsch, 1992a.

Alvheim, Atle, 1981. 'NSDs Kretsdatabank 1960-1970. Datainnhold og brukerveiledning' [NSD's Census Tract Data Bank 1960-1970. Data Contents and User Manual], *NSD rapporter* no. 45. Bergen: Norwegian Social Science Data Service.

Amer, Ramses et al. [8 authors], 1993. 'Major Armed Conflicts', ch. 3, pp. 81-130 in *World Armament and Disarmament. SIPRI Yearbook 1993*. Oxford etc.: Oxford University Press.

Anderson, Marion; M. Frisch & Michael Dee Oden, 1986. *The Empty Pork Barrel: The Employment Cost of the Military Build-Up 1981-1985*. Lansing, MI: Employment Research Associates.

Andreassen, Tormod, 1972. 'Forsvarets virkninger på norsk økonomi' [The Impact of the Defense on the Norwegian Economy], *Samfunnsøkonomiske studier*, no. 22. Oslo: Central Bureau of Statistics.

Anthony, Ian, ed., 1991. *Arms Export Regulations*. Oxford etc.: Oxford University Press for SIPRI.

Armington, Paul S., 1969. 'A Theory of Demand for Products Distinguished by Place of Production', *IMF Staff Papers*, no. 16, pp. 159-178.

Arms Control and Disarmament Agency, see US ACDA.

Arrow, Kenneth J., 1992. 'The Basic Economics of Arms Reduction', ch. 2, pp. 57-67 in Isard & Anderton, 1992a.

Aukrust, Odd & Petter Jakob Bjerve, 1945. *Hva krigen kostet Norge* [What the War Cost Norway]. Oslo: Dreyer.

Aune, Leif et al., 1991. *Forsvarets distriktspolitiske betydning – fase 2. Rapport fra et underutvalg av Forsvarskommisjonen av 1990 med oversikt over dagens virksomhet og konsekvenser av mulige endringer for et begrenset antall kommuner* [The Regional Impact of the Military Establishment – phase 2. Report from a Subcommittee of the Defense Commission of 1990 ...]. Oslo: Ministry of Defense.

Baek, Ehung Gi, 1991. 'Defence Spending and Economic Performance in the United States: Some Structural VAR Evidence', *Defence Economics*, vol. 2, no. 3, July, pp. 251-264.

Ball, Nicole, 1981. *The Military in the Development Process. A Guide to Issues.* Claremont, CA: Regina.

Ball, Nicole, 1983. 'Defense and Development. A Critique of the Benoit Study', pp. 39-56 in Tuomi & Väyrynen, 1983.

Ball, Nicole & Milton Leitenberg, eds., 1983. *The Structure of the Defense Industry. An International Survey.* London & Canberra: Croom Helm.

Baran, Paul & Paul Sweezy, 1966. *Monopoly Capital.* New York: Monthly Review Press.

Barker, Terry; Paul Dunne & Ron P. Smith, 1991. 'Measuring the Peace Dividend in the United Kingdom', *Journal of Peace Research*, vol. 28, no. 4, November, pp. 345-358.

Barth, Magne, 1982a. 'Internasjonal nedrustning er økonomisk fordelaktig for Norge' [International Disarmament is Economically Advantageous to Norway], *NAVFs kronikktjeneste*, Ukens kronikk, no. 19, September. *PRIO Inform* 6/82.

Barth, Magne, 1982b. *Norsk industriell militær eksport* [Norwegian Industrial Military Export]. Oslo: PRIO. *PRIO Inform* 2/82. Also in *Nordisk Forum*, no. 35/36/37, 1983, pp. 86-101.

Barth, Magne, 1982c. *Norwegian Military Consumption 1878-1980.* Oslo: PRIO. *PRIO Report* 2/82. [Data revised and included in Appendix A of this book.]

Bebermeyer, Hartmut & Christian Thimann, 1990. 'The Economic Impact of the Stationing of US Forces in the Federal Republic of Germany', ch. 6, pp. 97-131 in Sharp, 1990.

Beer, Francis A., 1981. *Peace Against War. The Ecology of International Violence.* San Francisco, CA: Freeman.

Belousov, Valeryi K.; Albert N. Panov & Andrei V. Uborsky, 1992. 'Economic Aspects of Environmental Problems Related to Conversion of Weapons and Military Industry', ch. 4, pp. 81-90 in Gleditsch, 1992a.

Benoit, Emile, 1962. 'The Economic Impact of Disarmament in the United States', pp. 134-157 in Melman, 1962 and pp. 643-665 in Richard A. Falk & Saul H. Mendlowitz, eds. *Disarmament and Economic Development*, vol. IV of *The Strategy of World Order.* New York: World Law Fund, 1966.

Benoit, Emile, ed., 1967. *Disarmament and World Economic Interdependence.* Oslo: Norwegian University Press/New York & London: Columbia University Press.

Benoit, Emile, 1973. *Defense and Economic Growth in Developing Countries.* Boston, MA: Heath.

Benoit, Emile, 1978. 'Growth and Defense in Developing Countries', *Economic Development and Cultural Change*, vol. 26, no. 2, January, pp. 271-280.

Benoit, Emile & Kenneth Boulding, eds., 1963. *Disarmament and the Economy.* New York: Harper & Row.

Berger, Manfred et al. [seven authors], 1991. *Produktion von Wehrgütern in der Bundesrepublik Deutschland* [The Production of Defense Goods in the Federal Republic of Germany]. *Ifo-Studien zur Industriewirtschaft*, no. 42. Munich: Ifo – Institut für Wirtschaftsforschung.

Bergsgard, Nils Asle; Jens Fredrik Nyhagen & Jarl Ove Ramsvik, 1989. *Teknologioverføringer fra militær forskning og utvikling til sivil industri* [Technology Transfers from Military R&D to Civilian Industry]. Oslo: PRIO. PRIO Report 1/89.

Bezdek, Roger H., 1975. 'The 1980 Economic Impact – Regional and Occupational – of Compensated Shifts in Defense Spending', *Journal of Regional Science*, vol. 15, no. 2, pp. 183-198.

Bischak, Gregory A., 1988. 'Facing the Second Generation of the Nuclear Weapons Complex: Renewal of the Nuclear Production Base or Economic Conversion?', *Bulletin of Peace Proposals*, vol. 19, no. 1, pp. 81-97. Reprinted pp. 111-137 in Dumas & Thee, 1989.

Bischak, Gregory A., ed., 1991. *Towards a Peace Economy in the United States. Essays on Military Industry, Disarmament and Economic Conversion.* London etc: Macmillan.

Bischak, Gregory A., 1992. 'Debt Reduction in Exchange for Arms Conversion: The Case for Linking Conversion, Development, and Debt Reduction', pp. 259-267 in Brunn et al., 1992.

Bischak, Gregory A. & Michael Oden, 1991. 'The INF Treaty and the United States Experience: The Industrial, Economic, and Employment Impact', ch. 7, pp. 123-156 in Paukert & Richards, 1991a.

Biswas, Basudeb & Rati Ram, 1986. 'Military Expenditures and Economic Growth in Less Developed Countries: An Augmented Model and Further Evidence', *Economic Development and Cultural Change*, vol. 34, no. 2, January, pp. 361-372.

Bjerkholt, Olav, 1965. 'Økonomiske konsekvenser av nedrustning i Norge' [Economic Consequences of Disarmament in Norway], *Tidsskrift for Samfunnsforskning*, vol. 6, no. 4, pp. 249-267. Reprinted in Artikler fra Statistisk Sentralbyrå, no. 17, 1966.

Bjerkholt, Olav, 1967. 'An Analysis of the Economic Consequences of Disarmament in Norway', pp. 146-153 in Benoit, 1967.

Bjerkholt, Olav, 1980. 'Nedrustning, utviklingshjelp og full sysselsetting' [Disarmament, Development Aid, and Full Employment], pp. 366-375 in Torbjørn Jagland et al., eds. *Atomvåpen og usikkerhetspolitikk* [Nuclear Weapons and Insecurity Policy]. Oslo: Tiden.

Bjerkholt, Olav & Svein Longva, 1979. 'MODIS IV – the Norwegian National Budget Model', *Samfunnsøkonomiske studier*, no. 43. Oslo: Central Bureau of Statistics.

Bjerkholt, Olav; Ådne Cappelen, Nils Petter Gleditsch & Knut Moum, 1980. *Disarmament and Development: A Study of Conversion in Norway*. Report prepared for the United Nations Group of Governmental Experts on the Relationship between Disarmament and Development. Oslo: PRIO.

Bjerkholt, Olav & Knut Moum, 1982. 'Nedrustning og økonomisk utvikling' [Disarmament and Economic Development], pp. 169-177 in Odd Andreassen, ed. *Nedrustning* [Disarmament]. Oslo: Norwegian University Press.

Bjerkholt, Olav; Ådne Cappelen, Nils Petter Gleditsch & Knut Moum, 1983. 'The Economic Effects of Conversion: A Case Study of Norway', pp. 225-258 in Tuomi & Väyrynen, 1983.

Bjerkholt, Olav & Jørgen Rosted, eds., 1987. *Macroeconomic Medium-Term Models in the Nordic Countries*. Contributions to Economic Analysis no. 164. Amsterdam: North-Holland

Bjerkholt, Olav; with Øystein Olsen & Jon Vislie, eds., 1990. *Recent Modelling Approaches in Applied Energy Economics*. London: Chapman & Hall.

Boulding, Kenneth, 1986. 'The Economics and the Noneconomics of the War Industry', *Contemporary Policy Issues*, vol. 4, no. 4, October, pp. 12-21.

Bowitz, Einar & Ådne Cappelen, 1990. 'Nullvekst i forsvarsutgiftene. En modellbasert analyse' [Zero Growth in Military Expenditure. A Model-Based Analysis]. Unpublished study for the Defense Commission. Oslo: Central Bureau of Statistics.

Bremer, Stuart, ed., 1987. *The Globus Model. Computer Simulation of Worldwide Political and Economic Developments*. Frankfurt am Main: Campus/Boulder, CO: Westview.

Brock, Lothar, 1991. 'Peace through Parks: The Environment on the Peace Research Agenda', *Journal of Peace Research*, vol. 28, no. 4, pp. 407-423.

Brömmelhörster, Jörn, 1991. *Abrüstung und Beschäftigung – Die Bedeutung der Konversion für die Wirtschaft des Landes Nordrhein-Westfalen* [Disarmament and Employment – the Impact of Conversion on the Economy of the State of North Rhine-Westphalia]. Study for the Ministry of Research in North Rhine-Westphalia. Bochum: Department of Economics, Ruhr University, Bochum.

Brömmelhörster, Jörn, 1992. 'Economic Aspects of Conversion in Germany', pp. 42-58 in Chai & Zhang, 1992.

Brown, Arthur J., 1964. *The Economic Consequences of Disarmament*. London: The David Davies Memorial Institute of International Studies.

Brown, Harold, 1983. *Thinking About National Security*. Boulder, CO: Westview.

Brundin, Hjalmar, 1985a. 'Samhällsekonomiska konsekvenser av nedrustning – en presentation av några beräkningar av finansdepartementet', pp. 227-263 in Thorsson, 1985a. [English translation in Brundin, 1985b]

Brundin, Hjalmar, 1985b. 'The Economic Consequences of Disarmament: A Presentation of Calculations made by the Ministry of Finance', pp. 233-271 in Thorsson, 1985b.

Brundtland, Gro Harlem et al., 1987. *Our Common Future. World Commission on Environment and Development*. Oxford etc.: Oxford University Press.

Brunn, Anke; Lutz Baehr & Hans J. Karpe, eds., 1992. *Conversion – Opportunities for Development and Environment*. Berlin etc.: Springer.

Buck, David; Keith Hartley & Nick Hooper, 1993. 'Defence Research and Development, Crowding-Out and the Peace Dividend', *Defence Economics*, vol. 4, no. 2, April, pp. 161-178.

Bundesministerium der Verteidigung, 1972. *Die Wehrstruktur in der Bundesrepublik Deutschland. Analyse und Optionen. Bericht an der Bundesregierung.* English-language edition: *The Force Structure in the Federal Republic of Germany. Analysis and Options. Report to the Federal Government.* Bonn: Force Structure Commission of the Government of the Federal Republic.

Buzan, Barry; Morten Kelstrup, Pierre Lemaitre, Elzbieta Tromer & Ole Wæver, 1990. *The European Security Order Recast. Scenarios for the Post-Cold War Era.* London & New York: Pinter.

Cappelen, Ådne, 1978. 'Makrokonsumfunksjonen i MODIS IV' [The Macro Consumption Function in MODIS IV], *Arbeidsnotat IO 78/6.* Oslo: Statistics Norway.

Cappelen, Ådne, 1986. 'Økonomiske sider ved nedrustning' [Economic Aspects of Disarmament], *Sosialøkonomen*, vol. 40, no. 5, May, pp. 34-39.

Cappelen, Ådne, 1992. 'MODAG: A Macroeconometric Model of the Norwegian Economy', pp. 55-93 in Lars Bergmann & Øystein Olsen, eds. *Economic Modeling in the Nordic Countries. Contributions to Economic Analysis* no. 210. Amsterdam: North-Holland. Also in Reprint series no. 61. Oslo: Central Bureau of Statistics.

Cappelen, Ådne; Olav Bjerkholt & Nils Petter Gleditsch, 1982. Global Conversion from Arms to Development Aid: Macroeconomic Effects on Norway. Oslo: PRIO. PRIO-publication S-9/82.

Cappelen, Ådne; Eva Ivås & Paul Sand, 1980. 'MODIS IV. Detaljerte virkningstabeller for 1978' [MODIS IV. Detailed Impact Tables for 1978], Report no. 80/16. Oslo: Central Bureau of Statistics.

Cappelen, Ådne; Nils Petter Gleditsch & Olav Bjerkholt, 1984a. Military Spending and Economic Growth in the OECD Countries. Oslo: PRIO. *PRIO Report* 6/84.

Cappelen, Ådne; Nils Petter Gleditsch & Olav Bjerkholt, 1984b. 'Military Spending and Economic Growth in the OECD Countries'. *Journal of Peace Research*, vol. 21, no. 4, November, pp. 361-373. Also in Reprint Series, no. 12. Oslo: Central Bureau of Statistics, 1985.

Cappelen, Ådne; Nils Petter Gleditsch & Olav Bjerkholt, 1992. 'Guns, Butter, and Growth: The Case of Norway', ch. 4, pp. 61-80 in Chan & Mintz, 1992. Also in Reprint series no. 59. Oslo: Central Bureau of Statistics, 1992.

Cappelen, Ådne & Svein Longva, 1987. 'MODAG A: A Medium-Term Macroeconomic Model of the Norwegian Economy', pp. 153-212 in Bjerkholt & Rosted, 1987.

(CDI), 1993. 'Cutting Unnecessary Military Spending: Going Further and Faster', *The Defense Monitor*, vol. 21, no. 3, entire issue, pp. 1-8.

(Centre for Studies ...), 1983. *The Economic Impact of Canadian Defence Expenditure.* Kingston, Ontario: Centre for Studies in Defence Resources Management, The Royal Military College of Canada.

Chai Benliang & Zhang Junping, eds., 1992. *Proceedings of the International Conference on International Cooperation in Peaceful Use of Military Industrial Technology* (22-25 October 1991 in Beijing). Beijing: International Academic Publishers.

Chalmers, Malcolm, 1985. *Paying for Defence: Military Spending and British Decline.* London: Pluto.

Chan, Steve, 1984. 'Defense Spending and Economic Performance: Correlates Among the OECD Countries', Paper Presented to the 25th Annual Meeting of the International Studies Association, Atlanta, GA, 27-31 March.

Chan, Steve, 1985. 'The Impact of Defense Spending on Economic Performance: A Survey of Evidence and Problems', *Orbis*, vol. 29, no. 2, Summer, pp. 403-434.

Chan, Steve, 1987. 'Military Expenditures and Economic Performance', pp. 29-37 in *World Military Expenditures and Arms Transfers 1986.* Washington, DC: US Government Printing Office, for United States Arms Control and Disarmament Agency.

Chan, Steve, 1988. 'Defense Burden and Economic Growth: Unraveling the Taiwanese Enigma', *American Political Science Review*, vol. 82, no. 3, September, pp. 913-920.

Chan, Steve, 1993. *East Asian Dynamism. Growth, Order, and Security in the Pacific Region.* Second edition. Boulder, CO: Westview. [Originally published 1990.]

Chan, Steve & Alex Mintz, eds., 1992. *Defense, Welfare, and Growth.* London & New York: Routledge.

Charlin, Marcelo & Augusto Varas, 1992. 'Conversion and Environment: The Role of Local Government in the Third World', ch. 18, pp. 291-305, in Gleditsch, 1992a.

Chatterji, Manas & Linda Rennie Forcey, eds., 1992. *Disarmament, Economic Conversion, and Management of Peace*. New York etc.: Praeger.

Chester, Eric, 1978. 'Military Spending and Capitalist Stability', *Cambridge Journal of Economics*, vol. 2, no. 3, September, pp. 293-298.

Chowdhury, Abdur R., 1991. 'A Causal Analysis of Defense Spending and Economic Growth', *Journal of Conflict Resolution*, vol. 35, no. 1, March, pp. 80-97.

Christensen, Arne Magnus, 1989. *Military R&D, Technological Change, and Civilian Economic Growth*. Oslo: PRIO. *PRIO Report* 2/89.

Christensen, Arne Magnus, 1990. 'Economic Consequences of SDI for the USA and Other Participating Countries', *Bulletin of Peace Proposals*, vol. 21, no. 1, March, 1990, pp. 104-112.

Christensen, Arne Magnus & Asbjørn Torvanger, 1986. 'Military and Civilian Research and Development and Growth'. Graduate thesis in Economics. Oslo: PRIO. *PRIO Report* 1/86.

Christensen, Arne Magnus & Asbjørn Torvanger. 1989. 'Godtgjeringssystem for vernepliktige mannskap – kva system bør vi velje?' [Salary System for Military Conscripts – What System Should We Choose?], *Sosialøkonomen*, vol. 43, no. 8, September, pp. 12-15.

Congressional Budget Office, 1983. *Defense Spending and the Economy*. Washington, DC: CBO.

Congressional Budget Office, 1992. *The Economic Effects of Reduced Defense Spending*. Washington, DC: CBO.

Cooper, Julian, 1991. *The Soviet Defence Industry: Conversion and Reform. Chatham House Papers*. London: Pinter & Royal Institute of International Affairs.

Cornwall, John, 1977. *Modern Capitalism*. Cambridge: Robertson.

Cypher, James, 1974. 'Capitalist Planning and Military Expenditures', *Review of Radical Political Economy*, vol. 6, no. 3, pp. 1-19.

Cypher, James M., 1987. 'Military Spending, Technical Change, and Economic Growth: A Disguised Form of Industrial Policy', *Journal of Economic Issues*, vol. 21, no. 1, March, pp. 33-59.

Daly, Herman E. & John Cobb, Jr, 1989. *For the Common Good*. Boston, MA: Beacon.

Davis, David R. & Steve Chan, 1990. 'The Security-Welfare Relationship: Longitudinal Evidence from Taiwan', *Journal of Peace Research*, vol. 27, no. 1, February, pp. 87-100.

Dedekam, Anders Jr, 1990. *Den sysselsettingsmessige betydningen av en reduksjon av Forsvaret i syv særlig forsvarsavhengige kommuner* [The Impact on Employment of a Reduction in Defense Activity in Seven Particularly Defense-Dependent Municipalities]. Molde: Møreforskning. [Appendix C to Aune et al., 1991.]

Dedekam, Anders Jr, 1992. 'På stedet, hvil!' [At ease!], *Norsk Økonomisk Tidsskrift*, vol. 106, no. 3, pp. 179-203.

Defense High Command, 1992. *Forsvarsstudien 1991* [The Defense Study 1991]. Unclassified version: Oslo: Chief of the Defense High Command, February. Released 13 March 1992.

Deger, Saadet & Ron P. Smith, 1983. 'Military Expenditures and Growth in Less Developed Countries', *Journal of Conflict Resolution*, vol. 27, no. 2, June, pp. 335-353.

Deger, Saadet & Somnath Sen, 1992. 'Re-orientation and Conversion of Military R&D towards Environmental R&D and Protection', ch. 9, pp. 165-194 in Gleditsch, 1992a.

DeGrasse, Robert W. Jr, 1983. *Military Expansion – Economic Decline*. Expanded edition. New York: M. E. Sharpe, for Council on Economic Priorities.

DeGrasse, Robert W. Jr, 1984. 'Military and Semiconductors', pp. 77-104 in Tirman, 1984a.

Diehl, Paul F. & Gary Goertz, 1985. 'Trends in Military Allocations Since 1816: What Goes Up Does Not Always Come Down', *Armed Forces and Society*, vol. 12, no. 1, Fall, pp. 134-144.

Dinneen, G. P. & F. C. Frick, 1977. 'Electronics and National Defense: A Case Study', *Science*, vol. 195, no. 4283, pp. 1151-55. Reprinted pp. 81-85 in Philip H. Abelson & Allen L. Hammond, eds. *Electronics: The Continuing Revolution*. Washington, DC: American Association for the Advancement of Science.

Duchin, Faye, 1983. 'Economic Consequences of Military Spending', *Journal of Economic Issues*, vol. 27, no. 2, June, pp. 543-553.

Duchin, Faye; Glenn-Marie Lange, Knut Thonstad & Annemarth Idenburg, 1992. *Strategies for Environmentally Sound Economic Development*. New York: Institute for Economic Analysis, New York University.

Duisenberg, Willem F., 1965a. *Economische gevolgen van Ontwapening* [Economic Effects of Disarmament]. Assen: van Gorcum.

Duisenberg, Willem F., 1965b. 'The Economic Consequences of Disarmament in the Netherlands', *Journal of Peace Research*, vol. 2, no. 2, pp. 177-186.

Duke, Simon, 1989. *United States Military Forces and Installations in Europe*. Oxford etc.: Oxford University Press.

Duke, Simon, 1990. 'The Economic Impact of a US Military Withdrawal from NATO's Northern Flank', pp. 154-178 in Sharp, 1990.

Dumas, Lloyd J., 1981. 'Disarmament and the Economy in Advanced Industrialized Countries – the US and the USSR', *Bulletin of Peace Proposals*, vol. 12, no. 1, pp. 1-10.

Dumas, Lloyd J., 1982a. *The Political Economy of Arms Reduction*. Boulder, CO: Westview.

Dumas, Lloyd J., 1982b. 'Military Spending and Economic Decay', pp. 1-27 in Dumas, 1982a. Also pp. 172-194 in Burns H. Weston, ed. *Toward Nuclear Disarmament and Global Security: A Search for Alternatives*. Boulder, CO: Westview, 1984.

Dumas, Lloyd J., 1986. *The Overburdened Economy. Uncovering the Causes of Chronic Unemployment, Inflation, and National Decline*. Berkeley, CA etc.: University of California Press.

Dumas, Lloyd J., 1989. 'Economic Conversion: The Critical Link', pp. 3-15 in Dumas & Thee, 1989.

Dumas, Lloyd J., 1990. 'Making Sense out of Nonsense'. Paper distributed at the United Nations Conference on Conversion, Moscow, 13-17 August.

Dumas, Lloyd J. & Marek Thee, eds., 1989. *Making Peace Possible: The Promise of Economic Conversion*. Oxford etc.: Pergamon.

Dunne, J. Paul, 1986. 'The Employment Consequences of Military Expenditure: A Comparative Assessment', *Working Paper*, no. 6. Geneva: International Labour Organization, Disarmament and Employment Program.

Dunne, J. Paul, 1990. 'The Political Economy of Military Expenditure: An Introduction', *Cambridge Journal of Economics*, vol. 14, no. 4, pp. 395-404.

Dunne, J. Paul, 1991. 'Quantifying the Relation of Defence Expenditure to Employment', ch. 2, pp. 11-26 in Paukert & Richards, 1991a.

Dunne J. Paul & Ron P. Smith, 1984. 'The Economic Consequences of Reduced UK Military Expenditures', *Cambridge Journal of Economics*, vol. 8, no. 3, September, pp. 297-310.

Dunne J. Paul & Ron P. Smith, 1990. 'Military Expenditure and Unemployment in the OECD', *Defence Economics*, vol. 1, no. 1, January, pp. 57-73.

Dörfer, Ingemar, 1983. *Arms Deal. The Selling of the F-16*. New York: Praeger.

Eberwein, Wolf-Dieter, ed. , 1992. *Transformation Processes in Eastern Europe. Perspectives from the Modelling Laboratory*. Frankfurt a.M. etc.: Peter Lang.

Eckhardt, William, 1989. 'Wars and War-Related Deaths, 1945-1989', p. 22 in Sivard, 1989.

ECON, 1991. *Evaluering av gjenkjøpsavtalene* [Evaluation of the Compensation Agreements]. Oslo: Center for Economic Analysis ECON. [Appendix 2 to Thulin et al., 1991.]

Economist Intelligence Unit, 1963. *The Economic Effects of Disarmament*. London: Economist Intelligence Unit.

Elsner, Wolfram & Gerhard Voss, 1991. *Bericht zu den Abrüstungsfolgen für das Land Bremen und zu den Handlungsmöglichkeiten* [Report on the Consequences of Disarmament for the State of Bremen and on the Policy Options], *Regionalwirtschaftliche Studien des Bremer Ausschusses für Wirtschaftsforschung*.

Engle, Robert F. & Clive W. J. Granger, 1987. 'Co-Integration and Error Correction: Representation, Estimation, and Testing', *Econometrica*, vol. 55, no. 2, March, pp. 251-276.

Eriksen, Tore & Jan F. Qvigstad, in cooperation with Tore Thonstad, 1978. 'Arbeidsmiljø og næringsstruktur' [Work Environment and Industry Structure], *Memorandum*. Oslo: Department of Economics, University of Oslo.

Erlandsen, Hans Christian, 1983. *Århundrets våpensalg* [The Arms Sale of the Century]. Oslo: Bedriftsøkonomens forlag.

Erlandsen, Hans Christian, 1987. *Toshiba/KV-saken* [The Toshiba/KV Affair]. Oslo: Bedriftsøkonomens forlag.

Evstafiev, Igor B. & Sergei G. Grigoriev, 1992. 'Ensuring Environmental Safety in the Elimination of Chemical Weapons', ch. 13, pp. 243-252 in Gleditsch, 1992a.

Fagerberg, Jan, 1988. 'International Competitiveness', *The Economic Journal*, vol. 98, no. 391, June, pp. 355-374.

Faini, Riccardo; Patricia Arnez & Lance Taylor, 1980. *Defense Spending, Economic Structure, and Growth: Evidence Among Countries and Over Time*. Cambridge, MA: Department of Economics, Massachusetts Institute of Technology. [Report prepared for the Thorsson Committee, cf. United Nations, 1982.] Revised version in *Economic Development and Cultural Change*, vol. 32, no. 3, April 1984, pp. 487-498.

Filip-Köhn, R.; R. Krengel & D. Schumacher, 1980. *Macro-Economic Effects of Disarmament Policies on Sectoral Production and Employment in the Federal Republic of Germany, with Special Emphasis on Development Policy Issues*. Report commissioned by the German Federal Foreign Office for the United Nations Group of Governmental Experts on the Relationship between Disarmament and Development. Berlin: Deutsches Institut für Wirtschaftsforschung.

Fogelström, Per Anders & Roland Morell. 1959. *Istedenfor atombomben* [Instead of Nuclear Weapons]. Oslo: Orientering. [Originally published in Sweden in 1958.]

Folta, Paul Humes, 1992. *From Swords to Plowshares?* Boulder, CO: Westview.

Fontanel, Jacques, 1980. *Formalized Studies and Econometric Analysis of the Relationship between Military Expenditure and Economic Development. The Examples of a Developed Country, France, and an Under-Developed Country, Morocco*. Report prepared for the United Nations Group of Governmental Experts on the Relationship between Disarmament and Development. Grenoble: University of Social Sciences: Centre for Security and Defence Studies. [Translated from the French.]

Fontanel, Jacques, ed., 1993. *Economistes de la paix* [Economists of Peace]. Grenoble: Presses Universitaires de Grenoble.

Fontanel, Jacques & Ron P. Smith, 1985. 'Analyse économique des dépenses militaires' [Economic Analysis of Military Expenditures], *Stratégique*, no. 3, pp. 73-116.

Forbord, Atle, 1976. *Norge og F-16* [Norway and the F-16]. Thesis in Political Science, University of Oslo. Oslo: PRIO.

Forsberg, Thomas & Leif Hedberg, 1978. *Undersökning av leveransströmmerna inom tillverkningsindustrin, särskilt försvarsindustrin, i Östergötlands län 1974 – en input-output-studie* [An Investigation of the Supply Flows within the Processing Industry, in Particular the Defense Industry in the District of Östergötland 1974 – an Input-Output Study; in Swedish]. Linköping: Länsstyrelsen i Östergötlands län & Department of Economics, University of Linköping, January.

Forssell, O., 1966. Tuotantotoiminnan ja kulutuksen kerrannaisvaikutukset tulojen muodostukseen, työllisyyteen ja tuontiin Suomessa [The Multiplier Effects of Economic Production and Consumption on Income Accumulation, Employment, and Imports in Finland]. Mimeographed. *Report* no. 17. Helsinki: Institute of Business Economics. [Cited from Joenniemi, 1970.]

Forssell, O.; L. Aarnio & J. Pietilä, 1968. *Puolustusmenojen vaikutus kansantalouden toimintaan* [The Impact Of Defense Expenditure on the Functioning of the National Economy]. Mimeographed report to the Finnish Council of Defense, Helsinki. [Cited from Joenniemi, 1970.]

Frydenlund, Knut, 1980. 'Introduction', *International Conference on Disarmament and Development, Sandefjord, May 6*. Oslo: Ministry of Foreign Affairs.

Førland, Tor Egil, 1988. *Vi sier intet. Norge i COCOM 1948-53* [We Say Nothing. Norway in CoCom 1948-53]. Oslo: Pax.

Førland, Tor Egil, 1991. '«Economic Warfare» and «Strategic Goods»: A Conceptual Framework for Analyzing COCOM', *Journal of Peace Research*, vol. 28, no. 2, May, pp. 191-204.

Gaddis, John Lewis, 1987. *The Long Peace. Inquiries Into the History of the Cold War*. New York & Oxford: Oxford University Press.

Galigan, C. G., 1984. *The Economic Impact of Canadian Defence Expenditures: FY 1982/83 Update*. Kingston, Ontario: Centre for Studies in Defence Resources Management, The Royal Military College of Canada.

Galtung, Johan, 1966. 'Attitudes Towards Different Forms of Disarmament. A Study of Norwegian Public Opinion', pp. 210-238 in *Proceedings of the International Peace Research Association Inaugural Conference*. Assen: van Gorcum.

Galtung, Johan, 1967. 'Public Opinion on the Economic Effects of Disarmament', pp. 171-180 in Benoit, 1967. Reprinted in Johan Galtung: *Peace, War and Defence. Essays in Peace Research*, vol. II, pp. 206-218. Copenhagen: Ejlers, 1976.

Galtung, Johan, 1968. 'Norge i verdenssamfunnet' [Norway in the World Community], pp. 445-491 in Natalie R. Ramsøy, ed. *Det norske samfunn* [Norwegian Society]. Oslo: Gyldendal. [English version pp. 385-427 in Natalie R. Ramsøy & Mariken Vaa, eds.: *Norwegian Society*. Oslo: Norwegian University Press. Also pp. 269-315 in Johan Galtung: *Peace and World Structure. Essays in Peace Research*, vol. IV. Copenhagen: Ejlers, 1980.]

Galtung, Johan, 1976. 'On the Strategy of Nonmilitary Defense. Some Proposals and Problems', pp. 378-426, 466-472 in Johan Galtung, *Peace, War, and Defense. Essays in Peace Research*, vol. II. Copenhagen: Ejlers.

Galtung, Johan, 1984. *There Are Alternatives. Four Roads to Peace and Security*. Nottingham: Spokesman. [Also editions in Norwegian, German, and other languages.]

Galtung, Johan & Nils Petter Gleditsch, 1975. 'Norge i verdenssamfunnet' [Norway in the World Community], ch. 17, pp. 742-811 in Natalie R. Ramsøy & Mariken Vaa, eds. *Det norske samfunn* [Norwegian Society], second edition. Oslo: Gyldendal. [First edition published 1968.]

Galtung, Johan & Per Hansen, 1981. *Totalforsvar* [Total Defense]. Oslo: Norwegian University Press.

Gansler, Jacques, 1980. *The Defense Industry*. Cambridge, MA: MIT Press.

Gansler, Jacques, 1989. *Affording Defense*. Cambridge, MA & London: MIT Press.

Gleditsch, Nils Petter, 1982. 'Utvikling, nedrustning, militarisering' [Development, disarmament, militarization], pp. 106-111 in Odd Andreassen, ed. *Nedrustning* [Disarmament]. Oslo: Norwegian University Press.

Gleditsch, Nils Petter, 1985. 'The Strategic Significance of the Nordic Countries', *PRIO Report* no. 14. Also in *Current Research on Peace and Violence*, vol. 9, no. 1-2, 1986, pp. 28-42. Shorter version as 'Europe's Northern Region between the Superpowers', *Bulletin of Peace Proposals*, vol. 16, no. 4, December 1985, pp. 399-411.

Gleditsch, Nils Petter, 1987. 'The Local Impact of Reduced Military Spending. A Case Study of Norway', pp. 213-235 in Jürgen Kuhlmann, ed. Edited Papers from Research Committee 01 'Armed Forces and Conflict Resolution', XI World Congress of Sociology, New Delhi, August 1986, in *Forum International*, vol. 7. München: Sozialwissenschaftliches Institut der Bundeswehr, 1987.

Gleditsch, Nils Petter, 1988. *Norge i verdenssamfunnet: En statistisk håndbok* [Norway in the World Community.] Second edition. Oslo: Pax. [First edition published 1970.]

Gleditsch, Nils Petter, ed., 1992a. *Conversion and the Environment. Proceedings of a Seminar in Perm, Russia, 24-27 November 1991. PRIO Report*, no. 2, May.

Gleditsch, Nils Petter, 1992b. 'Conversion and the Environment: An Overview', pp. 23-44 in Gleditsch, 1992a. Revised version as ch. 7, pp. 131-154 in Käkönen, 1994.

Gleditsch, Nils Petter, ed., 1992c. *The Future of Nordic Military Spending*, special issue of *Cooperation and Conflict*, vol. 27, no. 4, December.

Gleditsch, Nils Petter, 1992d. 'Defense Without Threat? The Future of Norwegian Military Spending', pp. 397-413 in Gleditsch, 1992c.

Gleditsch, Nils Petter, 1992e. 'Focus On: Democracy and Peace', *Journal of Peace Research*, vol. 29, no. 4, pp. 369-376.

Gleditsch, Nils Petter & Nils Ivar Agøy, 1993. 'Norway: Towards Full Freedom of Choice?', ch. 9, pp. 114-258 in Charles C. Moskos & John Whiteclay Chambers II, eds. *The New Conscientious Objection: From Sacred to Secular Resistance*. New York & Oxford: Oxford University Press.

Gleditsch, Nils Petter; Magne Barth, Ådne Cappelen & Rolf Skomsvold, 1989. *Prisindeks for innenlandsk bruk av varer og tjenester* [Price Index for Domestic Use of Goods and Services]. Oslo: PRIO.

Gleditsch, Nils Petter; Olav Bjerkholt & Ådne Cappelen, 1983. 'Conversion: Global, National, and Local Effects. A Case Study of Norway', *Cooperation and Conflict*, vol. 18, no. 3, September, pp. 179-195. Also in *Reprint Series*, no. 7. Oslo: Central Bureau of Statistics, 1985. Slightly revised version as: 'Conversion Effects: A Case Study of Norway', pp. 231-249 in Dumas & Thee, 1989.

Gleditsch, Nils Petter; Olav Bjerkholt & Ådne Cappelen, 1986. *Military Spending and Economic Structures: With Special Reference to Market Economies*. Report to Department of Disarmament Affairs, United Nations, April. A/Conf.130/PC/INF/14. *PRIO Publication* X-41/86. [Cf. also Gleditsch, Cappelen & Bjerkholt, 1986.]

Gleditsch, Nils Petter; Ingvar Botnen, Owen Wilkes & Sverre Lodgaard, 1978. *Norge i atomstrategien. Atompolitikk, basepolitikk, alliansepolitikk* [Norway in the Nuclear Strategy. Nuclear Policy, Base Policy, Alliance Policy]. Oslo: Pax.

Gleditsch, Nils Petter; Ådne Cappelen & Olav Bjerkholt, 1986. *Economic Incentives to Arm? Effects of Military Spending on Industrialized Market Economies*. Oslo: PRIO. *PRIO Report* 21/86. [Revised and expanded version of Gleditsch, Bjerkholt & Cappelen, 1986. Shortened version as Gleditsch et al., 1988.]

Gleditsch, Nils Petter; Ådne Cappelen & Olav Bjerkholt, 1988. 'Military R&D and Economic Growth in Industrialized Market Economies', pp. 198-215 in Wallensteen, 1988. [Shorter version of Gleditsch, Cappelen & Bjerkholt, 1986.] Also in *Reprint series*, no. 35. Oslo: Central Bureau of Statistics, 1989.

Gleditsch, Nils Petter; Arne Magnus Christensen & Asbjørn Torvanger, 1985. Sections 2.3, 2.4, 2.5, 2.6 + Appendix in Marek Thee et al. *Impact of the Arms Race on Education, Science and Technology, Culture, and Communication*. Report for UNESCO. Oslo: PRIO. Reprinted, pp. 1-173 in *UNESCO Yearbook on Peace and Conflict Studies 1987*. Westport, CT: Greenwood/Paris: UNESCO, 1989.

Gleditsch, Nils Petter & Sverre Lodgaard, 1970. *Krigsstaten Norge* [Norway as a Warfare State]. Oslo: Pax.

Gleditsch, Nils Petter & Olav Njølstad, eds., 1990. *Arms Races. Technological and Political Dynamics*. London etc.: Sage.

Gleditsch, Nils Petter; Kristen Nordhaug & Håvard Hegre, 1990. *Nasjonsdata. En lærepakke* [Nation Data. A Teaching Package]. Oslo: PRIO. [Third edition, revised by Nils Petter Gleditsch & Håvard Hegre, 1993.]

Gleditsch, Nils Petter; Rolf Skomsvold; Magne Barth, Ådne Cappelen & Olav Bjerkholt, 1987. *Local Effects of Conversion in Norway*. Oslo: PRIO. *PRIO Report* 5/87.

Gleditsch, Nils Petter; Håkan Wiberg & Dan Smith, 1992. 'The Nordic Countries: Peace Dividend or Security Dilemma?', pp. 323-347 in Gleditsch, 1992c.

Gleditsch, Nils Petter & Steingrim Wolland, 1991. 'Norway', pp. 287-291 in Frances D'Souza et al., eds. *Information Freedom and Censorship. World Report 1991*. London: Library Association Publishing for Article 19.

Goertzel, Ted G., 1985. 'Militarism as a Sociological Problem', pp. 119-139 in Richard Braungart & Philo Washburn, eds. *Research in Political Sociology*. New York: JAI Press.

Gold, David, 1990. *The Impact of Defense Spending on Investment, Productivity, and Economic Growth*. Washington, DC: Defense Budget Project.

Gold, David & Gordon Adams, 1990. 'Defence Spending and the American Economy', *Defence Economics*, vol. 1, no. 4, August, pp. 275-293.

Granger, Clive W. J., 1969. 'Investigating Causal Relations by Econometric Models and Cross-Spectral Methods', *Econometrica*, vol. 37, no. 3, May, pp. 424-438.

Griliches, Zvi, 1987. 'R&D and Productivity: Measurement Issues and Econometric Results', *Science*, vol. 237, no. 4810, July 3, pp. 31-35.

Griliches, Zvi & Frank Lichtenberg, 1984. 'R&D Productivity Growth at the Industry Level: Is There Still a Relationship?', pp. 465-501 in Zvi Griliches, ed. *R&D, Patents, and Productivity. National Bureau of Economic Research Conference Report*. Chicago, IL/London: University of Chicago Press.

Grobar, Lisa M. & Richard C. Porter, 1989. 'Benoit Revisited: Defense Spending and Economic Growth in LDCs', *Journal of Conflict Resolution*, vol. 33, no. 2, June, pp. 318-345.

Gronicki, Miroslaw & Lawrence Klein, 1992. 'Trade-Offs Between Military and Civilian Programs in the Warsaw Pact Countries', ch. 15, pp. 161-184 in Chatterji & Forcey, 1992.

Gummett, Philip & Judith Reppy, eds., 1988. *The Relationship between Defence and Civil Technologies. NATO Advanced Science Institute Series*. Dordrecht etc.: Kluwer.

Gurr, Ted Robert, 1990. 'Ethnic Warfare and the Changing Priorities of Global Security', *Mediterranean Quarterly*, vol. 1, no. 1, Winter, pp. 82-98.

Gurr, Ted Robert & James R. Scarritt, 1989. 'Minorities Rights at Risk: A Global Survey', *Human Rights Quarterly*, vol. 11, no. 3, August, pp. 375-405.

Hanoa, Rolf, 1976. *Militærtjeneste og helse. Hvem blir fritatt og hvem greier tjenesten?* [Military Service and Health. Who is Exempted and Who Manages to Serve?]. Oslo: Gyldendal.

Harildstad, Anders, 1989. 'Timeverks- og sysselsettingstall' [Person-hours and Employment Figures], *Økonomiske analyser*, no. 7, 1989. Oslo: Central Bureau of Statistics, pp. 21-23.

Harff, Barbara & Ted Robert Gurr, 1988. 'Toward Empirical Theory of Genocides and Politicides: Identification and Measurement of Cases Since 1945', *International Studies Quarterly*, vol. 32, no. 3, September, pp. 359-371.

Harris, Geoffrey; Mark Kelly & Pranowo, 1988. 'Trade-offs Between Defence and Education/Health Expenditures in Developing Countries', *Journal of Peace Research*, vol. 25, no. 2, pp. 165-177.

Harrison, Mark, 1988. 'Resource Mobilization for World War II: The USA, UK, USSR, and Germany 1938-45', *Economic History Review, Second Series*, vol. 41, no. 2, May, pp. 171-192.

Hartley, Keith & Nicholas Hooper, 1990a. *The Economics of Defence, Disarmament, and Peace. An Annotated Bibliography*. Aldershot & Brookfield, VT: Elgar.

Hartley, Keith & Nicholas Hooper, 1990b. 'Costs and Benefits to the United Kingdom of the US Military Presence', pp. 132-153 in Sharp, 1990.

Hartley, Keith & Pat McLean, 1978. 'Military Expenditure and Capitalism: A Comment', *Cambridge Journal of Economics*, vol. 2, no. 3, September, pp. 287-292.

Hartley, Keith & Todd Sandler, eds., 1990. *The Economics of Defense Spending. An International Survey*. London & New York: Routledge.

Heldt, Birger, ed., 1992. *States in Armed Conflict 1990-91. Report* no. 35. Uppsala: Department of Peace and Conflict Research, Uppsala University.

Heldt, Birger; Peter Wallensteen & Kjell-Åke Nordquist, 1992. 'Major Armed Conflicts', ch. 11, pp. 417-456 in *World Armaments and Disarmament. SIPRI Yearbook 1992*. Oxford etc.: Oxford University Press.

Hersh, Seymour M., 1991. *The Sampson Option. Israel's Nuclear Arsenal and American Foreign Policy*, New York: Random House.

Hickman, Bert G. & Kenneth G. Ruffing, 1991. 'Project LINK: Past, Present and Future', Paper Presented to the Tokyo Conference on Global Change and Modelling, United Nations University, 29-31 October 1991.

Hofmeister, Albert, 1976. *Input-Output Analyse und Multiplikatortheorie als Hilfsmittel der Regionalforschung, dargestellt an der militärischen Nachfrage in der Stadt Thun* [Input-Output Analysis and Multiplier Theory as Tools in Regional Research, as Exemplified by the Military Demand in the City of Thun]. Zürich: Schulthess.

Hofmeister, Albert, n.d. *Direkte, indirekte und induzierte Effekte militärischer Aktivitäten, ein Beitrag zur Verteidigungsökonomie mit Hilfe der Input-Output Analyse, dargestellt am Beispiel der Region Thun* [Direct, Indirect, and Induced Effects of Military Activities, a Contribution to Defense Economy using Input-Output Analysis, Exemplified by the Region of Thun]. Mimeographed. Place and publisher unknown.

Holm, Erling Dokk, 1989. 'Våpeneksportreglene liberaliseres' [Arms Exports: The Rules Are Being Liberalized], *Ikkevold*, no. 4, August 4, pp. 8-9.

Holst, Johan Jørgen, 1967. *Norsk sikkerhetspolitikk i strategisk perspektiv*. Bind I: *Analyse*, bind II: *Dokumentasjon* [Norwegian Security Policy in Strategic Perspective. Vol. I: Analysis, vol. II: Documentation]. Oslo: Norwegian Institute of International Affairs.

Holst, Johan Jørgen, 1978. *Vår forsvarspolitikk. Vurderinger og utsyn* [Our Defense Policy. Evaluations and Overview]. Oslo: Tiden.

Homer-Dixon, Thomas F., 1991. 'On the Threshold. Environmental Changes as Causes of Acute Conflict', *International Security*, vol. 16, no. 2, Fall, pp. 76-116.

Hove, Stein Inge, 1993. 'Nedrustning av forsvaret. En modellbasert analyse' [Disarming the military establishment. A model-ased analysis], *Notater*, no. 47. Oslo: Central Bureau of Statistics. [Summary in *Ukens statistikk* no. 3, 1994.]

Huang, Chi & Alex Mintz, 1990. 'Ridge Regression Analysis of the Defence-Growth Tradeoff in the United States', *Defence Economics*, vol. 2, no. 1, December, pp. 29-37.

Huang, Chi & Alex Mintz, 1991. 'Defence Expenditures and Economic Growth: The Externality Effect', *Defence Economics*, vol. 3, no. 1, December, pp. 35-40.

International Institute of Strategic Studies, annual. *The Military Balance*. London: IISS.

Isard, Walter & Charles H. Anderton, eds., 1992a. *Economics of Arms Reduction and the Peace Process. Contributions from Peace Economics and Peace Science*. Amsterdam etc.: Elsevier/North-Holland.

Isard, Walter & Charles H. Anderton, 1992b. 'Survey of the Peace Economics Literature', ch. 1, pp. 1-55 in Isard & Anderton, 1992a.

Joenniemi, Pertti, 1970. 'An Analysis of the Economic Consequences of Disarmament in Finland', *Papers, Peace Research Society (International)*, vol. 13, pp. 29-46.

Johansen, Ivar, 1984. 'NATO-stasjoner i Norge formidler signalene: NATOs atlantershavsflåte er forberedt til bruk av atomvåpen' [NATO Stations in Norway Relay the Signals. The Strikefleet Atlantic is Prepared to Use Nuclear Weapons], pp. 73-78 in Jørgen Johansen, ed. *Bombemålet Norge. Atomstrategi, ytringsfrihet og razzia* [Norway as a Bomb Target. Nuclear Strategy, Freedom of Expression, and a Raid]. Oslo: Folkereisning mot krig.

Johansen, Ivar et al., 1986. *S.O.S. U.S. Andøya. Ikkevoldssaken og amerikansk antiubåtkrigføring* [SOS US Andøya. The Case against Ikkevold and US antisubmarine warfare]. Oslo: Folkereisning mot krig.

Johansen, Leif, 1960. *A Multi-Sector Study of Economic Growth*. Amsterdam: North-Holland. [Second edition, 1974.]

Johansen, Steinar, 1990. 'Regionale effekter av en reduksjon av Forsvarets virksomhet, med vekt på sysselsettingen i Nord-Norge' [Regional Effects of a Reduction in the Activities of the Military Establishment, with Special Emphasis on the Consequences for Employment in Northern Norway]. Oslo: Norwegian Institute for Urban and Regional Planning. [Appendix B to Aamo et al., 1990.] Also as *Reduksjon av Forsvarets virksomhet – regionale konsekvenser. NIBR-rapport* no. 28. Oslo: Norwegian Institute for Urban and Regional Planning, 1990.

Kahn, Herman, 1979. *World Economic Development*. London: Croom Helm.

Kaldor, Mary, 1982. *The Baroque Arsenal*. London: Deutsch/New York: Hill & Wang.

Kaldor, Nicholas, 1966. *Causes of the Slow Rate of Economic Growth of the United Kingdom*. Cambridge: Cambridge University Press.

Kennedy, Gavin, 1975. *The Economics of Defence*. London: Faber and Faber.

Kennedy, Paul, 1987. *The Rise and Fall of the Great Powers. Economic Change and Military Conflict from 1500 to 2000*. New York: Random House.

Kielland, Arne, 1971. *Norsk gerilja og sivilmotstand* [Norwegian Guerrilla and Civilian Resistance]. Oslo: Det Norske Samlaget.

Kielland, Arne, 1979. 'Et forsvarsalternativ – heimevern og sivilmotstand' [A Defense Alternative. Home Guard and Civilian Resistance]. Bø, draft manuscript.

Kinsella, Davis, 1990. 'Defence Spending and Economic Performance in the United States: A Causal Analysis', *Defence Economics*, vol. 1, no. 4, August, pp. 295-309.

Kinsella, Davis, 1991. 'Defence Spending and Economic Performance in the United States: A Reply', *Defence Economics*, vol. 2, no. 3, July, pp. 265-267.

Kireev, Alexei, 1991. 'Price of the Peace Dividend', *International Affairs* (Moscow), no. 8, August, pp. 8-17.

Kiy, Manfred & Klaus Löbbe, 1990. 'Verteidigungsausgaben der Bundesrepublik und volkswirtschaftliche Auswirkungen verminderter Rüstungsausgaben' [Defense Expenditure in the Federal Republic of Germany and Macroeconomic Effects of Decreased Military Spending], *RWI-Mitteilungen* [Zeitschrift für Wirtschaftsforschung, Rheinisch-Westfälisches Institut für Wirtschaftsforschung], vol. 41, no. 4, pp. 331-360.

Klein, Lawrence R., 1971. 'The Role of War in the Maintenance of American Economic Prosperity', *Proceedings of the American Philosophical Society*, vol. 115, no. 6, December, pp. 507-516.

Klein, Lawrence R. & Miroslaw Gronicki, 1990. 'Conversion: The Trade-Off Between Military and Civilian Production in Warsaw Pact Countries', *Conflict Management and Peace Science*, vol. 1, no. 1, Spring, pp. 45-46.

Klein, Lawrence R.; Miroslaw Gronicki & Hiroyuki Kosaka; edited by Walter Isard, 1992. 'Impact of Military Cuts on the Soviet and Eastern European Economies: Models and Simulations', ch. 3, pp. 69-87 in Isard & Anderton, 1992.

Klein, Lawrence R. & Ken Mori, 1973. 'The Impact of Disarmament on Aggregate Economic Activity: An Econometric Analysis', pp. 59-77 in Udis, 1973.

Köllner, Lutz & Burkhardt J. Huck, eds., 1990. *Abrüstung und Konversion. Politische Voraussetzungen und wirtschaftliche Folgen in der Bundesrepublik* [Disarmament and Conversion. Political Preconditions and Economic Consequences in the Federal Republic of Germany]. Frankfurt & New York: Campus.

Käkönen, Jyrki, ed., 1994. *Green Securtiy or Militarized Environment*. Aldershot & Brookfield, VT: Dartmouth.

188   THE WAGES OF PEACE

Leitenberg, Milton, 1978. 'Base Closing in the United States: A Note on the Office of Economic Adjustment', pp. 135-139 in Peter Wallensteen, ed. *Experiences in Disarmament: On Conversion of Military Industry and Closing of Military Bases*. *Report* no. 19. Uppsala: Department of Peace and Conflict Research, Uppsala University.

Leontief, Wassily, 1978. *Preliminary Study of World-Wide Economic and Social Implications of a Limitation on Military Spending (An Input-Output Approach)*. New York: New York University, Department of Economics, Center for Applied Economics.

Leontief, Wassily, 1980. *Worldwide Implications of Hypothetical Changes in Military Spending (an Input-Output Approach)*. New York: Institute for Economic Analysis, New York University, for US Arms Control and Disarmament Agency.

Leontief, Wassily; Anne P. Carter & Peter A. Petri, 1977. *The Future of the World Economy. A United Nations Study*. New York: Oxford University Press.

Leontief, Wassily & Faye Duchin, 1983a. *Worldwide Economic Implications of a Limitation on Military Spending*. New York: Institute for Economic Analysis, New York University, for Centre for Disarmament, United Nations.

Leontief, Wassily & Faye Duchin, 1983b. *Military Spending. Facts and Figures, Worldwide Implications, and Future Outlook*. New York: Oxford University Press.

Leontief, Wassily W. & Marvin Hoffenberg, 1961. 'The Economic Effects of Disarmament', *Scientific American*, vol. 204, no. 4, April, pp. 47-55.

Leontief, Wassily W. & Marvin Hoffenberg, 1963. 'Input-Output Analysis of Disarmament Impacts', pp. 89-98 in Benoit & Boulding, 1963.

Leontief, Wassily W.; Alison Morgan, Karen Polenske, David Simpson & Edward Tower, 1965. 'The Economic Impact – Industrial and Regional – of an Arms Cut', *Review of Economics and Statistics*, vol. 47, no. 3, August, pp. 217-241. Reprinted pp. 184-222 in Wassily W. Leontief, *Input-Output Economics*. New York: Oxford University Press, 1966.

Lerner, Joshua, 1992. 'The Mobility of Corporate Scientists and Engineers between Civil and Defence Activities: Implications for Economic Competitiveness in the Post-Cold War Era', *Defence Economics*, vol. 3, no. 3, August, pp. 229-242.

Levy, Jack S., 1983. *War in the Modern Great Power System 1595-1975*. Lexington, KY: The University Press of Kentucky.

Lichtenberg, Frank R., 1988. 'Assessing the Impact of Federal Industrial R&D Expenditure on Private R&D Activity in the United States', chapter 4, pp. 68-87 in Gummett & Reppy, 1988.

Liew, L.H., 1985. 'The Impact of Defence Spending on the Australian Economy', *Australian Economic Papers*, vol. 24, no. 45, December, pp. 326-336.

Lim, David, 1983. 'Another Look at Growth and Defense in Less Developed Countries', *Economic Development and Cultural Change*, vol. 31, no. 2, January, pp. 377-384.

Lindelien, Knut, 1979. 'Fra L/70 til F-16: Norsk samproduksjon av våpen og militært materiell' [From L/70 to F-16: Norwegian Co-Production of Arms and Military Equipment], *NUPI-rapport* no. 42, August.

Lindén, Mikael, 1987. 'Varustelumenojen vaikutus taloudelliseen kasvuun ja investointeihin: Eräitä teoreettisia ongelmia ja empiirinen sovellutus Suomen ainestoon v. 1950-1984' [The Impact of Military Expenditures on Economic Growth and Investments: Some Theoretical Problems and Application to Finnish Data for the period 1950-84], in Finnish, with English abstract, pp. 138-159 in *Taloustieteellinen vuosikirja 1986/87* [Yearbook of the Finnish Society for Economic Research]. Taloustieteellinen seura, Vammala: Vammalan kirjipaino.

Lindgren, Göran, 1984. 'Armaments and Economic Performance in Industrialized Market Economies', *Journal of Peace Research*, vol. 21, no. 4, November, pp. 375-387. Updated version as 'Armaments and Economic Performance', ch. 8, pp. 169-197 in Wallensteen, 1988.

Lindgren, Karin, 1990. *Världens krig* [The Wars of the World]. Stockholm: Swedish Institute of International Affairs. *Världens Fakta*, no. 5.

Lindgren, Karin, 1991. 'Patterns of Armed Conflict', pp. 1-17 in Karin Lindgren, ed. *States in Armed Conflict 1989*. *Report* no. 32. Uppsala: Department of Peace and Conflict Research, Uppsala University.

Lindroos, Reijo, 1981. *Disarmament and Employment. A Study on the Employment Aspects of Military Spending and on the Possibilities to Convert Arms Production to Civilian Production*. Helsinki: Central Organization of Finnish Trade Unions.

Lindstøl, Aslak, 1978. *De 13. 'Protest mot atomvåpen' – et utenomparlamentarisk initiativ under atomdebatten i Norge våren 1961* [The 13. 'Protest against Nuclear Weapons' – an Extra-Parliamentary Initiative during the Nuclear Weapons Debate in Norway in Spring 1961]. Unpublished cand.philol. thesis in History, University of Oslo.

Lock, Peter, 1992. 'International Cooperation and Conversion: Overcoming the Inherited Environmental Hazards of the Arms Race', ch. 14, pp. 253-268 in Gleditsch, 1992a.

Longva, Svein; Lorents Lorentsen & Øystein Olsen, 1980. 'Energy in a Multi-Sectoral Growth Model', *Report* no. 80/1. Oslo: Central Bureau of Statistics.

Longva, Svein; Lorents Lorentsen & Øystein Olsen, 1985. 'The Multi-Sectoral Growth Model MSG-4. Formal Structure and Empirical Characteristics', pp. 187-240 in Finn R. Førsund, Michael Hoel & Svein Longva, eds. *Production, Multi-Sectoral Growth and Planning. Contributions to Economic Analysis* no. 154. Amsterdam: Elsevier. Also in *Reprint series*, no. 17. Oslo: Central Bureau of Statistics, 1986.

Looney, Robert E., 1992. 'Latin American Military Expenditures and Arms Production: The Environmental Consequences', ch. 11, pp. 209-228 in Gleditsch, 1992a.

Luard, Evan, 1986. *War in International Society: A Study in International Sociology*. London: Tauris.

Lumsden, Malvern, 1981. 'The Use of Raw Materials, Land, and Water for Armament and War', pp. 38-57 in Wendy Barnaby, ed. *War and Environment*. Stockholm: Liber, for the Environment Advisory Council.

McTague, John, 1987. 'Defense R&D and National Competitiveness: Past, Present, and Future Prospects', pp. 3-8 in Stewart Nozette & Robert Lawrence Kuhn, eds. *Commercializing SDI Technologies*. New York: Praeger.

Maneval, Helmut; Pasi Rautsola & Rolf Wiegert, 1991. 'Defense Spending and Economic Growth: A Comment on Cappelen, Gleditsch, and Bjerkholt', *Journal of Peace Research*, vol. 28, no. 4, November, pp. 425-430. [Comment on Cappelen et al., 1984b.]

Martin, Stephen; Ron P. Smith & Jacques Fontanel, 1987. 'Time-series Estimates of the Macroeconomic Impact of Defence Spending in France and the UK', pp. 342-361 in Schmidt & Blackaby, 1987.

Maxwell, Tom, 1984. 'The Economic Impact of Defence Spending', pp. 99-114 in Brian MacDonald, ed. *Guns and Butter: Defence and the Canadian Economy*. Toronto: Canadian Institute of Strategic Studies.

Mearsheimer, John J., 1990. 'Back to the Future: Instability in Europe After the Cold War', *International Security*, vol. 14, no. 4, Spring, pp. 42-64.

Melko, Matthew, 1990. *Peace in Our Time*. New York: Paragon House.

Melman, Seymour, ed., 1962. *Disarmament: Its Politics and Economics*. Boston, MA: The American Academy of Arts and Sciences.

Melman, Seymour, 1983. 'Twelve Propositions on Productivity and War Economy', *Armed Forces and Society*, vol. 1, no. 4, August, pp. 490-497.

Melman, Seymour, 1987. *Profits Without Production*. Philadelphia, PA: University of Pennsylvania Press.

Milward, Alan S., 1977. *War, Economy and Society 1939-45*. Berkeley, CA & Los Angeles, CA: University of California Press.

Ministry of Defense, annually. *Norwegian Defense. Facts and Figures*. Oslo: MoD.

Ministry of Defense, 1949. *Innstilling fra forsvarskommisjonen av 1946* [Report from the Defense Commission of 1946]. Oslo: Ministry of Defense, 3 vols.

Ministry of Defense, 1955. *Fra Boyesensutvalgets innstilling. Pressemelding fra Forsvarsdepartementet 14.7.1955* [From the final report of the Boyesen Committee. Press release from the Ministry of Defense, 14 July, 1955. The actual report remains classified.]

Ministry of Defense, 1981. *Sivil nytte av Forsvaret* [The Civilian Utility of the Defense Establishment]. Oslo: Ministry of Defense.

Ministry of Defense, 1990. *Miljøplan Forsvaret. Forprosjekt* [Environmental Plan for the Military Establishment, Trial project]. Oslo: Forsvarsdepartementet.

Ministry of Defense, 1991. *Strategi for norsk deltakelse i internasjonalt forsvarsmateriell- og teknologisamarbeid* [Strategy for Norwegian Participation in International Defence Materiel and Technology Cooperation]. Oslo: Ministry of Defense. [Appendix 1 to Thulin et al., 1991.]

Ministry of Defense, 1992. *Miljøplan Forsvaret. Styringsgruppens forslag fremlagt 25. mars 1992* [Environmental Plan for the Military Establishment. Report from the Steering Committee 25 March 1992]. Oslo: Ministry of Defense.

Ministry of Defense, 1993. *Hovedretningslinjer for Forsvarets virksomhet og utvikling i tiden 1994-98* [Main Directions for the Activity and Development of the Military Establishment 1994-98]. *St.meld.* no. 16 (1992-93).

Ministry of Foreign Affairs, 1985. *Forsvar mot ballistiske raketter. De tekniske og vitenskapelige sider ved USAs strategiske forsvarsinitiativ* [Defense against Ballistic Missiles. The Technical and Scientific Aspects of the US Strategic Defense Initiative]. Report Prepared for the Prime Minister's Office, June. Reprinted in *Aktuelle utenrikspolitiske spørsmål,* Norwegian Ministry of Foreign Affairs, September.

Ministry of Foreign Affairs, 1992a. 'Om utviklingstrekk i nord-sør forholdet og Norges samarbeid med utviklingslandene' [On Development Trends in the North-South Relationship and Norwegian Co-operation with the Developing Countries], *St.meld.* no. 51 (1991-92).

Ministry of Foreign Affairs, 1992b. 'Om Norges samarbeid med utviklingslandene i 1991 [On Norway's cooperation with developing countries in 1991], *St.meld.,* no. 66 (1991-92).

Ministry of Foreign Affairs, 1992c. *Melding fra Utenriksdepartementet. Utførsel* [Notice from the Ministry of Foreign Affairs. Exports]. Oslo: Ministry of Foreign Affairs.

Ministry of Justice, 1955. *Utkast til lov om fritakelse for væpnet militær tjeneste av overbevisningsgrunner. Tilråding fra Utvalget til revisjon av lovgivning om vernepliktige sivilarbeidere* [Draft Law on Exemption from Armed Military Service on Grounds of Conviction. Recommendation from the Committee for the Revision of the Legislation on Conscientious Objection]. Oslo: Ministry of Justice.

Mintz, Alex, ed., 1992. *The Political Economy of Military Spending in the United States.* London & New York: Routledge.

Mintz, Alex & Chi Huang, 1990. 'Defense Expenditures, Economic Growth, and the «Peace Dividend»', *American Political Science Review,* vol. 84, no. 4, December, pp. 1283-1293.

Mintz, Alex; Chi Huang & Uk Heo, 1992. 'Defense Spending and Economic Performance: A Disaggregate Analysis', ch. 2, pp. 21-35 in Chan & Mintz, 1992.

Moe, Johannes, 1985. 'Forskningens rolle i vår industrielle utvikling [The Role of Research in our Industrial Development], *Bergen Bank Kvartalsskrift,* no. 3, pp. 119-145.

Moskos, Charles C., 1988. *A Call to Civic Service. National Service for Country and Community.* New York: Free Press/London: Collier Macmillan.

Mosley, Hugh G., 1985. *The Arms Race: Economic and Social Consequences.* Lexington, MA: Heath.

Mueller, John, 1989. *Retreat from Doomsday. The Obsolescence of Major War.* New York: Basic Books. [Paperback version with new preface, 1990.]

Myrdal, Alva, 1976. *The Game of Disarmament. How the United States and Russia Run the Arms Race.* New York: Pantheon. [Paperback editions: New York: Pantheon, 1978; Nottingham: Spokesman, 1980.]

Møller, Bjørn, 1991. *Resolving the Security Dilemma in Europe. The German Debate on Non-Offensive Defence.* London etc.: Brassey's.

Nielsson, Gunnar & Ralph Jones, 1988. 'From Ethnic Category to Nation: Patterns of Political Modernization'. Paper presented to the 29th Annual Meeting of the International Studies Association, St. Louis, MO, March.

Nietschmann, Bernard, 1987. 'The Third World War', *Cultural Survival Quarterly,* vol. 11, no. 3, pp. 1-16.

Norman, Colin, 1981. *The God That Limps: Science and Technology in the Eighties.* New York/London: Norton.

NOU, 1972. *Tjenestetiden i Forsvaret* [The Length of Military Service]. *Norges Offisielle Utredninger,* no. 32.

NOU, 1978. 'Forsvarskommisjonen av 1974' [The Defense Commission of 1974], *Norges Offisielle Utredninger,* no. 9. Oslo: Norwegian University Press.

NOU, 1989. 'Godtgjøringssystemet for vernepliktige mannskaper' [The Renumeration of Conscripted Personnel], *Norges Offisielle Utredninger,* no. 3. Oslo: Norwegian University Press.

NOU, 1992. 'Forsvarskommisjonen av 1990' [The Defense Commission of 1990], *Norges Offisielle Utredninger*, no. 12. Oslo: Norwegian University Press.

Nyhagen, Jens Fredrik, 1989. 'Militær forskning – sivil nytte' [Military Research – Civilian Benefits], *NAVFs kronikktjeneste*, Ukens kronikk, no. 1, January.

Oden, Michael Dee, 1988. *A Military Dollar Really Different. The Economics Impacts of Military Spending Reconsidered*. Lansing, MI: Employment Research Associates.

OECD, annually. *Development Cooperation*. Paris: Organization for Economic Cooperation and Development.

Olson, Mancur, 1982. *The Rise and Decline of Nations: Economic Growth, Stagflation, and Social Rigidities*. New Haven, CT: Yale University Press.

Olson, Mancur, Jr & R. Zeckhauser, 1966. 'An Economic Theory of Alliances', *Review of Economics and Statistics*, vol. 48, no. 3, pp. 266-279.

Onishi, Akira, 1990. 'Impact of Disarmament on the Global Economy and Environment – FUGI Global Model Simulations'. Paper presented to the United Nations Conference on Conversion, Moscow, 13-17 August.

Onishi, Akira, 1991. 'FUGI Global Model: Simulations of Global CO_2 Cutbacks and Arms Reduction on the World Economy'. Paper presented to the United Nations University Conference on Global Change and Modelling, Tokyo, 29-31 October.

Organski, A.F.K. & Jacek Kugler, 1980. *The War Ledger*. Chicago, IL & London: Chicago University Press.

Owens, Susan, 1990. 'Defence and the Environment: The Impacts of Military Live Firing in National Parks', *Cambridge Journal of Economics*, vol. 14, no. 4, pp. 497-505.

Paukert, Liba & Peter Richards, eds., 1991a. *Defence Expenditure, Industrial Conversion and Local Employment*. Geneva: International Labour Office.

Paukert, Liba & Peter Richards, 1991b. Employment Impact of Industrial Conversion: A Comparative Analysis', ch. 11, pp. 205-228 in Paukert & Richards, 1991.

Payne, James E. & Kevin L. Ross, 1992. 'Defense Spending and the Macroeconomy', *Defense Economics*, vol. 3, no. 2, April, pp. 161-168.

Pite, Chris, 1980. 'Employment and Defence', *Statistical News*, no. 51, November, pp. 15-19.

Pivetti, Massimo, 1992. 'Military Spending as a Burden on Growth: An «Underconsumptionist» Critique', *Cambridge Journal of Economics*, vol. 16, no. 3, pp. 373-384.

Proost, Stef; Erik Schokkaert & Paul Van Elewijck, 1981. 'Enkele economische aspecten van de Belgische defensie-uitgaven [Some Economic Aspects of Belgian Military Spending], *Cahiers Economiques de Bruxelles*, vol. 92, no. 4, pp. 571-599. Brussels: Editions du DULBEA, Département d'économie appliquée de l'Université libre de Bruxelles.

Reich, Michael, 1972. 'Does the US Economy Require Military Spending?', *American Economic Review*, vol. 62, no. 2, May, pp. 296-303. Reprinted as ch. 4, pp. 85-102 in Steven Rosen, ed., *Testing the Theory of the Military-Industrial Complex*. Lexington, MA: Heath.

Renner, Michael, 1989.'National Security: The Economic and Environmental Dimensions', *Worldwatch Paper*, no. 96. Washington, DC: Worldwatch Institute.

Renner, Michael, 1990. 'Swords Into Plowshares: Converting to a Peace Economy'. *Worldwatch Paper*, no. 96. Washington, DC: Worldwatch Institute.

Renner, Michael, 1991. *Economic Adjustment After the Cold War*. Aldershot, etc: Dartmouth.

Ricardo, David, 1820. *Essay on the Funding System*. London.

Richardson, Lewis Fry, 1960. *Arms and Insecurity: A Mathematical Study of the Causes and Origins of War*. Pittsburgh, PA: Boxwood/Chicago, IL: Quadrangle.

Richardson, Peter, 1988. 'The Structure and Simulation Properties of OECD's Interlink Model', *OECD Economic Studies*, no. 10, Spring. Paris: Organization for Economic Cooperation and Development.

Ringdal, Kristen, 1977. 'Folkemeininga om utviklingshjelp' [Public Opinion on Development Aid], *Tidsskrift for Samfunnsforskning*, vol. 18, no. 1, pp. 47-75.

Ringdal, Kristen, 1979. *Folkemeininga og den tredje verda. Ein analyse av norske meiningar om u-landsspørsmål* [Public Opinion and the Third World. An Analysis of Norwegian Opinions on Issues Concerning Developing Countries]. Oslo: Solum.

Roland-Holst, David W.; Sherman Robinson & Laura D'Andrea Tyson, 1988. 'The Opportunity Cost of Defense Spending: A General Equilibrium Analysis', *Working Paper* no. 8871, Department of Economics, University of California, Berkeley, April.

Rothschild, Kurt W., 1973. 'Military Expenditure, Exports and Growth', *Kyklos*, vol. 26, no. 4, pp. 804-814.

Rummel, Rudolph J., 1994. 'Focus On: Power and Democide', *Journal of Peace Research*, vol. 31, no. 1, February, pp. 1-10.

Russett, Bruce M., 1970. *What Price Vigilance: The Burdens of National Defense*. New Haven, CT: Yale University Press.

Russett, Bruce, 1993. *Grasping the Democratic Peace. Principles for a Post-Cold War World*. Princeton, NJ: Princeton University Press.

Russett, Bruce M., 1982. 'Defense Expenditures and National Well-being', *American Political Science Review*, vol. 76, no. 4, December, pp. 767-777.

Say, Jean-Baptiste, 1803. *Traité d'economie politique*. Paris.

Schloenbach, Knut, 1973. 'Studies on the Structure of the Armed Forces with the Aid of Simulation: On the Quantitative Methods of Analysis Employed by the Force Structure Commission', *German Economic Review*, vol. 11, no. 4, pp. 361-368.

Schmidt, Christian & Frank Blackaby, eds., 1987. *Peace, Defence, and Economic Analysis*. Basingstoke: Macmillan/New York: St. Martin's.

Sharp, Jane M.O., ed., 1990. *Europe After an American Withdrawal. Economic and Military Issues*. Oxford & New York: Oxford University Press for SIPRI.

Sims, Christoper A., 1980. 'Macroeconomics and Reality', *Econometrica*, vol. 48, no. 1, July, pp. 1-48.

SIPRI, annually. *World Armaments and Disarmament. SIPRI Yearbook*. Oxford: Oxford University Press. [Previously: Stockholm: Almqvist & Wiksell/London: Taylor & Francis.]

Sivard, Ruth Leger, ed., annually. *World Military and Social Expenditures*. Washington, DC: World Priorities [earlier editions have other publishers].

Skaug, Reidar, 1991. *Forsvarets Forskningsinstitutts innflytelse på norsk teknologisk kompetanse-utvikling* [The Influence of the Norwegian Defence Research Establishment on the Development of Norwegian Technological Competence]. Kjeller: Norwegian Defense Research Establishment. [Appendix 3 to Thulin et al., 1991.]

Skogan, John Kristen, 1985. 'Fra Krag-Jørgensen-produksjon til Cuba-eksport og Pingvin-salg' [From Krag-Jørgensen Production to Exports to Cuba and the Sale of Penguin Missiles], *NUPI-rapport*, no. 90, June.

Skomsvold, Rolf; Ådne Cappelen, Nils Petter Gleditsch & Olav Bjerkholt, 1987. 'Regionaløko-nomiske konsekvenser av nedrustning i Norge' [Regional Economic Consequences of Disarmament in Norway], *Sosiologi i dag*, vol. 17, no. 3/4, pp. 113-130. Also in *Reprint series* no. 30. Oslo: Central Bureau of Statistics, 1988.

Small, Melvin & J. David Singer, 1982. *Resort to Arms. International and Civil Wars, 1816-1980*. Beverly Hills, CA & London: Sage.

Smith, Adam, 1776. *An Inquiry into the Nature and Causes of the Wealth of Nations*. London.

Smith, Dan & Ron P. Smith, 1980. *Military Expenditures, Resources, and Development*. London: Department of Economics, Birkbeck College, University of London.

Smith, Ron P., 1977. 'Military Expenditure and Capitalism', *Cambridge Journal of Economics*, vol. 1, no. 1, March, pp. 61-76.

Smith, Ron P., 1978. 'Military Expenditure and Capitalism: A Reply', *Cambridge Journal of Economics*, vol. 2, no. 3, September, pp. 299-304.

Smith, Ron P., 1980a. 'Military Expenditure and Investment in OECD Countries 1954-73', *Journal of Comparative Economics*, vol. 4, no. 1, March, pp. 19-32.

Smith, Ron P., 1980b. 'The Demand for Military Expenditure', *Economic Journal*, vol. 90, no. 360, December, pp. 811-820.

Smith, Ron P., 1987. 'The Demand for Military Expenditure: A Correction', *Economic Journal*, vol. 97, no. 388, December, pp. 989-990.

Smith, Ron P. 1989. 'Models of Military Expenditure', *Journal of Applied Econometrics*, vol. 4, no. 4, October-December, pp. 345-349. Reprinted as ch. 6, pp. 99-118 in Chan & Mintz, 1992.

Smith, Ron P., 1990. 'The Warwick ESRC Macroeconomic Modelling Bureau: An Assessment', in *International Journal of Forecasting*, vol. 6, no. 3, October, pp. 301-309.

Smith, Ron P., 1993. 'The Effects of Disarmament on the UK Economy', paper presented to the International Colloquium on Peace Economics/Economies in Peacetime, Grenoble, May.

Smith, Ron P. & J. Paul Dunne, 1993: 'Is Military Spending a Burden? A «Marxo-Marginalist» Response to Pivetti', submitted to *Cambridge Journal of Economics*.

Smith, Ron P. & George Georgiou, 1983. 'Assessing the Effect of Military Expenditure on OECD Economies: A Survey', *Arms Control*, vol. 4, no. 1, May, pp. 3-15.

Starr, Harvey; Francis W. Hoole, Jeffrey A. Hart & John R. Freeman, 1984. 'The Relationship Between Defense Spending and Inflation', *Journal of Conflict Resolution*, vol. 28, no. 1, March, pp. 103-122.

Stokke, Olav, 1975. *Norsk Utviklingsbistand* [Norwegian Development Assistance]. Oslo/Uppsala: Wennergren-Cappelen/Scandinavian Institute of African Studies.

Strand, Jon, 1980. 'Virkninger av utviklingshjelpen på norsk økonomi' [Effects of Development Aid on the Norwegian Economy], *Sosialøkonomen*, vol. 34, no. 1, pp. 13-19.

Ståhl, Ingemar, 1968. 'Försvarets samhällsekonomiske kostnader' [The Economic Costs of Defense], *Strategisk Bulletin*, vol. 4, no. 6, December, entire issue. Stockholm: Utrikespolitiska Institutet.

Szymanski, Albert, 1973. 'Military Spending and Economic Stagnation', *American Journal of Sociology*, vol. 79, no. 1, July, pp. 1-14.

Tamnes, Rolf, 1991. *The United States and the Cold War in the High North*. Aldershot etc.: Dartmouth/Oslo: Ad Notam.

Terleckyj, Nestor E., 1974. *Effects of R&D on the Productivity Growth of Industries: An Exploratory Study*. Washington, DC: National Planning Association.

Thee, Marek, 1986. *Military Technology, Military Strategy, and the Arms Race*. London & Sydney: Croom Helm/New York: St. Martin's.

Thomas, R. William; H. O. Stekler & G. Wayne Glass, 1991. 'The Economic Effects of Reducing US Defence Spending', *Defence Economics*, vol. 2, no. 3, July, pp. 183-197.

Thompson, Gordon, 1984. 'The Genesis of Nuclear Power', pp. 63-75 in Tirman, 1984a.

Thorsson, Inga, ed., 1985a. *Med sikte på nedrustning. Omställning från militär till civil produktion i Sverige*, vol. 1, *Huvudbetänkande*; SOU 1984: 62; vol. 2, *Särskilda rapporter*, SOU 1985: 43. Stockholm: Liber. [Almost complete English translation in Thorsson, 1985b.]

Thorsson, Inga, ed., 1985b. *In Pursuit of Disarmament. Conversion from Military to Civil Production in Sweden*, vol. 1 A, *Background, Facts and Analyses*; vol. 1 B, *Summary, Appraisals and Recommendations*; vol. 2, *Special Reports*. Stockholm: Liber. [Translation of Thorsson, 1985a.]

Thue, Rolf, 1969. 'Totalforsvar i Norge. Med spesiell vekt på sivilforsvaret' [Total Defense in Norway. With Special Attention to Civil Defense], *NATO-Nytt*, vol. 4, no. 3, July, 1969, pp. 21-28.

Thulin, Lars Uno et al., 1990. *Forsvarets næringspolitiske betydning. Rapport fra et underutvalg av Forsvarskommisjonen av 1990 med oversikt over Forsvarets næringspolitiske betydning samt betydning og konsekvens når det gjelder internasjonalt samarbeid på forsvarsmateriellsektoren* [The Impact of the Military Establishment on Industry. Report from a Subcommittee of the Defence Commission of 1990 ...]. Oslo: Ministry of Defense.

Thulin, Lars Uno et al., 1991. *Forsvarets næringspolitiske betydning. Rapport fra et underutvalg av Forsvarskommisjonen av 1990 med oversikt over Forsvarets næringspolitiske betydning samt betydning og konsekvens når det gjelder internasjonalt samarbeid på forsvarsmateriellsektoren – fase 2* [The Impact of the Military Establishment on Industry. Report from a Subcommittee of the Defense Commission of 1990 ...- phase 2]. Oslo: Ministry of Defense.

Thurow, Lester, 1978. 'Eight Imperatives for R&D', *Technology Review*, vol. 91, no. 1, January, pp. 64-71.

Tirman, John, ed., 1984a. *The Militarization of High Technology*. Cambridge, MA: Ballinger.

Tirman, John, 1984b. 'The Defense-Economy Debate', pp. 1-32 in Tirman, 1984a.

Tirman, John, 1984c. 'Conclusions and Countercurrents', pp. 215-235 in Tirman, 1984a.

Tuomi, Helena & Raimo Väyrynen, eds., 1983. *Militarization and Arms Production*. London: Croom Helm.

Udis, Bernard, ed., 1970. *Adjustments of the US Economy to Reductions in Military Spending*. ACDA/E-156. Washington, DC: US Arms Control and Disarmament Agency, December.

Udis, Bernard, ed., 1973. *The Economic Consequences of Reduced Military Spending*. Lexington, MA: Lexington Books.

Udis, Bernhard, 1978. *From Guns to Butter: Technology Organizations and Reduced Military Spending in Western Europe*. Cambridge, MA: Ballinger.

UK Ministry of Defence, 1987. *Statement on the Defence Estimates*. London: Her Majesty's Stationery Office.

Ullmann, John E., 1983. 'The Arms Race and the Decline of U.S. Technology', *Journal of Economic Issues*, vol. 17, no. 2, June, pp. 565-574.

UNESCO, 1978. 'Review of Research Trends and an Annotated Bibliography: Social and Economic Consequences of the Arms Race and Disarmament', *Reports and Papers in the Social Sciences*, no. 39. Paris: United Nations Educational, Scientific, and Cultural Organization.

UNIDIR, 1993. *Economic Aspects of Disarmament: Disarmament as an Investment Process*. UNIDIR/92/94. UN publ. no. A/47/150. New York: UN for United Nations Institute for Disarmament Research.

United Nations, annually. *Handbook of International Trade and Development Statistics*. New York: UN.

United Nations, annually. *Statistical Yearbook*. New York: UN.

United Nations, 1962. *Economic and Social Consequences of Disarmament*. New York: United Nations.

United Nations, 1965. *The United Nations and Disarmament 1945-1965*. New York: United Nations.

United Nations, 1968. *A System of National Accounts. Studies in Methods,* Series F, no. 2, rev. 3. New York: United Nations.

United Nations, 1972. *Economic and Social Consequences of the Arms Race and of Military Expenditures*. New York: United Nations. A/32/8469/Rev. 1. E.78.IX.1. [Originally issued in 1971.]

United Nations, 1973. *Disarmament and Development. Report of the Group of Experts on the Economic and Social Consequences of Disarmament*. New York: United Nations. ST/ECA/174. E.73.IX.1. [Originally issued in 1972.]

United Nations, 1978. *Economic and Social Consequences of the Arms Race and of Military Expenditures*. New York: United Nations. A/32/88/Rev. 1. E.72.IX.16. [Originally issued in 1977.]

United Nations, 1981. *Review of the Implementations of the Recommendations and Decisions Adopted by the General Assembly at its Tenth Special Session on Development and International Economic Co-Operation. Study on the Relationship between Disarmament and Development. Report of the Secretary-General*. New York: UN. October 5. A/36/356.

United Nations, 1982. *The Relationship between Disarmament and Development*. A/36/356. E.82.ix.1. *Study Series*, no. 5. New York: UN. [Originally issued in 1980 as the Report prepared for the United Nations Group of Governmental Experts on the Relationship between Disarmament and Development, i.e. the Thorsson Committee Report.]

United Nations, 1983. *Economic and Social Consequences of the Arms Race and of Military Expenditures*. New York: United Nations. A/37/386. E.83.IX.2. *Study Series* no. 11. [Originally issued in 1982.]

United Nations, 1985. *Disarmament and Development. Report of the Secretary-General*. New York: United Nations. A/40/618.

United Nations, 1986. *Disarmament and Development. Joint Declaration by the Panel of Eminent Experts in the Field of Disarmament and Development*. New York: United Nations. E.86.IX.5.

United Nations, 1987. *The Military Use of R&D, A Report Pursuant to General Assembly Resolution 37/99J*. New York: UN, Department of Disarmament Affairs.

United Nations. 1989. *Study on the Economic and Social Consequences of the Arms Race and Military Expenditures*. New York: United Nations. A/43/368. E.89.IX.2. *Study Series* no. 19. [Originally issued in 1988.]

US ACDA, annually. *World Military Expenditures and Arms Transfers*. Washington, DC: US Government Printing Office for United States Arms Control and Disarmament Agency.

US ACDA, 1962a. *Economic Impacts of Disarmament*. A Report of the Panel on Economic Impacts of Disarmament. Economic Series no. I, Publication no. 2. Washington, DC: US Government Printing Office for US Arms Control and Disarmament Agency, January.

US ACDA, 1962b. *The Economic and Social Consequences of Disarmament. US Reply to the Inquiry of the Secretary-General of the United Nations.* Washington, DC: United States Arms Control and Disarmament Agency, July.

US ACDA, 1990. *Report to the Congress on Defense Industry Conversion.* Washington, DC: United States Arms Control and Disarmament Agency, August.

US Bureau of the Census, 1976. *Statistical History of the United States.* New York: Bureau of the Census.

US Bureau of the Census, 1978. *Statistical Abstract of the United States.* New York: Bureau of the Census.

US Congress, 1973. *The Impact of Defense Cutbacks on American Communities.* Report of the President's Economic Adjustment Committee on Communities Affected by the Defense Facility and Activity Realinements. Announced on 17 April, 1973. Committee on Public Works, United States Senate. Washington, DC: US Government Printing Office.

US Congress, 1979. *Base Closures and Realignments Proposed by Department of Defense Fiscal Year 1979.* Hearings before the Subcommittee on Military Construction Appropriations of the Committee on Appropriations, House of Representatives, Ninety-Sixth Congress, First Session. Washington, DC: US Government Printing Office.

US Congress, 1985. *Base Closures.* Hearing before the Subcommittee on Military Construction of the Committee on Armed Services, United States Senate, Ninety-Ninth Congress, First Session, 12 May, 1985, Washington, DC: US Government Printing Office.

Ustvedt, Yngvar, 1979. *Velstand – og nye farer* [Affluence – and New Threats], vol. 2, 1952-61 of *Det skjedde i Norge* [It Happened in Norway]. Oslo: Gyldendal.

Venstre, 1980. *Innstilling fra Venstres forsvars- og sikkerhetshetspolitiske utvalg* [Report from the Defense and Security Policy Committee of the Left Party]. Oslo: Venstres opplysningsforbund.

Viguerie, Richard A, 1980. *The New Right: We're Ready to Lead.* Falls Church, VA: Vigurie co.

Väyrynen, Raimo, 1992. *Military Industrialization and Economic Development. Theory and Historical Case Studies.* Aldershot etc.: Dartmouth.

Wallensteen, Peter, ed., 1988. *Peace Research. Achievements and Challenges.* Boulder, CO/London: Westview.

Wallensteen, Peter & Karin Axell, 1993. 'Armed Conflict at the End of the Cold War, 1989-92', *Journal of Peace Research*, vol. 30, no. 3, August, pp. 331-346.

Wallensteen, Peter & Olof Frensborg, 1980. *New Wine and Old Bottles. Product versus Organization: Swedish Experiences in Changing from Military to Civilian Production.* Report prepared for the United Nations Group of Governmental Experts on the Relationship between Disarmament and Development. Uppsala: Department for Peace and Conflict Research, Uppsala University.

Wang Liguo, 1992, 'The Readjustment of the Defence Industrial Enterprises in Turning to the Civil Market', pp. 215-219 in Chai & Zhang, 1992.

Weede, Erich, 1983. 'Military Participation Ratios, Human Capital Formation, and Economic Growth: A Cross-National Analysis', *Journal of Political and Military Sociology*, vol. 11, no. 1, Spring, pp. 11-19.

Weidenbaum, Murray L., 1964. *The Economics of Peacetime Defense.* New York: Praeger.

Weiss, Ted, 1992. 'Public Law for Economic Conversion', ch. 14, pp. 155-159 in Chatterji & Forcey, 1992.

Wellmann, Christian, 1989. *Abrüstung und Beschäftigung – ein Zielkonflikt? Eine empirische Analyse finanzieller und ökonomischer Ausgangsbedingungen für Konversion in der Bundesrepublik Deutschland* [Disarmament and Employment – A Goal Conflict? An Empirical Analysis of the Financial and Economic Starting-Points for Conversion in the German Federal Republic]. *Studien der Hessischen Stiftung Friedens- und Konfliktforschung* Frankfurt: Campus.

Westing, Arthur H., 1988. 'The Military Sector vis-à-vis the Environment', *Journal of Peace Research*, vol. 25, no. 3, September, pp. 257-264.

Westing, Arthur H., 1989. 'Environmental Approaches to Regional Security', ch. 1, pp. 1-14 in Arthur H. Westing, ed. *Comprehensive Security for the Baltic. An Environmental Approach.* London etc.: Sage.

Westing, Arthur H. , ed., 1990. *Environmental Hazards of War. Releasing Dangerous Forces in an Industrialized World.* London etc.: Sage.

Wibberley, Leonard, 1955. *The Mouse that Roared.* Boston, MA: Little Brown.

Wicken, Olav, 1985a. 'Våpenimport eller egenproduksjon? Hvorfor Norge ikke bygde ut militær industri 1945-1950' [Weapons Import or Domestic Production? Why Norway did not Establish a Military Industry 1945-1950], pp. 186-224 in Rolf Tamnes, ed. *FORSVARSSTUDIER – Defense Studies IV. Årbok for Forsvarshistorisk forskningssenter – Forsvarets høgskole 1985* [Yearbook for The Research Centre for Defence History – The Military Academy 1985]. Oslo: TANO.

Wicken, Olav, 1985b. 'Arms and Expertise: Industrial Policy and Military Export in Norway', *Defense Analysis*, vol. 1, no. 2, pp. 111-129.

Wicken, Olav, 1987a. 'Norske våpen til NATOs forsvar. Norsk militærindustri under Koreakrigens opprustning' [Norwegian Weapons for NATO's Defense. Norwegian Military Industry in the Rearmament During the Korean War], *Forsvarsstudier*, no. 1.

Wicken, Olav, 1987b. 'Militære anskaffelser: Forsvars- eller industripolitikk?' [Military Procurement: Defense or Industrial Policy?], pp. 54-72 in Klaus-Richard Böhme, ed. *Krigsmaterialanskafning 1987*. Stockholm: Militära Högskolan.

Wicken, Olav, 1988a. 'Stille propell i storpolitisk storm' [Silent Propeller in High Politics Storm], *Forsvarsstudier* no. 1.

Wicken, Olav, 1988b. 'Adaptation of New Technology: The Case of Servo Technology in Norway 1947-1956', ch. 16, pp. 259-276 in Gummett & Reppy, 1988.

Wicken, Olav, 1990. 'Modernization through Military Industry: The Creation of a «Military-Industrial System» in Norway 1960-75', ch. 9, pp. 140-153 in Gleditsch & Njølstad, 1990.

Wicken, Olav, 1992. 'Moralens vokter eller våpenkremmer? Regulering av norsk våpeneksport 1935-1992 [Guardian of Morality or Merchant of Arms? The Regulation of Norwegian Arms Exports 1935-1952], *Forsvarsstudier*, no. 3.

Wilke, Peter & Herbert Wulf, 1986. 'Manpower Conversion in Defence-Related Industry', *Working Paper*, no. 4. Geneva: International Labour Organization, Disarmament and Employment Program.

Wilkes, Owen & Nils Petter Gleditsch, 1979. *Intelligence Installations in Norway. Their Number, Location, Function, and Legality*. Oslo: International Peace Research Institute, Oslo, February, PRIO Publication S-4/79. [Expanded Norwegian version in Wilkes & Gleditsch, 1981.]

Wilkes, Owen & Nils Petter Gleditsch, 1981. *Onkel Sams kaniner. Teknisk etterretning i Norge* [Uncle Sam's Rabbits. Technical Intelligence in Norway]. Oslo: Pax.

Wilkes, Owen & Nils Petter Gleditsch, 1987. *Loran-C and Omega. A Study of the Military Importance of Radio Navigation Aids*. Oslo: Norwegian University Press/Oxford etc.: Oxford University Press.

Wright, Quincy, 1965. *A Study of War. Second Edition with a Commentary on War since 1942*. Chicago, IL & London: University of Chicago Press. [First edition published 1942.]

Wulf, Herbert, ed., 1993. *Arms Industry Limited*. Oxford etc.: Oxford University Press for SIPRI.

Wängborg, Manne, 1979a. *Disarmament and Development: A Guide to Literature Relevant to the Nordic Proposal*. Stockholm: unpublished manuscript. Swedish Working Paper on Available Literature Relevant to the UN Study on Disarmament and Development.

Wängborg, Manne, 1979b. *Draft Bibliography. Appendix to Swedish Working Paper on Available Literature in the Field of Disarmament and Development*. [Unpublished Appendix to Wängborg, 1979a.]

Wängborg, Manne, 1979c. 'The Use of Resources for Military Purposes: A Bibliographical Starting-Point', *Bulletin of Peace Proposals*, vol. 10, no. 3, pp. 319-331.

Zegweld, Walter & Christian Enzing, 1987. *SDI and Industrial Technology: Policy Threat or Opportunity*. New York: St. Martin's.

Aalbu, Hallgeir, 1979. 'Statsansattes lokalisering. En statistikk-samling med regional og etatsvis stillingsoversikt' [The Geographical Distribution of Employment in the Public Sector, a Collection of Statistics], *Working Paper*, no. 10/79 from the Norwegian Institute for Urban and Regional Planning.

Aamo, Bjørn Skogstad et al., 1990. *Forsvarets distriktspolitiske betydning. Rapport fra et underutvalg av Forsvarskommisjonen av 1990 med oversikt over dagens virksomhet og konsekvenser av mulige endringer* [The Regional Impact of the Military Establishment. Report from a Subcommittee of the Defense Commission of 1990 ...]. Oslo: Ministry of Defense.

Aanesen, Margrethe, 1990. *Den sysselsettingsmessige betydning av en reduksjon av Forsvaret i sju særlig forsvarsavhengige kommuner. Datadel* [The Impact on Employment of a Reduction in

Defense Activity in Seven Particularly Defense-Dependent Municipalities. Data]. Tromsø: FORUT, University of Tromsø.

Årethun, Torbjørn, 1990. 'Fylkesfordelt nasjonalregnskap for forsvaret' [National Accounts for the Military, Distributed by District], *Interne notater*, no. 28. Oslo: Central Bureau of Statistics. [Also as Appendix A to Aamo et al., 1990.]

List of Figures

List of Tables

A Note on Terminology

As far as possible we have tried to use official terms in English for the names of Norwegian institutions, officials, etc. We initially used the following two standard works: *Statsforvaltningsordboka*. Oslo: Tanum, 1971; and Erik Næshagen: *Norsk-engelsk ordbok for utredningsterminologi og administrasjonsspråk*. Oslo: Norwegian University Press, 1977.

More recently, we have used: Patrick Chaffey, ed.: *Norsk-Engelsk Administrativ Ordbok* [Norwegian-English Administrative Glossary]. Oslo: Norwegian University Press, 1988; 2nd edn. The latter is a collaborative effort between the University of Oslo, the translation bureau of the Norwegian Ministry of Foreign Affairs, and others, and may be regarded as a quasi-official source. It is not complete, however. It is also oriented towards the UK, whereas our spelling and style generally follows US standards. Needless to say, responsibility for the final choice of terminology remains with the us.

For military terms the following book is useful: Ingvald Marm: *Engelsk-Amerikansk-Norsk militær ordbok* [English-American-Norwegian Military Dictionary]. Oslo: Fabritius, 1977.

To facilitate recognition, we have used English translations or short-hand terms for some Norwegian public document series which we refer to frequently. These include:

Defense Budget	*Forsvarsbudsjettet* or, more precisely, *Stortingsproposisjon* no. 1, *Forsvarsdepartementet*
Fiscal Accounts	*Statsregnskapet* or, more precisely, *Stortingsproposisjon* nos. 2 and 3 *Statsregnskapet* and *Trygderegnskapet*. (In Norwegian public documents, reference is sometimes made to Public Accounts or Central Government Accounts. In our own earlier work we have used the term State Accounts.)
Proposal to the Storting	*Stortingsproposisjon (St.prp.)*
Report to the Storting	*Stortingsmelding (St.meld.)*

For non-Norwegian readers it may be required to add that the *Storting* is the Norwegian Parliament.

We have tried to use gender-neutral language; hence employment is measured in *person-years* rather than in more traditional *man-years*.

The term *conversion* is frequently used to describe the process whereby a person, a firm, or an industry retools from swords to plowshares. Our own analysis concerns economic effects at the macro level. In our usage, conversion refers to the retooling for the economy as a whole, at the global, national, or local level. Others might prefer the word *reallocation* for this broad form of conversion.

In our previous work we have also sometimes used the word *model* for projected, hypothetical arms spending. We now consistently use the term *scenario* (or *policy alternative*), reserving the word model for a set of equations simulating the economy at the global, national, or local level.

Notes on the Authors

OLAV BJERKHOLT, b. 1942; Cand.oecon. (University of Oslo, 1968); Assistant Director General, Statistics Norway; Adjunct Professor of Energy Economics, University of Oslo (1986-92). Main areas of research: macroeconomic planning. energy economics. Recent books: *Macro-economic Medium-Term Models in the Nordic Countries. Contributions to Economic Analysis* no. 164 (co-edited with Jørgen Rosted). Amsterdam: North-Holland, 1987; *Recent Modelling Approaches in Applied Energy Economics*. London: Chapman & Hall, 1990 (co-edited with Øystein Olsen & Jon Vislie).

ÅDNE CAPPELEN, b. 1950; Cand.oecon. (University of Oslo, 1976); Research Director, Statistics Norway. Main areas of research: Large-scale macroeconomic models. Numerous articles and research reports on the economics of defense and macroeconomic models, including a study for the Norwegian Defense Commission (1990).

NILS PETTER GLEDITSCH, b. 1942; Mag.art. in Sociology (University of Oslo, 1968); Senior Research Fellow, International Peace Research Institute, Oslo (PRIO) (1968-); Director of PRIO (1972, 1977-78); Editor, *Journal of Peace Research* (1976-77, 1983-); Adjunct Professor of International Relations, University of Trondheim (1993-). Most recent books in English: *Arms Races: Technological and Political Dynamics* (co-edited with Olav Njølstad, Sage, 1990), *Conversion and the Environment* (edited, PRIO, 1992). Has also written extensively on Norwegian national security policy, and on the Norwegian struggle over membership in the Common Market 1970-72.

Acknowledgements

This book is the result of a research project of more than a decade's standing, with subprojects funded at various times by the Fridtjof Nansen Foundation for Science and the Humanities, the Norwegian Government's Advisory Committee on Arms Control and Disarmament, the Norwegian Ministry for Development Cooperation, and the Norwegian Research Council for Science and the Humanities (NAVF). The final grant for completing the book manuscript in 1990-92 came from the NAVF.

In various ways, the United Nations has played an important role in stimulating research on the topics at hand. Our first project was undertaken for the research program on disarmament and development initiated by the United Nations, and our first report (Bjerkholt et al., 1980) was one of the many background documents for the UN Group of Governmental Experts on the Relationship between Disarmament and Development – better known as the Thorsson Committee (United Nations, 1982). A later report (Cappelen et al., 1982) was prepared in connection with the Second Special Session of the General Assembly on Disarmament; a third (Gleditsch et al., 1985) was written for the *UNESCO Yearbook*; and a fourth (Gleditsch et al., 1986) was commissioned by the UN Department of Disarmament Affairs for the International Conference on the Relationship between Disarmament and Development. Our writings express only our own views, however. The United Nations and its agencies are in no way responsible for this book or our earlier reports.

Although two of the authors are affiliated with Statistics Norway (formerly called Central Bureau of Statistics), the work has been carried out as a project of the International Peace Research Institute, Oslo (PRIO). We are grateful to both institutions for direct and indirect support of the project during more than a decade. Statistics Norway also provided office space for Nils Petter Gleditsch for two weeks during a critical phase of the writing.

Computer programming and various forms of research assistance, word processing services, etc. have been provided over the years by Rasmus Bakke, Totto Befring, Nils Asle Bergsgard, Ingvar Botnen, Lasse Bockelie, Liv Buttingsrud, Margaret Chapman, Kåre Eltervåg, Eldbjørg Faye, Vigdis Fredriksen, Eva Grønmoe, Tor Andreas Gitlesen, Håvard Hegre, Erik Ivås, Eva Ivås, Kari Jensen, Ragnar Kristoffersen, Terje V. Larsen, Kristen Nordhaug, Jens Fredrik Nyhagen, Enrique Perez-Terron, Jarl Ove Ramsvik, Agnete Schjønsby, Jens Fredrik Selmer, Tor Skoglund, Knut Ø. Sørensen, Solveig Wiig, Åse Øyen, and Knut Øygard. We are grateful to all of them and particularly to Bakke, Hegre, Larsen, Nordhaug, and Selmer who assisted very ably in the final phases.

Susan Høivik edited the language in several of our original project reports and has also edited drafts of the present book. As usual, she has contributed plenty of good sense along with numerous stylistic remarks. Åshild Kolås prepared the indexes. At Sage, David Hill and Rowena Lennox guided the project through to completion.

Magne Barth, Arne Magnus Christensen, Stein Inge Hove, Knut Moum, Rolf Skomsvold, and Asbjørn Torvanger have not only served as research assistants but have also co-authored earlier publications, parts of which are incorporated here. While this book may not include much of their actual writing, their intellectual contributions have been very valuable in various phases of the work. Virtually all our earlier joint publications appear in the extensive bibliography. In Chapter 1 we have drawn to some extent on a joint publication between the first author, Dan Smith, and Håkan Wiberg, and in chapter 3 on a joint publication by the first author and Nils Ivar Agøy.

We would also like to acknowledge valuable comments on earlier drafts and oral presentations by Per Berg, Steve Chan, Paul Dunne, Bjørn Hagelin, Steinar Johansen, Milton Leitenberg, Göran Lindgren, Alex Mintz, Dan Smith, Ron Smith, along with other colleagues in Statistics Norway and at PRIO, as well as participants in various conference sessions where we have presented our work.

Kristen Ringdal and Jon Strand provided data from their own work for use in our first report. In that phase of our work Sten Lundbo, then Head of Division of the Norwegian Ministry of Foreign Affairs and a member of the Thorsson Committee, was a particular source of inspiration and support.

Some of the data used in Chapter 6 derive from the Census Tract Data Bank (Kretsdatabanken) operated by the Norwegian Social Science Data Services (NSD). NSD is neither responsible for the analysis nor for the interpretations of the data used.

For the purpose of linking the analysis of Norway to the World Model, as reported in Chapter 5, Bjerkholt and Cappelen visited the Institute for Economic Analysis at New York University in 1980. We are grateful to Faye Duchin and Daniel Szyld for help in computing most of the tables in Chapter 5 of this book, as well as comments on our design. Some of the work on the final manuscript was done while Gleditsch was a visiting professor in the Department of Peace and Conflict Research at Uppsala University in 1990-91 and 1993, and he expresses his gratitude to colleagues there for hospitality and intellectual stimulation.

Portions of Chapters 1 and 7 were presented at a conference on conversion, organized by the International Institute of Peace, Vienna, 24-27 January 1992, at the Fourteenth General Conference of the International Peace Research Association, Kyoto, 27-31 July 1992, and at the Inaugural Pan-European Conference in International Relations, Heidelberg, 16-20 September, 1992. Gleditsch would like to record his thanks to participants in the three meetings for comments on the presentations and to the Japan-Scandinavia Sasakawa Foundation for a travel grant to go to the Kyoto conference. He also thanks Björn Hagelin, Jyrki Käkönen, Olli-Pekka Jallonen, and Håkan Wiberg for their collaboration in a Nordic study of military expenditure and the Joint Committee of Nordic Social Science Research Council (NOS-S) for financial support of that study. The review of international research in Chapters 1 and 2 has also benefited from a grant from the Berghof Foundation in Germany – although the main results from that project will be reported later.

The book draws on our earlier writings previously published in articles in *Cooperation and Conflict* (Gleditsch et al., 1983, 1992), *Journal of Peace*

Research (Cappelen et al., 1984b), *Sosialøkonomen* (Cappelen, 1986) and *Sosiologi i dag* (Skomsvold et al., 1987) as well as in edited volumes published by Westview (Wallensteen, 1988), Routledge (Cappelen et al., 1992) and Dartmouth (Gleditsch, 1992b). We are grateful to the editors and publishers for permission to use the material in this book.

The first author is a sociologist and the other two are economists. This has of necessity led to a certain division of labor. Although this book is mainly written using the language and models of economics, we hope that it has also gained from an interdisciplinary perspective. This publication represents a joint effort for which we take collective responsibility.

Nils Petter Gleditsch
Ådne Cappelen
Olav Bjerkholt

Name Index

Subject Index

ACDA, *see* US, Arms Control and Disarmament
  Agency
Ace High communications system 142
aerospace industry 27
Afghanistan 1
Africa 110, 112-115
Air-raid shelters 48
Alaska 124
Andøy 135
Angola 38
armed conflict 2, 40, 145-146
arms expenditure, *see* military spending
arms exports, *see* military exports
arms industry, *see* military industry
arms race 1, 6, 10, 11, 15, 30, 67, 70, 78, 105,
  146
Asia 112-114
Aukra 122
Australia 5, 9, 13
Austria 67, 68

B-47 bomber 25
balance of payments, *see* international trade,
  balance of payments
balance of trade, *see* international trade, balance
  of trade
Bardu 135, 140
Barents Sea 106, 142
Belgium 5, 9, 13, 51
Boeing *707* 25
Boeing *747* 25
Bolivia 51

C-5 cargo plane 25
Canada 5, 9, 31-33, 49
capital inflow 21
capital stock 21, 32, 84, 93, 171, 175
Central America 53
CFE 2, 63, 64
chemical weapons 5, 105-106
China 3, 8, 28, 34, 40, 110, 112, 124, 142
  State Information Centre 110
CIS 2
COCOM 25, 52
Cold War 1-4, 7, 12, 15, 25, 30, 37, 45, 50, 57-
  59, 63, 66, 108, 121-125, 133, 141-150
Commonwealth of Independent States, *see* CIS
Congo 38
Congress of Vienna 36, 37
conscientious objectors 58, 66, 151
conscription 12, 20, 41, 44, 47-48, 56, 57, 58,
  61, 66, 94, 131, 133, 134, 135, 140, 150
  women 58, 66
Conventional Forces in Europe, *see* CFE

conversion 5-7, 12, 14, 22-28, 34, 56, 62-87,
  100-144, 149, 152, 173, 174, 201, 203
correlation studies 11, 14, 17
Costa Rica 4
countermeasures, *see* disarmament with
  countermeasures
Cross Fox communications system 122
Cross-sectional analysis 15-18, 20, 22, 32
crowding-out effect 5, 17, 25-28, 175
Cuba 51

defense expenditure, *see* military spending
Defense Commission 39, 46, 51, 64-66, 89, 106,
  126, 132-133, 136, 139, 151, 203
democracies 4, 23
Denmark 33, 36-38, 51, 57, 61, 67, 79, 132,
  133
developing countries 7, 16, 20-23, 80-81, 110,
  112, 115, 116, 129
development assistance 70, 75-83, 100, 106,
  112-115, 118-119, 137, 143-144, 152,
  169
disarmament,
  verification 5
  with countermeasures 75, 139
  with countermeasures, Health scenario 86-92,
    94-96, 98-101, 105, 129
  with countermeasures, Tax scenario 87-92,
    96-100, 105, 127
  without countermeasures 72-74, 100, 128,
    137, 144

'economic deterrence' 3
economic growth 5, 6, 10, 11, 14-26, 30-34, 70,
  73, 74, 78, 84, 89-93, 100, 104, 143-144,
  174-176
econometric models 19, 26, 109
economic zone 39, 42, 54, 59, 61, 149, 151
education, *see* public sector, education
EFTA 173
Egypt 115
employment, *see* unemployment or military
  employment
energy crisis 17
environment 3, 4, 7-8, 70, 75, 101-110, 121,
  138, 142, 144, 150, 152, 203
ethnic minorities 3
ethnic violence 3
Europe 1-4, 23, 25, 36-38, 40, 50, 54, 63, 66,
  67, 89, 101, 107, 110-114, 117, 122, 125,
  132, 141, 143-148, 173
Evje 135, 140

F-16 aircraft 29, 44, 51, 65, 151

Detailed Table of Contents